THE REGULATORY PROCESS

With Illustrations from Commercial Aviation

The Regulatory Process

With Illustrations from
Commercial Aviation

By EMMETTE S. REDFORD

UNIVERSITY OF TEXAS PRESS

AUSTIN AND LONDON

Printed by The University of Texas Printing Division, Austin
Bound by Universal Bookbindery, Inc., San Antonio

PREFACE

In 1958 I had the benefit of a Public Affairs Grant from the Social Science Research Council. It was a grant without application and without designation of subject. As I had written a book, *Administration of National Economic Control*, that described the powers, procedures, organization, responsibility, and problems of public regulatory agencies, I decided to utilize the grant in a study of a particular field of regulation but with perspectives broader than those in the earlier project. I would look at a system, not merely of administration nor even of government action, but of regulated private supply of a service. This would be a system composed of industrial, legislative, and public administrative structures. The perspectives for study of such a system were outlined in an initial essay. To get depth perception and to achieve results within the time available, I chose certain areas for interpretive analysis and case studies. Such analyses and studies would not answer all the questions that were presented by the broad perspective, but would, it was hoped, produce new insights and deeper understanding of the nature of a regulatory system.

In the course of the study I was asked to participate in panel discussions and to give a lecture at the University of Maryland which would be suitable for publication. In these instances, I gave attention to the problems of reform. The Maryland lecture led to a request in April, 1960, from the President's Advisory Committee on Government Organization to prepare for it a study on the relation of the President to regulatory commissions. I thus became involved in two kinds of study, one descriptive and analytical in its objectives, the other having a reform purpose.

With three exceptions, the studies of both types were all published from 1960 to 1962 as separate pieces. The one for the President's Advisory Committee was available for distribution only in multi-lithed form, and was subsequently revised and printed in the December, 1965, issue of the *Texas Law Review*. The other two—a study on the Air Transport Association and an evaluation of what is revealed about regulated private supply of service—are now printed for the first time.

The studies primarily intended to increase understanding are printed in this volume. They include the essay on perspectives, two other interpretive essays, three case studies, and the evaluation. The pieces on reform of the regulatory system are not included.

To all those who have helped me on these essays I am deeply grateful, and yet all cannot be named here. The Social Science Research Council's grant made possible the study. The University of Texas has assisted, not only through its Press, but by grants for a research assistant and for typing. Members of the Executive Board of The Inter-University Case Program, and Professors Edward A. Bock and James A. Fesler, in particular, suggested many improvements in the case studies included as Chapters 4 and 5. Mr. Robert Murphy, now a member of the Civil Aeronautics Board and earlier with Senator Mike Monroney, and Mr. Thomas Finney, also once on Senator Monroney's staff, offered files and gave many hours of help on the story of the passage of the Federal Aviation Act. Members of the CAB and its staff assisted on the General Passenger Fare Investigation case, and the Air Transport Association opened its records and generously assisted my research assistant and me on two of the cases. Professor Harvey C. Mansfield, Sr., commented on Chapter 7, offering many helpful suggestions for improvement. Dr. David Welborn, while a graduate student, helped on Chapter 3. I could not possibly overestimate the value of the help given by Dr. Orion White, Jr., first as my research assistant on the cases presented as Chapters 2 and 6, and after he became my colleague as reader of chapters and adviser on the project.

Finally, I express appreciation to the following for permission to reprint, with minor modifications, cases or articles:

The Inter-University Case Program, Inc., for "Policy Evolves: Congress, the Executive, and a Trade Association," printed by the University of Alabama Press, under the title "Congress Passes a Law: The Federal Aviation Act of 1958," copyright 1961 by the Inter-University Case Program; and for "An Administrative Center at Work: The CAB's General Passenger Fare Investigation," under the title "The General Passenger Fare Investigation" in *Government Regulation of Business: A Casebook*, edited by Edwin A. Bock, pp. 336–411 (New York: Prentice-Hall, Inc., 1965), copyright 1965 by the Inter-University Case Program.

The Journal of Politics, for "Congress and Regulation: Civil Aviation, 1957–1958," XXII (May, 1960), 228–258.

The Midwest Journal of Political Science, for "Perspectives for the Study of Government Regulation," VI (February, 1962), 1–18. Reprinted by permission of the Wayne State University Press. Copyright 1962.

The Western Political Quarterly, for "The Significance of Belief Patterns in Economic Regulation: The Civil Aeronautics Act of 1938," XIV (September, 1961), 13–25.

EMMETTE S. REDFORD

The University of Texas at Austin

CONTENTS

TABLES

PART I

Interpretive Essays

CHAPTER 1

Perspectives for the Study of Government Regulation

Much of the study of regulation has been focused on the activity of administrative agencies. Official and academic studies of this kind have been made frequently. The President's Committee on Administrative Management, the Attorney General's Committee on Administrative Procedure, task forces of the first and second Hoover Commissions, and James M. Landis, as President-elect Kennedy's agent, presented reports in 1937, 1941, 1949, 1955, and 1960, respectively. These reports have been supplemented by studies in congressional committees, such as those recently under way in the Government Oversight Subcommittee of the House Committee on Interstate and Foreign Commerce and the Carroll Subcommittee of the Senate Judiciary Committee. Academic interest in agency administration has been demonstrated in such studies as Herring's trail-blazing *Public Administration and the Public Interest* in 1936, Sharfman's monumental five volumes on the Interstate Commerce Commission from 1931 to 1937, Cushman's *The Independent Regulatory Commissions* in 1941, and, somewhat later, Bernstein's *Regulating Business by Independent Commission* in 1955, and my *Administration of National Economic Control* in 1952. In all of these studies attention has been centered primarily on administrative operations.

In what is perhaps the most useful single reference on regulation, Merle Fainsod in 1940 concentrated attention on whether the administrative agencies could have any independent force and effect; but he also explained other perspectives for study, namely interest

NOTE: Reprinted with minor modifications as published in 1962.

pressures and institutional forces.[1] I think it is time to consider again perspectives from which adequate understanding of the significance of government regulation can be obtained.

The perspectives need to be broader than those of agency administration alone. They should provide a view of all that happens when a decision to regulate is made: What fashioned this decision and the subsidiary decisions on scope and methods of public control? What has fashioned the subsequent lines of policy? What has been the content of policy? What techniques of regulation have been employed? Who got what out of the process? What have been the elements of determinism and what have been the possibilities for maneuverability? The answers to such questions will not be found by analysis of agency action alone. They will be found in a varied set of factors operating from outside and from within a structure of many interacting organizations.

A fruitful way to study these factors is to isolate an area of service to the public and then see what determines the course of action in this area. One such area of service, for example, is domestic commercial supply of air transport. This is a sufficiently distinct area of service to be viewed as a universe of social action. It does, of course, overlap with or merge into other universes of social action. Thus, it overlaps military air transport and merges into total aviation supply, domestic and international, and beyond that into total transportation supply. Yet there is a domestic commercial aviation industry and it is regulated, and these two facts create a universe of social action which can be studied as a sample of the regulatory process.

Such a universe of social action, that is, an area of economic function under public regulation, cuts across various institutional universes, such as Congress, the executive branch of the government, and the corporate system, and generates its own institutional mechanisms, such as companies, trade associations, public administrative agencies, and congressional subcommittees. In this enveloping universe, partially and vaguely independent of other economic universes, slicing across institutional forms and generating new ones, an elaborate complex of social phenomena develops. There

[1] Merle Fainsod, "Some Reflections on the Nature of the Regulatory Process" in Carl Joachim Friedrich and Edward S. Màson (eds.), *Public Policy, 1940,* Chapter 10.

will be responses to external stimuli, motivations crystallizing into institutional activities, and interaction among points of decision and action. The universe may be viewed as a system, relatively distinct from other systems, or sometimes as a subsystem, encompassed within broader systems defined by different criteria.

The study of the complex of phenomena in an area of economic supply under public regulation will transcend economics. It will be seen that activity within the universe will be determined quite meagerly by market forces. The study could be called political economics, indicating that the supply of the service was influenced by political forces; it could more appropriately be called political sociology, indicating that the supply of the service was encompassed in a complex of social forces, and that the focus of attention was the generation and impact of political intervention. It is this latter feature which puts the subject on the agenda of political science, though it can be on the agenda also of sociology and of economics.

The basic assumption behind the current statement of perspectives for study is that understanding of the governmental aspects of regulation is possible only by analysis of the whole complex of forces in which political structures operate. Other assumptions relate to the purposes of research for understanding. It is assumed that there are three. One is scientific, that is, to provide a basis for prediction of what will happen in this universe of social action or in other economic universes in which public regulation exists. Even though no methods of hard science—for example, no mathematical equations or no controlled experiments—are employed, depth in perception may bring understanding of the confines of possibility and the directions of movement. Thus, anyone who analyzes the belief patterns behind the system of regulation in this country, as revealed in separate economic universes, will be able to predict certain lines of action unless or until those belief patterns are altered. To be specific, as long as the belief pattern that regulation should be fair is accompanied by the tightly wedded belief that fairness is attainable ordinarily only by judicial processes, then the dampening hand of procedure will impair efficiency in regulation.[2] A second purpose is utilitarian. If an accumulation of analyses of regulation does not support unqualified determinism, this is no argument

___

[2] See Chapter 2, section titled "Regulation Should be Fair and This Requires Judicial Process."

that the studies should not have been made. Against the diminished opportunity for prediction, there may be an increased opportunity for utility. Where understanding produces knowledge of limits and possibilities of change, it serves the purpose of the policy maker. The third purpose is moral. To the extent that analysis reveals possibilities for maneuverability in human affairs, to this extent opportunity is provided for man to make choices in terms of his moral purposes—in terms of his concept of public interest or of other standards of public morality.[3]

Beyond the broad and general perspectives stated above, five particular perspectives for study may be outlined. If the first three of these conform to a biological model, this is, I believe, accidental. It implies no organismic assumption and, I trust, no effort to twist mechanically the analysis of social data into line with methods of inquiry in natural sciences. The use of two models in the discussion is itself recognition that we may draw from various analogies without yielding to any.

Ecology

Ecology is an essential element in study of behavior in the functioning of a regulated industry.[4] The basic environmental factors influencing behavior may be classified as technology, resources, general (societal) institutional organization, and belief patterns. Technology includes both the industrial arts and the managerial arts. The latter in turn include general managerial methodology and regulatory techniques. Resources include both materials and finances; involved also are special resources, such, for example, as availability or limitation of air space. Institutional organization encompasses the standing arrangements through which society has ordered its affairs—in essence the constitution of a society. Fused with these arrangements are the shared attitudes called "rules of the

---

[3] Compare the analysis of purposes of study in Richard C. Snyder and Glenn D. Paige, "The United States Decision to Resist Aggression in Korea: The Application of an Analytical Scheme," *Administrative Science Quarterly*, III (December, 1958), 342–344.

[4] John Gaus, particularly, among political scientists has emphasized the importance of ecology. See, for an example, his *Reflections on Public Administration*, Chapter 1.

game" by David Truman, "systems of belief" by Clyde Kluckhohn, and "general ideological consensus" by Gabriel Almond.[5]

Environmental factors may be almost as deterministic of regulatory activity as soil, water, and temperature are of the growth of animal or plant organisms. Consider, for example, the story Warner Mills tells of martial law in East Texas in 1931.[6] A vast new reservoir of oil resource is discovered, above this reservoir the rights of ownership are divided among thousands of small tract holders, the legal rule of capture gives each owner a right to sink wells for capture of the oil, the shallowness of the oil resource and the developments in technology make capture possible with a small investment, new refineries crop up quickly to purchase the oil and run it to independent filling-station operators, the results in six months are a decline in the price of oil from over a dollar to ten cents a barrel and the end is not yet in sight, a major industry of a state is demoralized and the solvency of the state treasury is threatened, and the Supreme Court of the United States has said that the powers of production control are reserved to the states. Under these conditions was it not inevitable that the responsible state officials would search for ways to limit the production of oil? One may say that to determine inevitability he would have to look at the interest configuration resulting from these factors. This is true, but the fact remains that the situational factors determined what the dominant interests would be. The perspective for research must, therefore, reach to the situational factors, to the setting from which a problem arose for those having political power or influence. Justification for control also was fashioned out of the setting. The courts found that the production of oil beyond market demand called for storage in earthen tanks and that this produced overground physical waste; subsequently, the engineers discovered that unlimited flow of oil from the field resulted in decline of the water pressure which forced out the oil, and hence that limitation of production was necessary to prevent underground waste. Thus, law and engineering science came to the side of the dominant interests. The point is that it was im-

[5] David B. Truman, *The Governmental Process: Political Interests and Public Opinion*, p. 512; Clyde Kluckhohn, *Mirror for Man*, p. 248 and *passim*; and Gabriel A. Almond, *The American People and Foreign Policy*, p. 158.
[6] Warner E. Mills, Jr., *Martial Law in East Texas*.

material who was governor or who sat on the regulatory commission. Environmental factors determined that proration would be the policy of Texas; all else was detail.

Another illustration of ecological determinism may be found in the influence of belief patterns. In Chapter 2, I will sketch the belief patterns that lie behind the system of regulation of commercial air transportation. The chapter leads to the conclusion that no fundamental alteration of regulation is possible unless basic belief patterns concerning the respective roles of public and private effort, economic organization, and the technology (procedure and organization) of regulation are modified.

It appears that civil air transport illustrates the possibilities for a larger mixture of determinism and opportunity for choice than existed in petroleum production. There were many significant environmental factors affecting the course of development. The basic one was burgeoning technology creating ever larger opportunities for transportation service and forcing in the industry a dynamism which produced instability and flux in regulatory policy. An additional factor was the existence of a business civilization which led to the choice of private enterprise as the means of supply of service and to an allocation of functions between private and public agents. Other factors were information about regulatory technique accumulated from experience and the ubiquitous patterns of belief inherited from the past which combined to forge the governing policies in the enabling legislation. Yet, on the stage set by these factors there was room for maneuvering. Choice was open on important issues of policy: How much competition should be authorized? What span of territorial service should be sought? If local service were to be authorized, should local-service airlines be kept separate from trunkline companies? What scope should be given to irregular-service airlines? Should airlines be encouraged by positive regulatory decisions to reach for a mass market? These were important issues of policy, and the amount of attention given to them—even more the changes in policy relating to them—indicates the existence of a realm of discretion for the regulators.

Responsible decision makers know that they must assess the factors in the situation which produce a problem and determine the limits and possibilities of action. The limits are the realm of determinism; the possibilities lie in the area of maneuverability within which human beings may at the moment have some opportunity for manipulation. Not all the factors are understood by a look only at the interests created; some lie deeper in the environment which creates and gives force to interests. The realistic student will look at all the factors which will be assessed by the decision maker and at all those factors which, whether known to the decision maker or not, will determine or confine his judgment. The response of men to environment is the first perspective of study in regulation.

Anatomy

Anatomy is a second element for study. Anatomy includes all the structural arrangements within the universe of social action. The study of the structure of a regulated sphere of economic service will aim toward discovery of the centers of decision and action, and toward determination of those which carry weight in the trend of events.

The most significant centers will ordinarily be organizational units representing social groupings. If a particular individual acquires influence it will usually be the result of his role in a strategic position as the representative of a group. Search may therefore be directed toward discovery of strategic organizational positions.

In studies of regulation it has usually been assumed that the commissions were strategic organizations worthy of study. This apparently is true, but it may also be true that the strength of their position can be exaggerated. There may at times be other organizational centers, within or outside the government, which will carry more weight in significant developments, even in government policy. Adequate understanding of government regulation can be attained only if the impact of the various organizational centers is considered.

The anatomy of a universe of social action will differ from that of an animal organism in at least two respects. The universe of social action within which the organizational centers operate is not a closed structure like an animal organism. In addition, there are no rigidly fixed positions of the organizational centers with relation to each other. Their positions are only loosely fixed and may shift with changes in the interaction of forces. They do have differentiated functions which to an extent fix positions with relation to other organizational centers; and they do contribute, through exercise of functions and through communication with other centers, to the activity of the universe.

By resorting to a different kind of model, we may visualize a society or culture as a sea of fluid substance. Its shore lines are set in the main by environmental factors, though these may be modified by action within the sea. Within this sea are whirlpools of activity.[7] Each whirlpool, with all the enveloping influences impinging upon it and effects issuing from it, is a universe of social action. Within and around, and generating, the whirlpool are floating, that is, active, organisms. The floating organisms are the structural aggregations of power and influence. Each of these organisms has some effect upon the whirlpool. Some are large and continuously active and move near the center of the whirlpool. Size, proximity, and activity are indexes of influence, though perhaps not the only indexes. Potentiality for influence on movement creates strategic position. Strategic positions are primary centers of influence on action. Beyond the strategic positions are other positions operating more remotely, less actively, or less continuously on the whirlpool. These may be primary centers of influence on other whirlpools of activity with only a secondary influence on the whirlpool of our interest. But all the organisms are floating, sometimes remote from the whirlpool or for other reasons unable to exercise strong influence on its motion, and at other times closer to the center of the whirlpool or exerting additional activity from their previous positions.

Each universe of social action is affected by a multitude of floating organisms. This is merely to say that in any continuous functional area, such as supply of an economic service, there are many centers of decision and action which have influence on the course of events. If one is to study the operation of the system, he must isolate the strategic centers from which most influence may be exerted.

It has been said that the organizational centers will have differentiated functions. The centers and their functions will have been established by formal and informal allocation. By deliberate (formal) action, or by the concurrence of events (informal) action, the centers will have been created and will have functions, power, and

[7] We are indebted to Ernest S. Griffith for the description of "government by whirlpools." See, as examples, his *The Impasse of Democracy*, p. 182, and *The American System of Government*, p. 127.

influence. The most familiar aspect of allocation is delegation through formal process. Congress allocates functions to a Civil Aeronautics Board and other administrative agencies, and to units within agencies—such as examiners. Within the agencies other allocations are made by internal delegation. Allocations are often the result of the formation of representative organization. Thus airlines form an Air Transport Association and pilots an Air Line Pilots Association, and these associations are allocated or assume functions. Other allocations issue from the constitutional and political system which produces such strategic centers as the Presidency, the Congress and its committees, and the courts. Still other allocations result from the background of institutional habit and belief patterns. Most significant of all perhaps is the allocation of functions between the corporations supplying service and the public regulatory agencies, and this allocation will be affected as much by the background of environmental factors as by the express terms of statutory delegations.[8]

Commercial air transport illustrates the multiplicity of centers of influence. There are many social groupings which may be classified as private groupings and public representative groupings. The private groupings include the following: (1) Communities, which are represented, as for example in route cases, by private representative organizations, such as chambers of commerce, and by public representatives, such as mayors and city managers.[9] (2) Direct service groups, such as airlines and air pilots, grouped in companies and/or in associations of great and continuing strength. Some of these groupings, like the Air Transport Association and the Air Line Pilots Association, occupy strategic positions and must be given continuous attention by the student of airline service. (3) Auxiliary service groups, such as manufacturers of airline equipment and research organizations. These too may have asso-

---

[8] There are many aspects of allocation which can be studied for their effect on the strength of centers of decision and action. For examples, note the importance of power to make authoritative in contrast to advisory or preliminary decisions, and the importance of sanctions. For discussion of allocation of power to regulatory agencies, see my *Administration of National Economic Control*, Chapters 4 to 8. Some aspects, such as delegation, have had much study; others, such as sanctions, have received little attention.

[9] The communities may not be represented solely by municipal corporations. They are, for this reason, listed as private groupings.

ciations. Their position appears to be more peripheral as to day-to-day activities but they can create new activity in the whirlpool, as, for example, through introduction of jet-propelled planes. (4) Professional groups, such as aviation writers, also organized in an association, and attorneys, organized in such associations as the American Bar Association and the Federal Bar Association. (5) Residual groups, such as political parties or ministers (who took an active part in the debate over service of liquor on commercial planes). (6) Collateral or opposition groups, such as those having functions in military air transport and railroad transportation. Among the public representative groupings are the Congress and its committees, the President and his advisors, the several national executive agencies (Federal Aviation Agency, Civil Aeronautics Board, Weather Bureau, armed services, and others), and the states (represented through such organizations as the Council of State Governments and the National Association of Railroad and Public Utility Commissioners).

Each of these centers of decision and action is itself a complex organization, exhibiting officers, committees, staffs, members, or other components. These internal centers become another level of strategic influences, carrying force both within an organization and beyond it to other organizations. Hence, the study of the anatomy of regulation extends into this internal structure of centers of influence as well as to the structure of the system as a whole. Their own organization or their degree of cohesiveness may affect their potential for influence. A worm's-eye view of their structure and of the interrelations among parts may be essential for a bird's-eye view of the functioning of the universe of action, in the same way that analysis of cell structure or of the structure of the atom may be useful to understanding the operation of larger physical entities.

Nevertheless, the internal study of the separate centers of influence will be meaningless unless related to the total complex of forces affecting the whirlpool of activity. This means, for example, that no center of influence—not even a regulatory commission—can be studied fruitfully without analysis of its position with respect to other structural centers. A regulated economic service is not supplied to the public under a monolithic structure. Pluralism is the central fact in the anatomy of regulation. It is argued later, for example, that if one is to understand the public control of commercial aviation he may usefully consider that the centers of influence are arranged in a parallelogram, with the influence coming from four corners, namely, community, congressional, executive, and industry aggregations.[10]

Physiology
(Function and Process)

The study of anatomy will unavoidably be interlaced with that of physiology. Physiology is function and process. It is activity. It is interaction among components. It is structure activated into movement.

In biological science there are many approaches to understanding life processes in organisms, such as study of physical process, of chemical substance, and of electrical impulse. Similarly, the state of our present knowledge supplies a number of avenues to understanding activity and movement within universes of social action.

One is the study of interests, including their generation and the ensuing processes of conflict and accommodation. The term "interest," as used here, refers to the concern which some individual or group of individuals has with respect to what occurs. Once a technological development occurs, there is a response from individuals. The development creates new visions of opportunity or of threat to existing status, and hence motivations, expectations (positive or negative), and impulses to activity. These result for some individuals in definitive interests to be revealed in lines of activity. The development results also in development of aggregations of interest and in crystallization of new centers of organization or use of existing centers. Thus, with the development of technology of air transport the motivations of individuals led to formation of companies and of trade associations. Almost as soon as the industry was born, there were these two levels of structure. Other interests, such as that of the national community in use of the technology for national defense or of the local communities in obtaining air service, use immediately existing structure, such as committees on interstate commerce in the Congress. Ultimately, the technological developments in a setting of adequate resources generated many new in-

10 Chapter 3.

terests which in turn pushed out a multitude of organizational centers. Ecology produced a new anatomy. This was accomplished by a physiological process in which interests were as vital as electrical impulses in the atom.

Each organizational entity itself becomes a center of two types of physiological process. One is internal, the other external. Roles established within the organization create cellular units within which motivations and impulses to action develop. These motivations and impulses may result from interests developed within the organization, but they may be supported by professional or other types of association with groups outside. At any rate, there will be a process of conflict and accommodation within the organization. Both the organization itself and the cells within will distribute impacts on the outside, thus contributing to the process of group conflict and accommodation in the universe of social action.

This whole process of interest generation and interest accommodation is perhaps the most important clue to understanding the process of regulation. It is, I submit, with apologies to some of my colleagues, not the only clue. Interests arise in a setting. The interests of the entrepreneurs in commercial aviation were generated by technological development, made possible by resources, and protected by the institutional habits and belief patterns of a capitalistic society. Once generated, every interest is, in turn, hedged not only by other interests but also by the confinements of evolved structure. There is restriction on interests as well as service to them in group aggregations formalized in organization. The impacts of environment and organization should also be studied.[11]

Once created, interest groupings become part of the environment which the policy maker must consider. It is possible, however, that the policy maker may find that interests are less deterministic than the more basic environmental factors. This is because of the variety of the interests and the complexity of interest groupings. This creates conflict or merely lack of concurrencies in interest, and out of this conflict or disparity comes the opportunity of the person or organ in a strategic position to influence the course of events. Determinism fades and human manipulative potential arises because a setting of multiple interest groupings is one of maneuverability.

---

[11] Also the impact of established policy, discussed in the next section.

Only if it were assumed that there were no individual free will would it be possible to postulate complete predictability and argue that a hard science based on causation could be substituted entirely for a utilitarian science.

A second approach to an understanding of activity is through study of communications. Communications erect a web of links between the structural units in the anatomical system—connections between the floating organisms in and around the whirlpool of activity. Where channels of communications are fixed and continuous they may be regarded as part of the anatomical system itself, but there is likely to be much fluidity in the communications network. Communications make the current of action in the whirlpool of activity dependent upon interaction among the influence centers. The complexity of the interaction system is enhanced by the fact that communication links will be established between component cells of the separate major organizational groupings. Some of these groupings are themselves highly pluralistic with limited, perhaps negligible, hierarchical control over the establishment of communication lines from cellular units to similar units in other organizations.

One effect of the communication system may be to blur the distinction between private and public action, for the resulting action may be compounded of influences from both sources. Moreover, where affinity on point of view exists, as among trial examiners, agency lawyers, and practitioner associations, then the communication channels may not need to be strong in order to create a consolidated effect of considerable weight.

The student of regulation will find that the foregoing lines of physiological research will combine with his anatomical research to produce a considerable amount of knowledge about the universe of social action and the impact of public representative groupings on it. The strength of centers of influence will depend primarily upon the interest aggregations they represent, the allocations through delegation or institutional practice, and the communications maintained. The student can isolate the strategic centers of influence and study their respective impacts on the currents of movement.

Yet there is another route to an understanding of the physiology of regulation which may produce profound knowledge about the regulatory process. This is an examination of the processes of policy formation and decision making. We have long been familiar with formal study of process flow, that is, the procedure through which actions are taken or decisions made. More recently we have been introduced to a case approach in which attention is focused on the making of a particular decision or a series of decisions. The merit of the method is that, since it encompasses the total flow of influence, it may increase depth of perception about all the factors—whether environmental, anatomical, or psysiological—which can be isolated by the researcher. The danger is that, unless skillfully used, it may not reveal typical situations and processes; and the limitation is that a case study by itself will often provide inadequate foundation for generalization.

I have tried to use forms of the case approach to determine where and how decisional influences are exerted. Chapter 3 assesses the impact of congressional participation in regulation by studying all that Congress did for a two-year period with respect to commercial civil aviation. Chapter 5 illustrates the internal process of decision in a regulatory agency by describing the process of decision in a rate-making case in the Civil Aeronautics Board. Chapter 6 summarizes the activity of a trade association with relation to public centers of influence on civil aviation. Chapter 4 presents a view of the complementary contributions of the strategic industrial, congressional, and executive centers in regulation by analysis of the framing of the Federal Aviation Act. In each case an effort was made to combine the look inward for detail with search for and suggestion of relevance and significance.

It will be recognized that a study of decision-making processes is only one method of getting a cut across reality. Much that occurs in a universe of social action is repetitive performance; some things are the results of slide or accumulation of experience not isolatable in decisions or a series of decisions. But the study of the processes of decision making is likely to yield knowledge of the most significant elements in the current of movement. This will be true if careful selection of case topics is made to show the most significant processes or the most significant decisions.

Policy

The fourth element for study is policy. Policy consists of outcomes. It is the substance of what develops from a universe of social action, or from larger encompassing universes. It is another dimension, different from process.

The search for policy is an important part of the analysis of regulation. Policy is the meaningful result of environment, anatomy, and physiology; policy is the index of development; policy is a determiner of the future. Policy is both the stage of development and a molder of activities. To find policy is merely to mark what is enduring, to mark points of regularity, order, and consistency. To find that there is a gap in policy is to find that there is no system, no rhythm, only activity, where that gap exists.

Policy may be inherent in institutional system and belief patterns and discoverable by study of these. It may be found in moments of decision or it may be discoverable out of a slide of events.

It may crystallize a tendency or it may fix a new line of development. One feature of policy is that it tends to be decisive. There is determinism in policy. It marks what is accepted, and thus what will be applied. When it is confirmed by consonance with other policies, by concurrence with the basic institutions and ideals of society, and by time and application, it becomes part of the hardened and durable substance of social control. It is, I suggest, a more significant clue than organization to the understanding of the molding and channeling of tendency. It is the result of forces, but a result that resists fundamental change and that influences lines of adaptive change; it is both measure and preserver of unity and continuity in the universe of action.

An important characteristic of policy development, as Lindblom has told us, is that it is incremental.[12] Ordinarily, each policy decision is an addition to policies determined before. This is the meaning of what Simon has called the decision tree.[13] Certain decisions build a trunk, others a major branch, and others smaller branches. If we vary the analogy, to blend with our previous model, we may say that choice and events create first the shore lines of the environmental sea in which the whirlpools of semiseparate universes of social action occur, then a policy stream moves out of the whirlpool,

---

[12] Charles E. Lindblom, "Policy Analysis," *American Economic Review*, XLVIII (June, 1958), 298–312. The anthropologist says, simply, that "Cultural change can be accumulative." See F. Stuart Chapin, *Cultural Change*, pp. 205–206.

[13] Herbert A. Simon, *Administrative Behavior*, pp. xxvii–xxxiii.

and subsequently a tributary system of minor policy develops as the stream moves onward. Lawyers would explain the phenomenon in terms of concepts and standards, then leading decisions, then refinements of these, and then applications of law.

The durability and the significance of policy may be determined by its place on the decision tree, as Simon puts it, or on the shore lines, as I put it. A small change in the current from the whirlpool may cause water down the stream to alter the boundaries of the tributary system; but only a major revolution in technology, interests, and/or beliefs can change the shore lines of the environmental sea or agitate the whirlpool enough to create new shore lines on the main policy stream.

It follows then that the person seeking understanding must be time conscious, that is, history conscious. This history consciousness will give perspective. It will place things in order. Thus, in seeking for understanding of the universe of action represented in regulated commercial aviation the student will seek understanding not only of whirlpools of activity but also of shore lines on the sea and down the stream of movement issuing from the whirlpool. He may find that certain policies were fixed by the belief patterns already existing when the universe began to develop—that the main ingredients of regulatory policy are imbedded in the nation's past and fixed by the shore lines of the sea. Beyond this he may look for policy issuing from the whirlpool and follow it through the tributary system. He may find historic moments, as when policy was crystallized in the Civil Aeronautics Act of 1938;[14] as when the Civil Aeronautics Board decided in 1941 that there were enough trunkline carriers already in existence;[15] as when the Board decided in 1955 to expand competition among the trunklines;[16] as when Congress determined that permanent certificates should be granted to local service airlines;[17] as when by the concurrent activities of industry, and of congressional and executive centers, a decision was made in the

[14] 52 Stat. 973 (1938).

[15] Delta Air Lines et al., Service to Atlanta and Birmingham, 2 CAB 447, 480.

[16] New York-Chicago Service Case, 22 CAB Reports 973 (September 1, 1955); Denver Service Case, 22 CAB Reports 1178 (November 14, 1955); Southwest-Northeast Case, 22 CAB Reports 52 (November 21, 1955).

[17] 69 Stat. 49 (1955).

Federal Aviation Act to have a common system of air traffic control for military and civil aviation.[18]

The aim of both analytical and historical perspectives is to fix attention on major elements and trends. Analytical perspectives which fix the strategic points in anatomy and the meaningful processes of interest accommodation, communications, and decision making may keep the student close to the center of the whirlpool of activity which he seeks to explain. Historical perspectives may lead him away from the streamlets at the end of the tributaries—back to the shore lines of institutional patterns, beliefs, and basic policy, and enable him to see lines and stages of development.

Evaluation

The final element in perspectives for study is evaluation of results of activity and movement in the universe of social action. This will form the basis of Chapter 7, but a few aspects of the perspective may be noted summarily.

The student of the universe of social action will be able on the basis of his analysis of setting, structure, and operation to define the attributes of the system he is studying. The system is one which combines in some way private and public activity in the supply of an economic service. It conforms to a general model of sociopolitical action which is referred to as regulated economic service and stands somewhere on a continuum, as Dahl and Lindblom have put it,[19] between polar systems of public and private enterprise. It will exhibit certain special characteristics defined by such things as the allocation of function between public and private structures, the means by which public functions are exercised, and the interrelations among the parts of the system. Its features will be subject to specification.

The results of the system may have two types of meaning. The first is the significance of the system for the purposes it serves, and the second is its significance as a pattern for organization of other services.

[18] 72 Stat. 731 (1958).

[19] Robert A. Dahl and Charles E. Lindblom, *Politics, Economics, and Welfare,* p. 10.

There are two complementary sets of questions which are central to the inquiry on significance. The first set relates to beneficence: Is the stream of movements, insofar as it is determined by public policy, beneficent? Are there parts of the stream which are beneficent and others which are not? Should the system as a whole, or parts of the system, be copied, or be avoided in other areas of service? The second set of questions relates to potentials for modification: Are defects correctable? Are lessons of experience in the universe of action transferable to another universe? Are there areas of maneuverability and, if so, what are the conditions prerequisite to manipulation within such areas?

These questions may be answered in part—in large part—by reference to process. Has the process been one by which new technology could be absorbed? Has it been one by which interests could be reconciled in a way which appeared to them to be fair—in other words, has there been due process? Has the process been one which has not aroused criticism and demand for change?

The student, however, may justifiably seek for answers in substance of action as well as in process of action. Even the statement of process questions assumes substantive goals: absorption of technology, fairness, avoidance of revolutionary methods of change.[20] In addition, specific aims of policy may be touchstones of evaluation. If "fair and reasonable" price is stated by statute to be an objective of policy, may the student not be interested in knowing whether the objective is attained? Or whether it can be attained under the system of social action which exists? If the technology of air transportation offers potential for safe, speedy, convenient, inexpensive service for most long distance transportation of passengers, then the student may justifiably see if the sociopolitical system of supply has provided such service. He may do this, not because he assumes it is his business to determine goals, but because as a researcher he is searching for significance and believes that whatever has significance may have utility for those who have responsibility for policy.

The search for significance leads inevitably to the search for standards of judgment. The standards of judgment, relating to

---

[20] For recognition that process (so-called "Realist") theory is based on substantive (Normative: "Idealist") assumptions, see Glendon Schubert, *The Public Interest: A Critique of the Theory of Political Concept*, pp. 204–205.

process and substance, will constitute some view of public benefits worthy of attainment.

Illustrative Studies

The perspectives of study set forth in this chapter may appear to be too broad for practicable use. It need not, however, be assumed that perspectives for study should be stated in terms of what one individual can do in a brief span of time, though I must say that I have seen at least three students accomplish in dissertations a considerable part of what is here sketched. Moreover, studies of segments of a universe of social action will be most fruitful when pursued with comprehension of the full dimensions of meaningful inquiry. Finally, partial and reasonably accurate knowledge about big things may be more significant than complete and fully accurate knowledge about little things.

The chapters which follow in this book offer no complete view of, and no quantitative knowledge on, the regulatory process. They do not attempt to follow up on all the lines of inquiry suggested in this chapter, even for a single universe of social action. They are illustrative essays offered in the hope that they, along with this chapter, will deepen insights, and in the belief that this is all that is possible.

CHAPTER **2**

The Significance of Belief Patterns in Economic Regulation: The Civil Aeronautics Act of 1938

Beliefs determine social action. It is true, of course, that if beliefs are the chicken, there are many eggs in its lineage, and that these have yolks of social interaction and whites of environment. Beliefs may be rationalizations of need, symbols for interests, or links in a chain between the forging of interests and the institutionalization of behavior. It is true, nevertheless, that our concepts are guides for our action. It may be, as Justice Holmes remarked, that "the decision in a particular case will depend on a judgment or intuition more inarticulate than any major premise";[1] but behind a decision or a line of decisions there are some thought formations, vague or precise, about fairness, reasonableness, efficiency, duty to decide, and other matters.

Some beliefs are deeply rooted in the cultural heritage and are called traditions, some are interpretations of recent experience, others are responses to current need. Some are frozen, others are fluid under the press of circumstance. Some yielding to environmental factors may normally be expected, and also some compromising with competing beliefs. Yet they are crystallizations and therefore clues to tendencies. They are consensus for the present and direction setters for the future. They are one source of understanding about a series of decisions, a trend in policy, or the evolution of a social program.[2]

NOTE: Reprinted with minor modifications as published in 1961.

[1] Lochner v. New York, 198 U.S. 45, 76 (1905).

[2] The outstanding analysis of the influence of opinion on law is A. V. Dicey, *Lectures on the Relation between Law and Opinion in England, During the Nineteenth Century.*

This chapter reflects my search for belief patterns behind a system of economic regulation—that for domestic commercial air transport. The analysis is limited to this single area of regulation, but one may see in it explanations of a larger complex of social behavior —the whole system of public regulation of private economic activity.

The beliefs have all been stated repeatedly, though perhaps not in the same words used in this volume. My contribution, if such there is, lies in isolation of the beliefs from total reality, in imputations of significance, in elaborations on what is explicit and implicit in belief and circumstance, and in the ordering of these beliefs to facilitate comprehension of the regulatory process. The beliefs, or patterns of belief, will be stated categorically under seven headings and grouped in rather loose areas of correlation.

Basic Assumption

PUBLIC NEEDS ARE DOMINANT

In our basic thinking economic purpose and political purpose are the same. The public as consumer must be king. It is occupants of houses, not architects and builders, whose needs are to be satisfied. It is the common needs of people in the community, not the purposes of wielders of public power, which legitimize the efforts of the state. Not gain for capital and labor, not power, is the ultimate business of economics and politics, respectively. Not even economic and political freedom solely for their own ends. Abstract impressionism may have a big place in the arts, but the accounting is largely on the other side of the ledger in economics and politics. The basic belief for both unregulated and regulated enterprise is that public needs are dominant.

Our public records—notably judicial opinions, congressional committee reports, and preambles of statutes—provide us abundantly with explicit statement of accepted public needs. In the case of civil aviation the needs were defined out of both experience and prospect. Mail—carried by air since 1918—was the first need met by civil aviation. In the twenties passenger service was required of mail carriers by the Postmaster General and the vision of a new transportation system expanded. The importance of civil aviation as an "adjunct of defense" was also recognized. Consequently, in the organic statute for civil aviation passed in 1938 the objectives were stated to be "the present and future needs of the foreign and domestic commerce of the United States, of the postal service, and of the national defense."[3]

In the committee hearings preceding the passage of the Civil Aeronautics Act these needs were regarded as so important that frequent references were made to the need for law which, as the father of the organic law—Senator Pat McCarran—put it, would "encourage and promote aviation."[4] In five of the six statements of purpose in the Act of 1938 the words "encouragement," "development," or "promotion" appear and they are implicit in the sixth statement.

A further need was inherent in the nature of the service. Safety was recognized as interrelated with the development of air transportation, and hence was both stated as a statutory objective and supported by an extensive system of regulation.

The belief that public needs are dominant led, under the conditions which existed, to the development of a public policy. The nature of the policy was dependent, however, on other beliefs. These were part of our economic and our legal and political-administrative traditions.

Economic Assumptions

PRIVATE ENTERPRISE IS SUPERIOR

From the classical tradition came the idea that private enterprise was more efficient than public enterprise. Smithian economics and utilitarian philosophy supplied the arguments and these have been parroted by politicians, journalists, and academicians. The issue was changed when it was recognized that for some industries the choice, if choice there was, was between public management and regulated corporate management. John Stuart Mill saw defects in both systems, though less in regulated corporate management,[5] and the so-

---

[3] Civil Aeronautics Act of 1938, 52 Stat. 973, 980, Title 1, Section 2; the Act of 1938 was replaced by the Federal Aviation Act of 1958, in which the same words appear, 72 Stat. 731, 740, Section 102.

[4] *Hearings before a Subcommittee of the Committee on Interstate Commerce*, U.S. Senate, 75th Cong., 1st Sess. 38 (March 8, 1937).

[5] John Stuart Mill, *Principles of Political Economy*, edited by W. J. Ashley, pp. 960–963.

cialists argued the advantages of public enterprise. But in this country, where private capital was plentiful and government was amateurish, most commentators saw no reason to ponder the issue. Public enterprise would be accepted only when private capital was not attracted or where gross abuses were revealed. Yet rarely, except for electric supply, would the issue between regulated corporate enterprise and public enterprise be presented as one for choice. Private enterprise was ready and superior; regulation, its necessary complement, would be accepted, whatever its limitations and defects.

For air transportation—which is public enterprise almost universally in the rest of the world—private enterprise was confirmed in this country in a series of events. Although the government initially flew the mail, the Kelly Act of 1925 inaugurated a system of private flying of mail under government contract. When fraud was revealed, the government flew the mails.[6] This, however, was intended to be temporary, and a series of tragic accidents brought an abrupt end to the venture. The government returned to the contract system, and the first decisional position in the development of civil air transport was irrevocably fixed: it would be a private system.

This initial position set circumferences for further moves in public policy. Public service would be dependent upon attainment of business goals. There was new technology which could be used for a universal air mail system, a mass national transportation service, and greater national security. These objectives could be attained, however, only to the extent that profit could be anticipated by private investors. The rate and timing of use of technology for public ends were conditioned by the balance sheets of private companies. Private enterprise could take great risks in the reach for markets, but its reach would be limited by the chance for profit. All moves in public regulation would be conditioned by this ubiquitous business fact.

This conditioning of regulation can be overlooked or misinterpreted. By overlooking it, the defects in regulation may be attributed entirely to weakness in regulatory mechanism or in the men chosen as regulators. Through misinterpretation, the conditioning of regulation may be imputed entirely to the influence of the regulated upon the regulators. Though these factors may indeed be very sig-

[6] See Paul D. Tillett, *The Army Flies the Mails.*

nificant, the conditioning of regulation is inherent in the basic institutional system of regulated private enterprise. When the institutional arrangement of private supply of a service with regulation as a supplement is chosen, then the regulators must give attention to the welfare of the companies supplying the service. This is certainly true when the public goal is expansion of service, when the investment required is large and must be renewed recurrently because of rapid depletion and obsolescence, when continuity of service is desired, and when high maintenance standards are necessary for safety—all of which were conditions in civil air transport. The result is that planning turns inward to business facts. That this inward pull of regulation may obscure vision of public goals and call for compensations in regulatory approaches is part of the realities to be faced, not a reason for denying the existence of conditioning fact.

The public had, for air transport, certain tools through which it could reconcile public and business needs. It could grant subsidies, presumably to any extent necessary to supply the amount of service desired. Subsidy was an inevitable point of policy, just as deficit would have been in public ownership and operation. A second tool was the certificate system. This system was the logical replacement for the contract system for determining scope of service when passenger service became as important as mail service. It had, moreover, definite advantages for government and business. For government it was the means of channeling and limiting subsidy. For business it was the route to stability. This leads to the third belief.

REGULATED COMPETITION IS THE MEANS OF PROMOTING
PUBLIC SERVICE

The term "regulated competition" has had two meanings in American usage. Woodrow Wilson and Louis Brandeis used it to apply to restrictions necessary to maintain competition.[7] In this

---

[7] For use of the term by Brandeis, see *The Curse of Bigness: Miscellaneous Papers of Louis D. Brandeis*, edited by Osmond K. Frankel, p. 130; by Wilson, see *The Crossroads of Freedom: The 1912 Campaign Speeches of Woodrow Wilson*, edited by John Wells Davidson, p. 183. The concept as used by them has been discussed in James E. Anderson, *The Emergence of the Modern Regulatory State: A Study of American Ideas on the Regulation of Economic Enterprise, 1885–1917*, pp. 133ff.

usage it would include laws against combination and unfair methods of competition. Those who discuss regulated industries use the term to refer to controls over such things as entry, mergers, and rate agreements. In this usage, the term means control of the amount of competition.

There was apparently universal agreement among the legislative fathers of aviation regulation that competition was desirable.[8] A few favored or looked with sympathy on unlimited competition. During committee hearings extending through five legislative sessions Congressman George Sadowski repeatedly questioned the desirability of limiting entry through certificates of public convenience and necessity.[9] Amelia Earhart thought limitation "now would be really a little premature . . ."[10] Spokesmen for the Post Office Department, straining to retain jurisdiction, feared monopoly for various reasons.[11] Nevertheless, the near-unanimous opinion was that limited competition, that is, regulated competition, was the desirable objective for commercial aviation.

Belief in regulated competition was the result of several factors. One was interpretation of railroad experience. Mr. Joseph E. Eastman, long-time member of the Interstate Commerce Commission and venerated as a statesman of regulation, figured prominently in the events leading to the enactment of the Civil Aeronautics Act of 1938. He found in the facts of railroad history and the techniques of railroad regulation the pattern of regulated competition that should be adopted for air transportation.[12] Senator McCarran and

[8] See the comments in Hardy K. Maclay and William C. Burt, "Entry of New Carriers into Domestic Trunkline Air Transportation," *Journal of Air Law and Commerce*, XXII (Spring, 1955), 131–156.

[9] For examples see *Hearings before the Committee on Interstate and Foreign Commerce on H.R. 5234 and H.R. 4652*, 75th Cong., 1st Sess. 40 (March 30, 1937), 70 (March 31, 1937), 112–113 (April 1, 1937); *ibid.*, on H.R. 9738, 188 (March 24, 1937).

[10] *Hearings before a Subcommittee of the Committee on Interstate Commerce on S. 3027*, 74th Cong., 1st Sess. 103 (July 31, 1935).

[11] See, for example, letter from James A. Farley, Postmaster General, and testimony of Karl A. Crowley, Solicitor, Post Office Department, *Hearings before the Committee on Interstate and Foreign Commerce on H.R. 5234 and H.R. 4652*, 75th Cong., 1st Sess. 119ff. and 149 (April 2, 1937).

[12] *Hearings before a Subcommittee of the Committee on Commerce on H.R. 5234 and H.R. 4652*, 75th Cong., 1st Sess. 15–21 (March 30, 1937).

Congressman Clarence F. Lea, leaders in the development of the
legislation in the Houses of Congress, both regarded the existence
of the certificate system in railroad regulation as sufficient reason
for its use in air transport regulation.[13] In fact, we have here an outstanding example of how institutional history fixes an idea which in
turn becomes determinative of future policy.[14] Another influence
was the experience with airmail contracts. It was repeatedly argued
that the award of contracts to the lowest bidder favored the strong,
who could stand temporary losses and hence could bid at unre-
munerative prices. Senator McCarran called it a "vicious method
of awarding new routes" which should be changed "to allow intel-
ligent selection of the routes to be served and of those best qualified
to operate them economically and safely."[15] Finally, the air transport industry favored regulated competition. Mr. Edgar S. Gorrell,
president of the Air Transport Association, pointed out that only
$60,000,000 of $125,000,000 invested in the industry remained; he
strongly urged limited entry and protected investment as the foun-
dations for stable advance of the industry.[16]

The hearings, reports, and debates on a regulatory measure are
replete with condemnations of "unbridled," "cut-throat," "disastrous," "destructive," "wasteful," "unregulated" competition and
of "chaotic conditions," "unsound ventures," "haphazard growth,"
"blind economic chaos," and industry sowing of "wild oats." What
was favored was "orderly and sound growth," "orderly planning,"
"a measure of stability," and "financial stability."[17]

[13] *Hearings before a Subcommittee of the Committee on Commerce on S.
3659,* 75th Cong., 3d Sess. 156 (April 7, 1938) (McCarran); *Hearings before the
Committee on Interstate and Foreign Commerce on H.R. 5234 and H.R. 4652,*
75th Cong. 3d Sess. 159 (April 2, 1937) (Lea).

[14] Senator McCarran: "I want to say that in the preparation of this bill I
have followed the Interstate Commerce Act, and I have selected the best out of
it that I thought applied to this science with a view to the future development
of the science itself" (*Hearings before the Committee on Commerce,* U.S. Senate,
73d Cong., 2d Sess. 5 [April 12, 1934]).

[15] In Senate Debates, 83 *Cong. Rec.* 6635 (May 11, 1938).

[16] *Hearings before the Committee on Interstate and Foreign Commerce on
H.R. 5234 and H.R. 4652,* 75th Cong., 1st Sess. 51ff. (March 31–April 1, 1937).

[17] For examples of use of these latter terms see House of Representatives,
83 *Cong. Rec.* 6507 (May 9, 1938) (Congressman Jennings Randolph); *Hearings
before the Committee on Interstate and Foreign Commerce on H.R. 5234 and*

This pattern of belief was accepted by the regulatory agency. The first *Annual Report* of the Civil Aeronautics Authority declared: "For the first time air carriers and the public are safeguarded against uneconomic, destructive competition and wasteful duplication of services by the statutory requirement that no person or company may engage in air transportation without first receiving a certificate of public convenience and necessity."[18]

The result is that management of the system of competition has been the chief task of regulation. The Board first moved into a period of restricted competition. It declared in the Delta case in 1941[19] that there were enough passenger trunklines already in the business, and it followed a restrictive policy with respect to service by the airlines offering irregular service. Then in 1955 it adopted a policy of expanded competition.[20] The jet age in turn—producing higher per mile transportation cost—brought an end to this policy.

The mechanisms of regulation have been developed to meet this belief in regulated competition. With the exclusion of new companies from trunkline service, the Board's task became the apportionment of opportunities for large-city service among about a dozen companies. Balanced competition among those in the industry has been an objective. To meet this objective an elaborate set of rights and restrictions are couched in certificate terminology dealing with stopover, turnabout, through, and other forms of service. The time of the Board and its staff is devoted in large part to the refinements of balanced competition and stable growth. And the inwardness of the system of regulation has been increased as the refinements of balanced competition have become more complex.

H.R. 4652, 75th Cong., 1st Sess. 18 (March 30, 1937) (Eastman); *ibid.*, 66 (March 31, 1937) (Gorrell); 83 *Cong. Rec.* 6407 (May 7, 1938) (Lea).

[18] Civil Aeronautics Authority, *Annual Report*, 1939, p. 2.

[19] Delta Air Lines et al., Service to Atlanta and Birmingham, 2 *CAB Reports* 447, 480. On competition generally, see *The Role of Competition in Commercial Air Transportation*, Report of the Civil Aeronautics Board submitted to the Subcommittee of Monopoly, Senate Select Committee on Small Business, Subcommittee Print No. 9, U.S. Senate, 82d Cong., 2d Sess.

[20] New York-Chicago Service Case, 22 *CAB Reports* 973 (September 1, 1955); Denver Service Case, 22 *CAB Reports* 1178 (November 14, 1955); Southwest-Northeast Case, 22 *CAB Reports* 52 (November 21, 1955). For decision at the same time on irregular carriers see Large Irregular Carrier Investigation, 22 *CAB Reports* 853 (November 15, 1955).

PRIVATE RESPONSIBILITY SHOULD BE PRESERVED

Years ago Justice Brewer in an opinion for the Supreme Court of the United States said:

It must be remembered that railroads are the private property of their owners; that while from the public character of the work in which they are engaged the public has the power to prescribe rules for securing faithful and efficient service and equality between shippers and communities, yet in no proper sense is the public a general manager.[21]

It can be argued that government regulation has now been extended to the extent that it is in fact comanager of regulated industries.[22] Yet the fact remains that there is a prevailing opinion that government action should be minimal and should not intrude too deeply into managerial and policy judgments.

The concept of private managerial responsibility was recognized by the fathers of air transport regulation. It was more assumed than expressed.[23] It is implicit in the allocation of public and private responsibility embodied in the law and has been influential in its execution.

The law rings public power with restrictions, substantive as well as procedural. Foremost perhaps is the denial of any public administrative control over scheduling.[24] This is limitation of vast significance on public power to insure adequate service. It leaves to private judgment the decisions as to hours of departure, even though such decisions affect community interests, and even though they may, in competitive rendition of service, result in some duplication

[21] I.C.C. v. Chicago G. W. Ry. Co., 209 U.S. 108, 118–119 (1908); for an equally positive statement fifteen years later, see State of Missouri ex rel. Southwestern Bell Telephone Co. v. Public Service Commission of Missouri, 262 U.S. 276, 288 (1923).

[22] For such an argument see F. F. Blachly and Miriam E. Oatman, *Federal Regulatory Action and Control*, especially pp. 19–25, and Emmette S. Redford, *Administration of National Economic Control*, pp. 16ff.

[23] Though Eastman said, concerning leaving in a bill under consideration a salary limitation for airline officers of $17,500 per year, ". . . what becomes of the theory of private management and why not have direct Government management?" (Letter to Senator B. K. Wheeler, printed in *Hearings before a Subcommittee of the Committee on Interstate Commerce on S. 3027*, 74th Cong., 1st Sess. 69 [July 31, 1935]).

[24] Civil Aeronautics Act, Section 401(f); Federal Aviation Act, Section 401(e).

in schedules at the best hours while there is lack of service at others. In addition, the Act grants no authority to the Civil Aeronautics Board over security issues, the framers of the Act of 1938 having accepted only the protection given through the Securities and Exchange Commission. It has been held also that the Board has no power to regulate depreciation allowances through uniform reporting requirements,[25] and argued in rate proceedings that management must be allowed a wide range of discretion in determining depreciation expenses.[26]

Private judgment is the foundation on which airline service has been developed. This is true because the initiative rests with the private companies. In addition to decisions on scheduling, private judgments are reached on the adoption of new types of service, such as coach service; the development of rate structure, through which choices are made between favoring high-price or low-price transportation; the addition of fringe, perhaps luxury, benefits; and, most significant, the development of the route system. In all these cases, and many others, the initiative rests usually with the companies.

The powers granted to the Civil Aeronautics Board by the regulatory act are primarily enabling (granting or withholding consent), rather than directive (by order) on its own initiative.[27] It normally acts on petition, though this does not necessarily prevent advance planning by the agency. It could develop route patterns and service patterns to guide its judgment in decision on petitions from companies. It also does have considerable powers of action on its own initiative. Nevertheless, circumstances of various types have prevented public planning from being a dominant factor. One circumstance is that the "in" basket of petitions is accepted in considerable measure as the determinant of work priority; another is that action on petition is a normal outgrowth of the use of private enterprise; but still another is the belief that public action should be minimal and corrective, and private judgment broad. The result is that most of the planning of the airline system is done by com-

[25] Alaska Airlines v. Civil Aeronautics Board, 257 F.2d 229 (1939).
[26] For example, by the commercial airlines in The General Passenger Fare Investigation. See Chapter 5.
[27] On the distinction see Ernst Freund, *Administrative Powers over Persons and Property*, particularly pp. 10–18.

pany staffs and that the perspectives of planning are, in large measure, those set by company objectives.

Legal and Administrative Assumptions

BUSINESS AFFECTED WITH A PUBLIC INTEREST SHOULD BE
SUBJECT TO UTILITY-TYPE CONTROLS

The term "affected with a public interest" has ceased to have significance as a criterion of constitutional law. The words, however, have had another significance. They have been a form of expression denoting that the American people think of some industries as being of such a nature that certain types of control are appropriate for them. The appropriate form of control is the utility type, and this type of control is both an institutional system and a pattern of beliefs.

This pattern of beliefs arose in the formative period of railroad and utility regulation and has now been institutionalized through nearly one hundred years of experience in regulation. Through this experience the American people have been provided with a ready-made set of techniques in which they place much of their hope for implementing the basic belief that public needs should be dominant.

The National Association of Railroad and Public Utility Commissioners was represented on several occasions in the hearings on the aviation act. It was stated to be the view of the "association that any important public utility industry requires regulation in the public interest."[28] Congressman Lea said that regulation should have "two economic fundamentals"—issuance of certificates and control of rates.[29] These obviously are the core of utility regulation. To Mr. Gorrell a system based on certificates was "rooted in very early common-law conceptions."[30]

The details of the Civil Aeronautics Act followed closely those of the railroad and public utility acts. The same or similar types of provisions were included with respect to suspension of, hearings on, and setting of, rates, to grant or denial of certificates, and to allowance of mergers.

[28] *Hearings before the Committee on Interstate and Foreign Commerce on H.R. 5234 and H.R. 4652,* 75th Cong., 1st Sess. 163 (April 6, 1937).

[29] 83 *Cong. Rec.* 6407 (May 7, 1938).

[30] *Hearings before a Subcommittee of the Committee on Interstate Commerce on S.2,* 75th Cong., 1st Sess. 502 (April 12, 1937).

As in some other regulated industries, there were special objectives different from those behind utility regulation. One was safety—called the "keystone of the entire situation."[31] Another was the promotional objective. This was strongly and repeatedly emphasized in the legislative history of the Civil Aeronautics Act; it has been stressed also by the Civil Aeronautics Board. Reporting to Congress in 1956 the Board said that in use of the certificate power "the Board must apply the specified standards so as to maintain an appropriate equilibrium between the two major policies of the Act —that of controlling the air transport industry along the traditional lines of public utility regulation and that of fostering and promoting air transportation."[32] Belief in utility-type controls is therefore one, but only one, of the background ideas.

REGULATION SHOULD BE FAIR AND THIS REQUIRES JUDICIAL PROCESS

In American thinking about regulation, fairness is probably a stronger concept than efficiency. In fact, fairness is essential for efficiency when private enterprise is chosen as the instrument of service—for without fairness to the regulated the springs of initiative and the streams of investment go dry. Yet fairness is sought for its own sake and is protected both by the power of the regulated industry and by judicial and popular conceptions of due process.

The thing that gives special significance to the belief in fairness is that it is married to another belief: fairness is achieved only through judicial processes. Note the history of rate making as an example. It is called, in some of its manifestations at least, legislative; but it is believed to have some judicial attribute; it must, therefore, be done in a proceeding similar to that of a court. This is the pattern of beliefs in which fairness and judicial procedure lie bedded together.

The experience in air transport regulation is similar to that in other fields where utility-type controls are imposed. Provisions of the regulatory act and of the Administrative Procedure Act, judicial

---

[31] *Hearings before the Committee on Interstate and Foreign Commerce on H.R. 9738*, 75th Cong., 3d Sess. 259 (March 24, 1938).

[32] *Materials Relative to Competition in the Regulated Civil Aviation Industry*, 1956, transmitted by the Civil Aeronautics Board to the Select Committee on Small Business, U.S. Senate, 84th Cong., 2d Sess. 8 (April 18, 1956).

decisions or administrator's assumptions on what the judiciary would decide, and administrative practice follow the deeply set belief that judicial procedure is the only sure route to fairness.

In the development of regulatory process great emphasis was placed on the idea that proceedings of administrative agencies would be simpler than those of courts. Yet experience shows a tendency to round the circle and move toward the same point from which departure was sought.

The significance of the judicialization of processes is patently revealed in recent studies. James M. Landis has described the "inordinate delay" which "characterizes the disposition of adjudicatory proceedings before substantially all of our regulatory agencies," and the backlog of pending cases which confronts them.[33] Louis J. Hector, former member of the Civil Aeronautics Board, has shown how decisions on determination of community route needs are merged with and submerged in the judicial consideration of which carrier will be awarded the route.[34] My study of the General Passenger Fare case in the Civil Aeronautics Board shows a similar merging of consideration of policy standards with that of application of standards, and the serious impairment, if not virtual destruction, of rate-making authority through procedural involvements.[35]

Correctives for deficiencies in technique are essential for successful operation of a system based on the first two beliefs set out above —one in which public needs are dominant but private enterprise is used to supply them. The routes toward correction have been indicated in many discussions of regulatory technique: use of informal methods, simplication of formal procedure in judicial proceedings, and use of other types of process, whether called planning, policy making, or legislative proceedings. Innovations along these lines are inhibited, nevertheless, by the underlying belief that in regulatory matters there is only one certain route to fairness.

[33] *Report on Regulatory Agencies to the President-Elect* (Committee Print, Subcommittee on Administrative Practice and Procedure, Committee on the Judiciary, U.S. Senate, December, 1960), pp. 5–6.

[34] *Problems of the CAB and the Independent Regulatory Commissions* (Memorandum to the President of the United States, September 10, 1959), pp. 4–9.

[35] See Chapter 5.

REGULATION SHOULD BE NONPOLITICAL

The idea that regulation should be nonpolitical is a complex of many beliefs. Regulatory work is rationalized as judicial or legislative. It is easy to conclude, therefore, that it is not executive *in any sense* and should be independent from presidential direction and control. It seems obvious that judicial work should be performed with freedom from any external influence. It is *not* on its face self-evident that policy elaboration within the limits of statutory delegation should be nonpolitical or is nonexecutive, but the conclusions have been drawn nevertheless. The conclusions satisfy leaders in the congressional committees dealing with regulatory agencies because they support their jurisdictional claims; they satisfy industry because it fears novelty in policy; they have not been strongly challenged from the executive branch; they were embalmed by the judicial hand in *Humphrey's Executor v. United States* three years before the charter for commercial aviation became law.[36]

In the development of aviation legislation the representative of the commercial industry asked for legislation that would "place aviation behind an insulated wall, where politics cannot get at it, where the quasi-legislative features will be handled by the Commission without interference from politics, and where also the quasi-judicial functions will likewise be so handled."[37] Senator McCarran summarized his view when the final bill was under debate: "I have stood for a policy throughout this contest . . . whereby the air industry would be independent, and not under the subjugation and control of political agencies."[38] He referred specifically to merger controls as something which should be "in a non-partisan, quasi-judicial body,"[39] and wished "to keep the element of safety [which had executive aspects] clear of any political influence, clear out of politics."[40] Congressman Lea in the final debates said the board being created had been limited "as far as possible" to "quasi-

[36] 294 U.S. 602 (1935).
[37] *Hearings before a Subcommittee of the Committee on Interstate Commerce on S. 3659*, 75th Cong., 3d Sess. 25 (April 6, 1938).
[38] 83 *Cong. Rec.* 6726 (May 12, 1938).
[39] *Hearings before a Subcommittee of the Committee on Interstate Commerce on S. 2 and S. 1760*, 75th Cong., 1st Sess. 115 (March 11, 1937).
[40] *Ibid.*, 451 (April 12, 1937).

judicial and quasi-legislative functions," and summarized the prevailing view: "We desire that this commission, being a regulatory
commission, shall be as independent as we can make it."[41]

The Administration's position on regulatory organization was
clarified in January, 1938. The President originally favored delegation of regulation to the Interstate Commerce Commission, but
now supported the original McCarran view for separate regulation
of air transport. The Administration had received the Brownlow
Report in 1937, which recommended placing executive and policy-
determining functions under executive control,[42] and had approved
this recommendation in a message to Congress.[43] But the belief
pattern of the Brownlow Committee gained little acceptance. The
Administration chose in 1938 to recommend that only "executive"
functions in aviation regulation be under presidential direction.
Mr. Clinton M. Hester, the Administration's spokesman, told a
congressional committee: "In the exercise of its quasi-legislative,
or so-called quasi-judicial functions . . . the agency would sit as an
administrative court entirely independent of the executive branch
of the government."[44]

The draft of legislation supported by the Administration in
1938 contained no limitation on the President's power of removal
and provided that the exercise of powers "which are not subject to
review by the courts of law shall be subject to the general direction
of the President."[45] Hester explained that this provision was designed to ensure that "the executive work of this agency shall not
be placed beyond the constitutional control of the President . . ."[46]
The bill also protected the President's control over international
relations by providing for approval by him of foreign and overseas
air permits. The latter provision remained in subsequent drafts and

[41] 83 *Cong. Rec.* 6407 (May 7, 1938).

[42] President's Committee on Administrative Management, *Report of the Committee with Studies of Administrative Management in the Federal Government*
(Washington, 1937), 39–42, 207–243.

[43] "Reorganization of the Executive Departments" (Sen. Doc. 8), 81 *Cong.
Rec.*, Pt. I, 187–188 (January 12, 1937).

[44] *Hearings before the Committee on Interstate and Foreign Commerce on
H.R. 9738*, 75th Cong., 3d Sess. 37 (March 10, 1938).

[45] *Ibid.*, 25.

[46] *Ibid.*, 39. The executive functions related primarily to safety. Hester thought
they would be 90 percent of the work of the agency (*ibid.*, 49).

is in the Act, but the provision for presidential direction on executive duties was removed. In both Houses, moreover, a provision was added stating that the President could remove members of the agency for "inefficiency, neglect of duty, or malfeasance in office," which was construed as a limitation on his power of removal. In the Senate, then-Senator Harry Truman proposed an amendment to remove this provision, and it was argued in debate that the provision should come out because of the executive functions of the agency. Although the amendment was vigorously opposed by Senator McCarran, the Senate adopted it. Nevertheless, the provision limiting the President's removal power remained in the House bill, and the House view for limitation of the power of removal prevailed in conference committee and in the two houses.

It is clear that the prevailing belief pattern was that quasi-legislative and quasi-judicial functions should be exercised independently. The so-called executive functions related by and large to safety regulation; and by executive order separating these functions, the Civil Aeronautics Board came to have functions regarded generally as quasi-legislative and quasi-judicial. Tradition has supported the notion of independence for these functions.

The significance of the tradition is to obscure the function of policy development. The notions that regulation should be nonpolitical and that the process should be judicial have tended to make regulation a pragmatic process of searching for the appropriate answer in each particular case with only vaguely defined policy guides. Independent boards are drawn away from policy by their absorption in day-to-day business and by their isolation from the policy-making departments of the government. Also, the view that regulation should be nonpolitical contributes to inattention to the substantive problems of regulation in the office of the President and in the executive departments. The result is that the trend toward inwardness inherent in a system of regulation of private enterprise is enhanced—in my opinion greatly enhanced—by the organizational arrangements chosen for regulation.

Conclusions and Comments

Of what relevance is the above description to the study and improvement of the regulatory process?

First, it may remind us that any universe of political phenomena can be understood only if a variety of approaches to its study is used. Interest-group analysis has served as one useful approach in study. The role or behavior of individuals has been another. Legal rules for ordering relationships and processes have been still another, and indeed the one used most extensively. Yet it seems clear that a full understanding of the system of regulation, or of any other system of political action, must extend beyond the immediacies of group pressures and personal actions, and behind the legal rules, to the wider canvas of technological dynamics, which this chapter has only assumed, and of institutional framework and societal belief, which this chapter has revealed as interacting in one system.

Second, it is clear that the directions of regulatory policy are fixed, not alone by response to needs and pressures, but also by the belief patterns in a culture. Beliefs may be employed as tools of manipulation by legislators and administrators; they are also part of the limitations on regulators. Proposals, to be practical, must either operate within the interstices of belief patterns or modify or overcome these patterns; the meeting of needs for effective public action is dependent upon the feasibility of using or developing favorable belief patterns. Those who search for feasibilities in government policy must, to be realistic, discern existing beliefs, estimate their potency, and determine whether to use them or seek to overcome or alter them.

CHAPTER 3

Congress and Regulation: Civil Aviation, 1957–1958

There are many ways to gain insights into the role of Congress in the regulatory process. This chapter takes one route to such an understanding: an analysis of the activity of Congress and its parts with relation to one subject-matter field, and for one Congress, through one type of research source. The field is civil aviation, the Congress is the eighty-fifth, and the source is the official documents of Congress.

Congressional Interest and Organization

There are certain peculiarities about civil aviation which affect Congress' relations to it. First, aviation is characterized by its visibility and immediate personal interest to Congressmen. There is no veil of secrecy or dimming of view by distance; aviation and its facts are open and near. Congressmen ride planes and make references in debates and committee hearings to their own discomforting experiences. Second, the local, community interests in civil aviation are strong. Third, there is a nexus between civil and military aviation which creates many special problems. Fourth, the allocation of primary administrative functions is to various types of agencies, economic regulation being vested in the Civil Aeronautics Board (CAB), or in international matters shared between it and the President, and safety control being divided, until near the end of the Eighty-fifth Congress, between the CAB, the Civil Aeronautics Administration (CAA), and the military departments. The congressional committees refer frequently to the regulatory commissions and boards, including the CAB, as "arms of Congress," with obvious

NOTE: Reprinted with minor modifications as published in 1960.

implication of a kind of special responsibility of Congress for reviewing their performance.

The responsibilities in the Congress with respect to civil aviation were fixed by party victory and jurisdictional allocations. The Democrats had a majority in both houses, and hence also the chairmanship and a majority of each committee and subcommittee. Jurisdiction over bills affecting civil aviation was in the Senate and House Committees on Interstate and Foreign Commerce. Such bills were usually referred in the House to the Subcommittee on Transportation and Communications and in the Senate to the Subcommittee on Aviation. Appropriations for the CAB and the CAA were considered in the House and Senate Subcommittees on the Department of Commerce and Related Agencies of the Committees on Appropriations. These four subcommittees were the primary centers of activity within the Congress on civil aviation. Other important activity centers for civil aviation in this Congress were a special Subcommittee on Legislative Oversight of the House Committee on Interstate and Foreign Commerce, created on February 5, 1957, to study the policies and administration of a large number of agencies to which the legislative jurisdiction of the committee extends;[1] the Senate and House Committees on Government Operations; the Senate Judiciary Committee; a special subcommittee of the House Armed Services Committee; and certain subcommittees of the Committees on Appropriations: in both houses the Subcommittees on Department of Defense Appropriations, in the House a Subcommittee on the Department of Air Force, and in each house one special subcommittee. In this Congress no hearings were held with respect to aviation by the Small Business Committees, but one letter was filed with another committee by the chairman of the Senate committee. The bulk of the work on civil aviation was done in the subcommittees of the Senate and House Committees on Interstate and Foreign Commerce; but, as will be seen, when a subject became one of vital concern, activities with respect to it spilled over into several activity centers, leading to much duplication in hearings and much repetition in testimony.

One important feature of this organizational system was the existence in the Senate of a subcommittee for the aviation industry

[1] 103 *Cong. Rec.* 1555 (February 5, 1957).

only. The Subcommittee on Aviation of the Committee on Interstate and Foreign Commerce was composed of a chairman and four associates, two from each party. Its existence provided for the aviation industry a focal point of interest in its affairs and for the Congress a working group "informed by experience" on all aspects of civil aviation.

The organization created a relatively small number of strategically important positions. The chief of these was the chairmanship of the Subcommittee on Aviation in the Senate. This position was held by Senator Mike Monroney of Oklahoma. For Monroney, aviation had been a life-time interest. While a cub reporter on an Oklahoma newspaper he had gone to St. Louis to witness Lindbergh's return after his flight over the Atlantic and had gone to Ohio to fly in on the first commercial plane to land in Oklahoma. He represented an inland state to which aviation was important. His interest was supplemented by an amazing knowledge of aviation facts and problems apparent to any reader of the record of hearings conducted by the Subcommittee on Aviation. Monroney presided at most hearings of the Subcommittee and asked most of the questions, with frequent interspersing of comments on the conditions being studied. His strategic position, interest, and competence helped make him a strong and effective leader on all matters affecting civil aviation in the Senate and, in fact, have made him one of the dominating figures in the national aviation picture. One is led to surmise that his position as a leader in civil aviation may be much more important than that of a member of the Civil Aeronautics Board.

A set of strategically important positions were held by Congressman Oren Harris of Arkansas. Harris was chairman of the House Committee on Interstate and Foreign Commerce, of its Subcommittee on Transportation and Communications, and after February, 1958, of its special Legislative Oversight Subcommittee. Harris' interest, however, was not concentrated on aviation to the extent Monroney's was. His attention was divided among a number of industries and functions, both as committee and as subcommittee chairman. Nevertheless, from his positions he exercised important influence on policy and administration.

In the Senate, the four associates of Monroney on the Subcommittee on Aviation all had strong interest in civil aviation. They were, on the Democratic side, Senators George Smathers

(Florida) and Alan Bible (Nevada), and on the Republican side, Senators Andrew Schoeppel (Kansas) and Frederick Payne (Maine). They regularly attended committee hearings, and, although their interests in aviation were not as special as those of Monroney, they did show real interest in the subject. Senator Warren Magnuson (Washington) occupied the strategic position of chairman of the Senate Committee on Interstate and Foreign Commerce and was also a member of the Appropriations Committee. The chairman of the Subcommittee on the Department of Commerce and Related Agencies of the Appropriations Committee was Senator Spessard Holland (Florida). This small group of men occupied, with Monroney, the strategic positions in the Senate.

In the House, the Subcommittee on Transportation and Communications was composed of six Democrats and six Republicans in addition to Congressman Harris. The Subcommittee on the Department of Commerce and Related Agencies of the Appropriations Committee was chaired by Congressman Prince Preston (Georgia). Of the other members of the Subcommittee, Congressmen Albert Thomas (Texas), Sidney Yates (New York), and Daniel J. Flood (Pennsylvania) continuously showed active interest. But only Harris and Preston occupied really strategic positions in the House of Representatives.

Congressional Activity in 1957–1958

The discrete actions taken within the congressional system can be summarized with respect to the quantity and nature of the output, the subjects of interest, and the centers of activity. Attention can at the same time be given to results achieved.

The formal output of the Congress consists of its laws and resolutions. A summary at the end of this chapter shows that ten acts relating directly to aviation became law. This average of 5 acts per year compares with an average of 3.55 acts or executive orders amending aviation regulatory law for the twenty-year period from 1939 to 1958. Of the ten acts passed in the Eighty-fifth Congress, two—the Airways Modernization Act of 1957 and the Federal Aviation Act of 1958—dealt with the same problem: the need for an improved system of control over use of navigable airspace by civil and military aviation. This was major legislation, the Federal

Aviation Act being one of the most important pieces of legislation enacted in 1958. The Act not only created a new Federal Aviation Agency to control airspace use but it also amended and replaced the Civil Aeronautics Act of 1938. In addition, it incorporated four other measures which had passed the Senate. Of the other eight acts, the last three listed in the summary were local legislation, the one preceding these on the list was designed to meet the needs of a very small group, while the other four made significant alterations in regulatory policy. Six of the ten acts dealt with issues of policy of concern to the industry generally or major segments thereof: Airways Modernization Act, Federal Aviation Act, and the acts relating to guaranteed loans, capital gains, equipment trusts, and permanent certification of United States-Alaska airlines. Though the latter appears to be of limited significance, it should be viewed as part of a series of three acts relating to permanent certification of local, territorial, and overseas carriers passed in the Eighty-fourth and Eighty-fifth Congresses.

In addition to these ten acts, one joint resolution was passed and also a significant rider (to the appropriation for armed services) directing larger use of civil aviation, particularly of small companies, for military transport. Also, one bill of real significance— that amending the Federal Airport Act to extend time for grants and for other purposes—was vetoed by the President and was to become a major subject for legislative consideration in the succeeding Congress.

There were in all eight pieces of major legislation going through Congress. Three of these—Airways Modernization Act, Federal Aviation Act, and amendments to the Federal Airport Act—were organic legislation, that is, they dealt with basic organization and rules for the public system of regulation and promotion of civil aviation. Two acts—that relating to certification of United States-Alaska airlines and the appropriation rider—could be called corrective policy determination, for they expressed Congress' dissatisfaction with the way the administrative agencies had operated. Three acts—those on guaranteed loans, equipment trusts, and capital gains—were supplemental policy determination. Thus a single term of Congress reveals a considerable amount of legislation directly appertaining to civil aviation.

The total volume of congressional activity is indicated in additional ways. The Senate passed four bills and four resolutions which did not reach floor consideration in the House of Representatives; House hearings were held on only one of them. A House committee reported one House bill which did not get floor consideration, and hearings were held on three which were not reported. The House Committee on Interstate and Foreign Commerce reports that fifty-two bills on civil aviation were referred to it in the first session.[2] In the Senate, forty-three bills on aviation went to the Committee on Interstate and Foreign Commerce in the two sessions. These bills do not include the large number of bills which dealt with subjects other than aviation but which also applied to civil aviation or agencies regulating it along with other industries or agencies.

A further index of the quantity of aviation work is that of the number of days devoted to hearings. In the Senate, there were, in the Committee on Interstate and Foreign Commerce, open hearings extending over 19 days in the Subcommittee on Aviation, 3 days in a special subcommittee to study civilian participation in military air transport (MATS), 5 days of legislative hearings in the full committee in addition to hearings on three presidential nominations, making a total of 30 days on which there were hearings on aviation matters. In addition, hearings relating to aviation were held by a Government Operations subcommittee on 4 days, by a Judiciary Committee subcommittee on 1 day, by a special subcommittee of the Appropriations Committee (airport facilities for Washington, D.C., area) on 5 days, and by a regular subcommittee on appropriations on 2 days—a total of 12 days. In the House, there were, in the Committee on Interstate and Foreign Commerce, 23 days of hearings by the Transportation and Communications Subcommittee, 3 by the Legislative Oversight Subcommittee, and 4 by the full committee on civil aviation matters—a total of 30 days. In addition, hearings relating to the subject were held by the Judiciary Committee on 1 day, by two Government Operations subcommittees on 25 days (on safety and on MATS), by a subcommittee of the Armed Services Committee on 3 days (on MATS), and in two appropriations subcommittees on 5 days, making a total

[2] *Activity of the Committee on Interstate and Foreign Commerce*, House Report No. 1276, 85th Cong., 1st Sess. (September 23, 1957).

of 34 days.[3] The total for all committees in both houses for both sessions was 106 days.

In all, the volume of work revealed by the above summaries is quite impressive and indicates that the quantity of work within the Congress for a single regulated and promoted industry is quite substantial.[4]

The span of this activity, and also its concentration and dispersion, can be better indicated by discussion of the major subjects of congressional interest, which was primarily in the following subjects: competition, operation of regulatory agencies, certification, financial support of airlines, airport construction, civil aviation's share in military transport, safety, and appropriations.

During the Eighty-fourth Congress the Antitrust Subcommittee of the House Committee on the Judiciary under the chairmanship of Congressman Emanuel Celler (New York), conducting a broad study of monopoly problems in regulated industries, held hearings on "Airlines" extending to 24 days between February and June, 1956. A comprehensive report on most phases of CAB policy was released on April 5, 1957.[5] No formal congressional action is directly traceable to this investigation; moreover, the investigation, conducted in a mood favorable to competition, followed the year in which the CAB had, in a series of decisions, brought new competition over major airline routes. It seems clear, however, that the inquiry and the pressure of Chairman Celler in open hearings led the CAB to institute its General Passenger Fare Investigation on May 10, 1956.[6]

There were a number of inquiries into operations of agencies.

[3] Figures for the Senate Committee on Interstate and Foreign Commerce and its subcommittees are taken from the Committee's report, *Activity of the Committee on Interstate and Foreign Commerce, 85th Congress* (Committee Print), 85th Cong., 2d Sess. (September 5, 1958). The other figures are from the author's research assistant, counting hearings on apportionment of MATS business as related to civil aviation, and counting all days on which civil aviation was the major and exclusive item on consideration for all or most of a half-day or full-day sitting.

[4] Several of the matters had been considered in previous Congresses.

[5] *Report of the Antitrust Subcommittee of the House Committee on the Judiciary*, 85th Cong., 1st Sess., Airlines (April 5, 1957).

[6] For this story see Chapter 5.

A subcommittee of the Senate Committee on Government Operations conducted an investigation of leaks of information in the CAB and issued a report, which was followed by introduction of bills relating to external influence and to employee leaks of information.[7] The House Interstate and Foreign Commerce Committee listened to representatives of the CAB and the CAA at "Agency Hearings" on January 16 and 17, 1957. The hearings were designed to acquaint the committee, particularly the new members, with the personnel and the problems of the agencies. The special House Subcommittee on Legislative Oversight conducted hearings on October 17, 1957, on "Right of Access to CAB Files" and on November 24, 1958, on "Civil Aeronautics Board: Procedural Matters and Examination of Certain Cases of the Application of CAB Standards." Its investigations of regulatory commissions and boards were followed by the issuance of a report on "Independent Regulatory Commissions"[8] and by introduction of an omnibus bill on improper influence and other matters affecting commission independence.[9]

Interest in certification arose in the main because of airline and community dissatisfaction with temporary certification of service. Although trunklines (companies supplying interstate service between major traffic points) and companies rendering scheduled international service had been granted permanent certificates of public convenience and necessity, several groups of smaller carriers had been certificated by the CAB on a temporary basis subject to renewal periodically. These carriers were displeased due to the insecurity in their service rights and the difficulties in financing resulting therefrom, as well as to the necessity of petitioning CAB for renewals of certificates. The Eighty-fourth Congress granted permanent certification to local service and territorial carriers.[10] The Eighty-fifth Congress extended permanent certification to the United States-Alaska carriers, and a bill for permanent certification of air-cargo carriers rendering domestic service passed the Senate

[7] S. 2461 and S. 2462, 85th Cong., 1st Sess. (July 2, 1957).

[8] House Report No. 2711, 85th Cong., 2d Sess. (January 3, 1959).

[9] H. R. 4800, by Congressman Harris, 86th Cong., 1st Sess. (February 19, 1959).

[10] 69 Stat. 49 (1955), 70 Stat. 591 (1956).

in the first session and was the subject of hearings in the House in the second session.

Another cause for attention to certification was CAB's desire to obtain an amendment to the Civil Aeronautics Act to make it clear that the Board could grant limited-service certificates. Such certificates, limiting the number of runs or flights on a route, could be granted to supplemental-service carriers. Hearings on the proposal were held by the Subcommittee on Aviation on April 4 and 5, 1957.

The objective of the acts for financial support was to strengthen the smaller carriers. The guaranteed-loan act applied only to "local or feeder," metropolitan helicopter, and territorial service, and certain specified short overseas services.[11] The equipment-trust legislation[12] amended the Bankruptcy Act to provide that the title of an owner of air equipment leased or conditionally sold to an air carrier should not be subject to the provisions of the Act. Such protection of the interest of the owner in case of bankruptcy of a carrier was designed to make financing easier for the smaller carriers. The capital-gains bill was significant to the lines on subsidy, which are primarily the local-service lines.[13] The bill provided that capital gains from the sale of flight equipment, if reinvested or set aside for reinvestment in such equipment, should not be counted as income in determining the amount of subsidy to be paid.[14] Altogether, legislation on permanent certification, guarantee for loans, and equipment trust and capital gains materially strengthened the credit position of the local airlines.

A number of bills relating to airport construction were introduced in the Eighty-fifth Congress. The primary purposes of the bill passed in the Senate and the House in 1958 were to extend the time for making grants under the Federal Airport Act of 1946, as amended, and to increase the amounts authorized for grants. Such grant-making authority had been due to expire at the end of the fiscal year

---

[11] 71 Stat. 629 (1957).

[12] 71 Stat. 617 (1957).

[13] Whether Pan American World Airways would benefit was uncertain. It appeared that no domestic trunklines, and no international lines except those serving Latin America, would, under existing conditions, benefit from the act. See Senate Report No. 1144, 85th Cong., 1st Sess. (August 26, 1957).

[14] 72 Stat. 84 (1958).

1959. Certain changes in the definition of facilities on which national funds could be expended were included.

Although these several matters were of interest to many congressmen, their consideration in committees was confined in each house, in the Eighty-fifth Congress at least, to one working center—in this case the Committee on Interstate and Foreign Commerce in each house. This was not true of two other areas of interest: civil aviation's share of military air transport and safety.

A controversy over civilian sharing of military air transport (MATS) illustrates wide dispersion of activity. Prior to the Eighty-fifth Congress there had been a build-up of interest in diverting MATS traffic to civilian lines over a period of years. Favorable to the civilian carriers were reports of the Air Coordinating Committee (1955), the Hoover Commission (1955), and the Comptroller General (1955), as well as the position of the CAB.[15] Several committee reports in the Eighty-fourth Congress gave attention to the matter. The Senate committee report accompanying the Department of Defense appropriation recommendations for the fiscal year 1957 declared in favor of use of private carriers "to the fullest extent possible when it was more economical" and the similar House report suggested that the Air Force consider handling its business (MATS business) in such a way as "to assist in keeping the nonscheduled and other airlines in a reasonably sound financial and operating position."[16] In August, 1956, the staff of the House Committee on Appropriations was directed to make a study of MATS.

The staff report was made early in the Eighty-fifth Congress with recommendations for promotion of commercial airlift and for holding of military airlift to the minimum needed for war. The study was the basis for hearings, presided over by Congressman George Mahon (Texas), in a House subcommittee of the Committee on Appropriations on March 13, 1957.[17] The Senate report accom-

[15] See summary in *Military Air Transportation*, Subcommittee of the House Committee on Government Operations, House Report No. 2011, 85th Cong., 2d Sess. 34–37 (June 26, 1958).

[16] Senate Report No. 2260, 84th Cong., 2d Sess. (June 18, 1956), and House Report No. 2104, 84th Cong., 2d Sess. (May 3, 1956).

[17] "Department of Defense Appropriations for 1958," *Hearings before Subcommittee of the House Appropriations Committee*, Part 2, 85th Cong., 1st Sess. (February and March, 1957).

panying the Department of Defense appropriation recommendations for 1958 reaffirmed the policy statement of the previous year
and stated that it was "the wish of the Committee" that the Department of Defense reprogram expenditures for MATS so as to give, as
nearly as possible, 40 percent of the passenger and 20 percent of the
cargo business to civil carriers. The conference committee report,
while deleting the main substance of the Senate committee report,
"emphasizes the importance of the Senate committee report on
use of commercial carriers and calls on the Department of Defense to carry out the full intent."[18] In debate in the House of
Representatives, Congressman Flood discussed the matter with Congressman Mahon to make clear the intent of Congress.[19]

In January and February, 1958, the Military Operations Subcommittee of the House Committee on Government Operations held
hearings for fifteen days on "Military Air Transportation." Congressman Chet Holifield (California), chairman, announced that
the hearings were held because of opposition of commercial carriers
to the announced intention of the Air Force to undertake operation
of MATS aircraft with commercial crews under MATS direction.
At Holifield's request the Air Force postponed this program. In the
course of the hearings commercial carriers voiced opposition to
MATS operations, and Department of Defense officials defended
the operations at length. The history of the matter and the positions
of the parties were comprehensively summarized in a report of the
Committee on Government Operations, which concluded that the
Department of Defense should take immediate steps to "expand and
stabilize the procurement of commercial air service."[20]

In the meantime, dissatisfaction mounted in Congress over failure
of the Air Force to follow what was regarded, by some at least, as a
"directive" from the Senate Committee on Appropriations to reprogram on the 40–20 formula. Pursuant to a request from the Senate
Appropriations Committee, the assistant secretary of defense for
supply and logistics reported by letter of January 14, 1958, to Senator Carl Hayden (Arizona), chairman of the Appropriations Committee, on the first half-year (July–December, 1957) of MATS

[18] *Conference Report, Department of Defense Appropriation Bill, 1958*, House
Report No. 841, 85th Cong., 1st Sess. (July 23, 1957).

[19] 103 *Cong. Rec.* 7734–7735 (May 27, 1957).

[20] *Military Air Transportation* (1958).

operations. Senator Dennis Chavez (New Mexico), chairman of the Senate Subcommittee on Department of Defense Appropriations, replied that the report was not consistent with the request of the committee and reaffirmed the committee's intent. Thereafter, a letter from the department said that "the wishes of the Committee" would "be given fullest consideration," but a further report to Senators Hayden and Chavez in April sought to justify the failure of the department to reprogram MATS operations.[21] The Committee on Government Operations criticized the "military diehard position."[22] A special subcommittee of the Senate Interstate and Foreign Commerce Committee held hearings on MATS on May 19 and June 12 and 13. In these hearings Senator Monroney criticized MATS operations extensively. Also, he testified at the hearings on MATS conducted by the Department of Defense Subcommittee of the Senate Appropriations Committee. At these hearings, a letter was presented from Senator John Sparkman (Alabama), chairman of the Senate Select Committee on Small Business, favoring "set-aside of MATS business for the small-business element of the air-transport industry."[23] In these hearings, Senator Chavez, chairman, referred to the 40–20 formula and said, "This year, unless something is done, we will write it in the law. . ."[24] In the meantime, on the House side, Congressman Flood had circulated a questionnaire to airlines on their opinions on MATS, and had received replies which, as anticipated, were in favor of the business being assigned to them. A further review of the problem was made in the House Appropriations Committee hearings on the Department of Defense appropriations for 1959.

All in all, the support for greater use of private airlines was quite impressive. The Hoover Commission and official groups outside Congress, the House Government Operations Committee, and the

[21] On these events see "Department of Defense Appropriations for 1959," *Hearings before Subcommittee of House Appropriations Committee,* 85th Cong., 2d Sess. 908ff. (April 14, 1958).

[22] *Military Air Transportation,* p. 57.

[23] "Department of Defense Appropriation for 1959," *Hearings before Subcommittee of Senate Appropriations Committee,* 85th Cong., 2d Sess. 1198 (July 8, 1958). Sparkman's committee had been concerned with the problem in an earlier Congress.

[24] *Ibid.,* 1091.

Senate Appropriations Committee had taken a strong stand for larger use of private industry, and additional support had come from the House Appropriations Committee, Senator Monroney, and the Senate Small Business Committee. Yet the force of this pressure was blunted by activity in strategic centers related to another universe of public action—national defense. The Senate Preparedness Subcommittee recommended in January, 1958, that military airlift be built up.[25] More significant, the House Armed Services Committee was roused to defense of MATS. A few weeks after the conclusion of hearings by the Government Operations Committee a special subcommittee of the House Committee on Armed Services held hearings on MATS. With a reference to "offbrand committees," apparently meaning the Government Operations Committee, Congressman Mendel Rivers, chairman, emphasized that the Committee on Armed Services was the only committee that could sponsor legislation for the military. The subcommittee report argued "that the size and peacetime operation of MATS are purely military considerations which should be and are properly reviewed and authorized by the Congress by the same process used for all military requirements." The subcommittee heard sympathetically the military, impatiently the only industry spokesman, and reported unreservedly and positively in defense of MATS and its operations.[26]

Congressional committees often try to give directions or suggestions to administrators. Some in Congress considered the 40–20 statement in the Senate committee report in 1957 to be a "directive." To the military, on the other hand, the statement only required "fullest consideration" by it of the feasibility of transferring traffic but did not impair its responsibility for maintaining emergency airlift. The experience seems to illustrate that, in a contest between competing needs and viewpoints represented in legislative and

[25] This was pointed out by Congressman Mahon in "Department of Commerce and Related Agencies Appropriations for 1959," *Hearings before Subcommittee of House Appropriations Committee,* 85th Cong., 2d Sess. 121 (April and May, 1958).

[26] "Investigation of National Defense, Phase II," *Hearings before Special Subcommittee No. 4 of the House Committee on Armed Services,* 85th Cong., 2d Sess. (on MATS), particularly 132ff. (March 27, April 15, and July 16, 1958); *Investigation of National Defense, Phase II,* Report of the Subcommittee, 1958, particularly p. 8.

administrative centers, it may take a law, as Senator Chavez saw, to change the course of administrative action. The result of the activity in 1958 was a provision in the Department of Defense appropriation for 1959 setting aside $80,000,000 of MATS appropriations for commercial service with the proviso that small-business carriers be used to the "fullest extent found practicable."[27] This appears to be a compromise between military opposition to a percentage allocation and the commercial airlines' desire for more business. The effect and desirability of the provision remained for consideration in the succeeding Congress.

It may be noted that there were cases where "suggestions" of committees apparently had some weight. Reference has already been made to the institution of the General Passenger Fare Investigation. The administrator of CAA acknowledged that an agreement between the CAA and the Department of Defense on joint use of certain facilities resulted from a suggestion by the House Subcommittee on Appropriations for the Department of Commerce and Related Agencies.[28] Also, this House subcommittee recommended in its report in 1957 that a study be made of the classification of air-traffic controllers, and the CAA reported the following year that this had been done.[29] On the other hand, the subcommittee was dissatisfied that certain steps had been taken by the CAA which established or tended to establish a committal for expenditure, and it reminded the CAA's administrator that members of the subcommittee were available for consultation at all times.[30]

Safety was the most important aviation subject before the Eighty-fifth Congress. (The story of the enactment of safety legislation will be told in Chapter 4.) The necessary supplement to this legislation was appropriation of funds for construction and operation of airway facilities. This was being done in appropriations to CAA prior

[27] Pub. L. No. 85–724, Sec. 634, approved August 22, 1958.

[28] "Department of Commerce and Related Agencies Appropriations for 1959," *Hearings, House* 121.

[29] *Department of Commerce and Related Agencies Appropriations Bill, Fiscal Year, 1958*, House Report No. 308, 85th Cong., 1st Sess. 4; "Department of Commerce and Related Agencies Appropriations for 1959," *Hearings, House* 126.

[30] "Department of Commerce and Related Agencies Appropriations for 1958," *Hearings before Subcommittee of the House Appropriations Committee*, 85th Cong., 1st Sess. 288–293 (March, 1957).

to its replacement by the Federal Aviation Agency at the end of 1958.

In opening the hearings on the 1958 budget for CAA on March 14, 1957, Congressman Preston said, "The 1958 budget marks a new era in spending on the part of CAA."[31] The spending involved establishment of air navigation facilities and their operation. In regard to the first of these, the CAA had asked Congress for $250,000,000 over a five-year period in its submittal of 1957 appropriation requests, and had later returned to Congress with the request that the program be compressed into a three-year period. Congress responded with a $75,000,000 appropriation for the purpose. Subsequently, in August, 1956, the years-old controversy between the CAA and the military over whether to use the VOR/DME or TACAN system was resolved by a decision of the Air Coordinating Committee in favor of a combination of VOR with TACAN into a new system called VORTAC. Thereafter, CAA developed plans calling for an expenditure of $810,000,000 in the six years from 1957 to 1962. The first effect on the appropriation subcommittee is indicated by this statement from Senator Holland:

But I confess that the avidity of the approach to this thing is somewhat startling when you find that last year we were working on the entire program consisting of $250 million to be expended over 5 years which was regarded at the time as quite revolutionary, and this year you come back for $175 million in this 1 year, the second year of 5, and tell us the program is now up around $810 million.[32]

The subcommittee, recalling that money had been spent earlier for DME, was concerned over whether the new VORTAC system had been adequately tested. The skepticism of committee members was voiced by Congressman Cliff Clevenger (Ohio), ranking minority member of the House subcommittee, who had "a strong feeling that everything is not strictly 'Kosher' on that shotgun wedding between TACAN and our VOR."[33]

[31] "Department of Commerce and Related Agencies Appropriations for 1958," *Hearings, House* 254.

[32] "Department of Commerce and Related Agencies Appropriations, 1958," *Hearings before the Subcommittee of the Senate Committee on Appropriations*, 85th Cong., 1st Sess. 345 (April and May, 1957).

[33] "Department of Commerce and Related Agencies Appropriations for 1958," *Hearings, House* 529.

The increased requirements for operations were also astounding. For 1958, CAA requested funds for approximately 6,000 new employees and, for 1959, funds for about 5,000 more.

The requests for 1958 led Congressman Preston to allege that CAA officials wanted "to develop a utopian situation."[34] Yet the subcommittee saw "no alternative but to go along with the program for VORTAC facilities endorsed by the Executive Branch and all segments of the aviation industry,"[35] and Preston remarked a year later that the requests were for a technical operation on which the subcommittee had "to operate more on the basis of faith" in the responsible officials.[36] For 1958, the House subcommittee recommended, and Congress granted, the requests for VORTAC, a substantial part of the other increases for air facilities, and funds for over 4,200 additional employees. For 1959, the full amount of the requests—$230,000,000 for "operation and regulation" and $175,000,000 for air navigation facilities—was approved by both Appropriations Committees and by the Congress. In addition, the CAA received a supplemental appropriation of $11,735,000.

Some members of the House subcommittee thought that a portion of this cost should be recovered from users.[37] They expressed interest in the study of user charges being made by the CAA. Moreover, the subcommittees recommended and Congress provided for $21,500,000 of the 1958 cost and $16,500,000 of the 1959 cost of air facilities to be transferred from military appropriations.[38]

Influences on Congress: External and Internal

What was the array of forces, of identifications and antagonisms? Who backed and who opposed what? Who had the initiative? Who contributed to the results which were achieved?

Aviation is both a technological system and a control system, the

[34] *Ibid.* 262.

[35] *Department of Commerce and Related Agencies Appropriations Bill, Fiscal Year, 1958*, House Report No. 308, 5.

[36] "Department of Commerce and Related Agencies Appropriations for 1959," *Hearings, House* 111.

[37] See, particularly, Clevenger's and Preston's comments in "Department of Commerce and Related Agencies Appropriations for 1958," *Hearings, House* 226, 257.

[38] The subcommittees considered other items of expenditure for CAA, as well as CAB appropriations, granting funds for additional positions in both years.

latter composed of the institutions and groups which affect the management or manipulation of the technological system. The institutions and groups directly related to civil aviation form a complex, pluralistic net. The major elements in the net make a quadrilateral, with radiations from congressional, public executive, business and occupational, and community corners.

As has been seen, the public-executive influence was largely from the CAB, the CAA, and the executive overhead, with some military impingement, and the congressional influence was largely, but by no means exclusively, from four activity centers. The business influence was exerted through many individuals and associations but dominantly through the one association which represents the core of the industry—the Air Transport Association (ATA). This association represents the certificated industry, though some parts of this industry have also been represented through other associations. ATA is actively interested in every phase of civil aviation and engages in all the usual activities of trade associations, including research, promotion, and representation before government. It is competently manned and is respected by all groups interested in civil aviation. The occupational groups were represented by several associations, the most important of which was the Air Line Pilots Association. The final corner of the quadrilateral—the communities—were represented by some associations but primarily through the responsiveness of the congressional membership itself.

There were certain prevailing attitudes within the Congress. One was that airline traffic should be safe. In fact, there was universal recognition, inside and outside Congress, that safety was an element of the public interest. There was almost no recognizable spirit of compromise on this issue; whatever was necessary for safety must be provided. Within Congress there was mounting impatience over the failure of the administrative system to provide adequate safety measures and over delays in the Executive Office in the recommendation of solutions.

Second, there was interest in local airline service. Mr. James R. Durfee, chairman of CAB, frequently referred to the number of letters received from congressmen on route cases; and some congressmen testified in committee hearings in favor of the airport aid bill. A number sent letters to the House appropriations subcommittee in favor of appropriations sufficient to allow needs of their districts to be met; for example, Congressman Preston of Georgia, while presiding as subcommittee chairman, told Durfee that he (Preston) would soon be knocking at the door for better service at Savannah, Georgia. Many congressmen made statements showing concern over the service within their respective districts.

The interest in local service accounted in large part for the concern for the well-being of the airlines. The bills on capital gains, guaranteed loans, and United States-Alaska certificates all reflected an interest in local service through stable, financially sound airline companies. A parallel reason for concern for healthy companies was the ever-present consciousness of Congress of subsidy payments. There is strong desire on the part of Congress to avoid recurrence of subsidy need for the trunkline carriers. This apparently explains, in part at least, the interest in use of civilian carriers for military transport. In the case of capital gains the aid for airlines did, of course, mean increase in subsidy.

It would be incorrect to interpret the actions of Congress as showing an excessive industry orientation. Rather, the intertwining of local service, the avoidance of increase of subsidy, and the benefits of sound airlines as motivations for Congress is obvious. At the same time that Congress was showing concern for airline finance and traffic growth there were frequent expressions of dissatisfaction over failure of the CAB to exercise its rate-making powers for protection of the public.

There were scattered indications of some viewpoints at variance with the prevailing attitudes. Congressman Errett Scrivner expressed sympathy for the Air Force and MATS,[39] Congressman John Heselton (Massachusetts) opposed the capital gains legislation in a minority report from the House Committee on Interstate and Foreign Commerce,[40] Congressmen John Moss (California) and John Dingell (Michigan) submitted a minority report on the Airways Modernization Bill,[41] Senator Homer Capehart (Indiana) supported a fare increase for the carriers,[42] Congressman Preston spoke disparagingly of the Air Coordinating Committee's recom-

[39] "Department of Defense Appropriations for 1959," *Hearings, House* 831.
[40] House Report No. 980, 85th Cong., 1st Sess. (August 2, 1957).
[41] House Report No. 836, 85th Cong., 1st Sess. (July 19, 1957).
[42] 104 *Cong. Rec.* 1534 (February 3, 1958).

mendations on safety measures without reference to cost,[43] and
Congressman Preston and Senator Frank Lausche (Ohio) were
concerned over the failure to assign more of airport costs to the
users of airport services.[44]

There appeared to be no dissatisfaction in the Congress with the
basic features of economic regulation under the Civil Aeronautics
Act. The policies of promotion of air transport and protection of
the financial solvency of the airline industry embodied in the Act
were accepted. Moreover, there was no criticism of the commission
system of economic regulation. There were particular criticisms of
CAB's performance, but no expressions of dissatisfaction with economic regulation by a board which could be called an "arm of
Congress."

Among individual members of Congress only Senator Monroney
revealed comprehensively his basic ideas about air transport and
government's relation to it. He was sympathetic to the needs of the
smaller, weaker carriers, and had a particularly strong interest in
the local service airlines. He suggested consideration of more favorable route structures for these lines so that they could "work their
way off subsidy." He suggested also that routes should not be regarded as exclusive property of those presently serving them, and
that entirely new carriers meeting the required standards should
be considered eligible.[45] He believed strongly in liberal national
support for construction of airports and airport facilities, and recognized the need for industry cooperation, particularly on technical
problems in making safety rules. He believed that airline pilots
should be consulted more in airport planning and on other matters,
and felt strongly that the job performed by the tower operators in

[43] "Department of Commerce and Related Agencies Appropriations for 1958,"
Hearings, House 263.

[44] *Ibid.* 257, 265; *Operating the Jet: A Symposium Presented to the Subcommittee on Aviation of the Committee on Interstate and Foreign Commerce
Together with a Report of Progress and Development on Jet Age Planning by
the Civil Aeronautics Administration of the U.S. Department of Commerce,*
Senate Committee on Interstate and Foreign Commerce (Committee Print),
85th Cong., 2d Sess. 71–72 (May 9, 1958).

[45] For the foregoing views see "Miscellaneous Nominations," *Hearings before
the Senate Committee on Interstate and Foreign Commerce,* 85th Cong., 1st and
2d Sess. 47–49 (1958).

large traffic centers was of such importance and difficulty that they should be rewarded by supergrade classification. He expressed concern that too much political influence existed in selection of top CAA personnel. He had a strong belief in a great future for air-cargo transportation and showed his impatience with the CAB for its failure to encourage more effectively this development. He felt that Air Force planning for MATS did not meet the strategic military needs of the nation and that more of the business of air transportation could be given to civil airlines without interfering with military needs. He came to have a deep conviction that the Department of Commerce restrained the development of CAA's services and that no real solution to the problems of air space use and air traffic management could be effected without placing control of these in an agency which was free of departmental control. He wanted unified administrative control over air safety with adequate protection of civilian interests. Though opposing the CAB on some matters, he also defended it against attack.

Community interests, though represented directly by congressmen, were also presented through cities and associations of public officials. The bill for permanent certification of United States-Alaska airports was supported in hearings by cities of the Pacific Northwest. The bill (S. 3502) to amend the Federal Airport Act was supported by numerous letters from state and local officials and by appearances at committee hearings by the American Municipal Association, United States Conference of Mayors, National Association of County Officials, National Association of State Aviation Officials, Alaska Aeronautics and Communications Commission, and directors and other officials of airports. The bill to increase the federal share of money for acquisition of runways was supported by appearances from some of the same groups.

Air transport, in its institutional organization, reflects a pluralism of interests: international and overseas carriers, domestic trunklines, local-service carriers, supplementary-service companies, "general aviation" (business-owned and personal aircraft), pilots, stewardesses, airport operations personnel, and others. Within these groups there are real differences of interests. The industry is regularly or frequently represented at hearings by the Air Transport Association, Air Line Pilots Association, Association of Local and Territorial Airlines, Conference of Local Airlines, Independent

Airlines Association, Aircraft Owners and Pilots Association, National Business Aircraft Association, and the National Aviation Trades Association. Separate carriers also are represented at hearings. Almost invariably the ATA appears and, almost as frequently, the Air Line Pilots Association.

In the Eighty-fifth Congress, there was a substantial amount of unity in the positions of these groups. All were for safety, expanded civilian service, government aid through airport facilities, and government action to assure financial stability. In general, the industry was in accord with the position taken by the ATA on these matters. The ATA favored establishment of a new agency for control of air space and air traffic, extension and liberalization of provisions for airport construction, more MATS business for civilian lines, guaranteed loans for smaller airlines, and exemption of capital gains from income determinations for subsidies. It did not oppose the civil-penalties bills (not applicable to economic violations), which became part of the new Federal Aviation Act.

There were matters which were not of interest to all. The ATA, for example, took no position on permanent certification of United States-Alaska airlines or on the certification of all-cargo carriers. There were also some divisions within the industry. The ATA opposed authorization of limited-service certificates; supplementary-service carriers favored it. Though there was substantial unity on the major provisions of the Federal Aviation Act, the ATA opposed, and the Air Line Pilots Association favored, appeal to the CAB from decisions of the administrator on safety rules.[46] The ATA opposed, while the associations representing pilots, stewards, and stewardesses favored, the bills prohibiting the serving of alcoholic beverages on planes.

It is interesting to note that the peripheral labor and business groups normally supported the position of airline industry groups. AFL-CIO, with definite industry orientation, supported the airport construction bill, permanent certification of United States-Alaska carriers and domestic all-cargo carriers, the guaranteed-loan and

[46] *Hearings before the Subcommittee on Aviation of the Senate Committee on Interstate and Foreign Commerce*, 85th Cong., 2d Sess. 32ff., 90ff, (June 4 and 5, 1958); *Hearings before a Subcommittee of the House Committee on Interstate and Foreign Commerce*, 85th Cong., 2d Sess. 176ff., 215ff. (June 26 and 27, 1958).

capital-gains bills, and quick action for effective safety controls. The Transport Workers Union of America appeared separately at committee hearings in favor of some of these. The Highway Contractors Division of the Associated General Contractors of America and the American Road Builders Association appeared for the airport-construction bill. Plane manufacturers supported the guaranteed-loan bill and the Aviation Securities Committee of the American Bankers Association endorsed the guaranteed-loan and capital-gains bills. Wide indeed are the peripheral groupings interested in a single industry and its regulation.

The special contributions of the ATA to aviation policy were considerable. Mr. Stuart G. Tipton, its president, was the originator of the 40–20 formula for allocation of MATS business which the Senate Appropriations Committee tried unsuccessfully to put into effect. Although Monroney had already decided that a new federal aviation agency was needed, a move in that direction had to await organized industry support, which came in a change of position by the Board of Directors of the ATA in December, 1957. Thereafter, Monroney, lacking staff for the purpose, asked the ATA to prepare a draft of a bill for a federal aviation agency. That draft, though greatly changed in the first draft prepared by Monroney's staff, did serve as a point of beginning. Moreover, the ATA contributed to the marshalling of industry support for the Federal Aviation Act.

Within the executive branch there was the Administration position and the CAB position. The CAB was required to submit its legislative proposals to the Bureau of the Budget, but it did not consider that it, as an "arm of Congress," was bound to follow the Administration's position. The CAB drafted the guaranteed loan bill; it was opposed by the Department of Commerce, the Treasury Department, and the Bureau of the Budget. The CAB favored the extended airport-construction program; the Department of Commerce and the Bureau of the Budget opposed it, and the veto of the President killed it in this Congress. The CAB took no position on the capital-gains problem, because of an investigation underway into the matter;[47] the Department of Commerce favored it and the Bureau of the Budget accepted its position. The CAB opposed, but the Ad-

[47] In the Eighty-fourth Congress the CAB had been unable to take a position because it was split two to two.

ministration favored, the transfer of the function of making safety rules to the Federal Aviation Agency. The CAB favored legislation to state that the Department of Defense should not compete with commercial airlines; the Department was protective of MATS policies. It may be added that the Comptroller General also had an independent position: in opposition to the Administration, he favored the guaranteed-loan bill and opposed the capital-gains legislation.

The influence of the CAB—viewed often as an "arm of Congress" —was weak in the Eighty-fifth Congress. Its annual reports in this period contain a long list of recommendations of legislation. Some of the more substantial of these, such as the authority to regulate contract carriers and international rates, had been included in omnibus bills and given extensive committee hearings in the Eighty-fourth Congress, but were not considered in the Eighty-fifth. One which had been included in the omnibus bills, namely civil penalties for economic violations, was the subject of hearings in the Subcommittee on Transportation and Communications but faced the opposition of the ATA and was not reported from committee. The CAB's recommendation for limited certification of supplementary carriers was considered in Senate hearings in April, 1957, but got no further than this. The CAB opposed bills for permanent certification of United States-Alaska airlines and all-cargo carriers, the first of which became law and the second of which passed the Senate. The several measures for permanent certification, including those for local service and territorial airlines in the Eighty-fourth Congress, are instances in which Congress has overridden the policy of the CAB. A pending proceeding prevented the CAB from taking a stand on capital gains. Two measures which it proposed—guaranteed loans and continuation of members' terms until successors were qualified—did become law.

The most severe treatment of the CAB was in the provisions of the Federal Aviation Act. Seldom is a regulatory agency criticized as severely as was the CAB by W. A. Patterson, president of United Air Lines, in the Senate hearings on this measure, in which Patterson in effect dared the CAB to oppose the bill.[48] The CAB, never-

[48] *Hearings on S. 3880 before the Subcommittee on Aviation of the Senate Committee on Interstate and Foreign Commerce*, 85th Cong., 2d Sess. 72ff. (June 5, 1958).

theless, as is typical of administrative agencies, sought to retain its jurisdiction in safety matters. But the sentiment in Congress in favor of a single authority for making safety rules was so strong that the CAB's opposition was unavailing.

The initiative for the various measures which became law was scattered. The CAB, as appears above, originated the guaranteed-loan and term-of-office proposals. The Administration sponsored two civil-penalty, dealers' certification, and Alaska-airport bills which became law. The initiative on the capital-gains and the United States-Alaska–airlines measures came from within the Congress, the first being framed by Congressman Harris and the second coming from two members whose constituencies were affected— Congressman Joseph O'Hara of Minnesota and Delegate E. L. Bartlett of Alaska. The initiative for the federal airport amendments likewise came from within the Congress.

On the major pieces of legislation dealing with air traffic control —the Airways Modernization Act and the Federal Aviation Act— the initiative came first from the Administration and was later seized by Monroney. Although congressional committees had been studying the problem for several years, the Airways Modernization Act was the direct result of studies in the Executive Office and a recommendation from the President.[49] The Administration's bill provided for an Airways Modernization Board with tenure for three years to permit the executive to plan further organizational adjustments. To Congress this looked like an unnecessary amount of delay, and it provided in the Airways Modernization Act that the President should report a plan by January 15, 1959.[50] The accidents in 1958 and the opportunity to obtain industry support spurred Monroney to action. He took the initiative in getting a bill framed and in resolving the differences between his bill and Administration amendments thereto, and he pushed his bill to enactment in an unusually short period. His ability to get enactment of the bill resulted from a number of factors: the background of education of the Congress on the problems through successive hearings in previous years, the Brunswick accident, the support of the ATA and

<hr/>

[49] For a summary of these steps taken in the Executive Office of the President, see Message of the President to Congress, 104 *Cong. Rec.* 11149 (June 13, 1958).
[50] 71 Stat. 349 (1957), Sec. 7.

Mr. Patterson in marshalling public opinion in favor of action, and his own strategic position and competence in aviation matters.

Within the Congress, jurisdictional allocations determined the opportunities for influence. Although activity with respect to MATS and safety was widely dispersed, action was possible only on the initiative of the primary working centers. The control of these over their jurisdictions was jealously guarded. Rivers, it will be recalled, referred to "off-brand" committees. Harris severely criticized the report of the Antitrust Subcommittee, saying the report went beyond the subcommittee's function and that its conclusions were not supported by the facts. Spokesmen for the House Appropriations Committee opposed provisions of the Federal Airport, Airways Modernization, and Federal Aviation bills which invaded the jurisdiction of the Committee. On the other hand, Monroney, being a member of the Post Office and Civil Service Committee, was conscious of its sensitivity on supergrade positions, and informally cleared with the committee the provisions of the Federal Aviation bill which related to that matter.

On the whole, the consensus necessary for congressional action, when obtained, was achieved at the committee level and most frequently at the subcommittee level. A number of bills were passed without discussion and without a record vote. Even on major legislation the debate was short and the differences at this stage were few in number. However, in the case of the Federal Aviation bill, a solution was worked out on the floor of the Senate for a very difficult problem which had created a deep cleavage between the Executive Office and the majority of the Subcommittee on Aviation. The conference committees were much more important centers of decision on issues than were the houses. The record of the Eighty-fifth Congress with respect to civil aviation brings sharply into focus the influence over policy which may be exerted by a few individuals.

Conclusions

A number of conclusions can be drawn from the foregoing analysis of congressional experience with respect to civil aviation in the Eighty-fifth Congress.

1. Civil aviation, like any regulated service, is affected immediately and directly by the operation of three institutional systems— the industry, the executive-administrative, and the congressional.

Each of these is pluralistic, consisting of an aggregation of primary activity centers and peripheral influences. Each is within itself a complex of varied forces. And none of the three is self-contained. In spite of the distinctiveness of each arising from its own functions, habits, and motivations, there is interweaving of influences from all parts of the field of civil aviation, and from other fields of human endeavor.

2. The Congress contains one set of activity centers with respect to civil aviation. Some of these centers are specialized with respect to this subject (the Subcommittee on Aviation) or to this and related subjects (Committees on Interstate and Foreign Commerce, Subcommittee on Transportation and Communications, and Subcommittees on Appropriations for the Department of Commerce and Related Agencies). These are the primary working centers for civil aviation. There are other centers which occasionally focus attention on the subject or which affect it peripherally through consideration of matters encompassing but not limited to aspects of civil aviation.

3. The primary working centers and their leadership posts are strategic positions. Congress as a whole is a primary strategic position and reveals itself as such when it passes a law or resolution, but it is also a loose holding company within which working centers also become strategic positions; even within these centers themselves leadership posts (like that of Senator Monroney) develop into strategic centers of influence. The working centers and their leadership posts create opportunities for initiation, influence, and leadership. They differentiate the positions of congressmen and concentrate upon a limited number of them the responsibilities and opportunities with respect to a particular subject.

4. There is, however, considerable overlapping of jurisdictions and of interests among congressional centers. This leads to much duplication of work within Congress and for persons appearing before it. It also affects the impact of the primary working centers with respect to a particular subject. There are, first, the opportunities for conflict or lack of agreement among the primary working centers—between those in the two houses or between legislative and appropriation committees in the same house. There was, for example, in the first session of the Eighty-fifth Congress a lack of precise agreement between House and Senate appropriation subcommittees

with respect to MATS. There are, second, opportunities for conflict with other committees with different specializations and, hence, different orientations. Thus, while the primary centers for aviation are industry focused, those working on national defense are oriented toward the military services; the conflict positions with respect to MATS resulted from these orientations growing out of specializations in interest. On the other hand, work in different activity centers may have complementary effects. The work of committees— for example, Government Operations, Judiciary, and Small Business—which are led from a peripheral position into active consideration of aviation matters may have an educative and stimulative effect, resulting in activation of or support for the primary working centers. In sum, the congressional organization has created primary working centers for each subject, and leadership posts within these, but both must operate within a pluralistic system of multiple and overlapping jurisdictions.

5. The staffing of congressional centers is small in comparison with that of the industry and administrative centers. This leads inevitably to selectivity as to subjects of consideration and may lead to considerable dependence upon outside centers for information and technical assistance. Also, it places a limitation on the number of items which may be considered and acted upon in a session or term.

6. Congressional activity with respect to a field of policy and congressional oversight of administrative agencies working therein are spotty, spasmodic, and sometimes cursory. The working centers are equipped for intermittent intervention, not for systematic and comprehensive surveillance.

7. Nevertheless, the quantity of activity and the quantity of output of Congress with respect to even a relatively small subject, such as civil aviation, may be substantial, and the quality of the deliberations may be quite impressive.

8. The records of the Eighty-fifth Congress on civil aviation do not reveal substantial influence on policy from the working centers of Congress except through the enactment of legislation. One committee influenced the CAB to initiate a rate investigation; a House subcommittee on appropriations made suggestions which carried weight; another committee was unsuccessful in its efforts to obtain a reprogramming of MATS business.

9. It is, however, impossible to determine the influence exerted

through informal relationships. Those holding leadership posts in the primary activity centers are in frequent contact with administrators. The latter are hypersensitive to every real or imagined nuance of emotion and opinion in the occupants of the leadership positions. Congressmen expect deference and are upset if they do not receive it. Yet administrators have problems to solve and institutions to represent. Crosstalk may not solve the problems or break through institutional interests and habits.

10. Congress is materially dependent upon administrative organizations when it is considering technical matters. The effect of congressional supervision and restraint is severely limited, even on amount and uses of money, when the business of government is so technical that lay comprehension is difficult.

11. The primary working centers for aviation were obviously sympathetic not only to the aviation industry but also to public needs. This may be the anticipated result of the compromise system of private supply of service under public sponsorship and regulation.

12. As for civil aviation in the Eighty-fifth Congress, beyond the universal interest in safety the most influential public considerations were those arising from community needs and interests, and the greatest sympathy was for the industry elements most directly connected with meeting these.

13. Initiative for congressional actions may come from industry, executive-administrative, or congressional centers. This analysis illustrates both the multiple sources of initiative and the potentialities which still exist for initiative and leadership within the Congress. It may also indicate limitations on congressional leadership, for in the most significant instance the leadership within Congress awaited spectacular incidents and industry support and was dependent upon industry aid in obtaining public attention and support.

14. Theories concerning congressional activity must take account of the factors of pluralism in the industry and in executive-administrative and congressional institutions, and of multiple patterns of relationships among institutions and their components; of the specializations and strategic positions within the Congress; of the limitations on congressional oversight and the nature of intermittent intervention; and of the multiple sources of initiative and the com-

plex patterns of support and resistance in policy consideration. Any recommendations with respect to conduct of public business must be grounded in recognition of these present realities.

A Summary of Legislative Action, 1957–1958

Acts Passed

1957 P.L. 133, August 14, 1957, to establish Airways Modernization Board.

P.L. 307, September 7, 1957, to guarantee loans of certain air carriers for purchase of aircraft and equipment.

P.L. 166, August 26, 1957, to amend Section 401 (e) of Civil Aeronautics Act to provide for permanent certification of United States-Alaska air carriers.

P.L. 295, September 4, 1957, to amend Federal Bankruptcy Act to make equipment-trust provisions applicable to aircraft and air carriers.

1958 P.L. 726, August 23, 1958, to create a Federal Aviation Agency.

P.L. 373, April 9, 1958, to amend Section 406(b) of Civil Aeronautics Act to provide that reinvested capital gains derived from sale of flight equipment shall not be counted as income in determining subsidy payments.

P.L. 817, August 28, 1958, to amend Communications Act to authorize issuance of licenses to noncitizens for radio stations on aircraft.

P.L. 503, July 3, 1958, to amend Alaska Airports Act to extend period for which real property on airports may be leased.

P.L. 511, July 11, 1958, to amend the act which had authorized additional airport for District of Columbia.

P.L. 835, August 28, 1958, to provide for sale of property acquired for construction of Burke Airport.

Acts Passed Senate and Incorporated in Federal Aviation Act

S. 3016, passed Senate, March 3, 1958, to provide for issuance of dealers' aircraft registration certificates.

S. 1749, passed Senate, March 3, 1958, to amend Civil Aeronautics
Act to authorize civil penalties in certain additional cases.

S. 1380, passed Senate, March 6, 1958, to authorize civil penalties
for violation of security provisions of Civil Aeronautics Act.

S. 1718, passed Senate, June 26, 1957, to provide for continuance of
terms of members of Civil Aeronautics Board until successor appointed.

Senate Joint Resolution Enacted

P.L. 448, June 4, 1958, to authorize appropriation for meeting of
International Civil Aviation Organization in the United
States.

Rider, Appropriation Bill

In Department of Defense Appropriation Bill. Eighty million
dollars to be spent for civil aviation and small business, to be used
to the "fullest extent possible."

Vetoed

S. 3502 (and S. 3533 incorporated therein), to amend Federal Airport Act to extend time for grants, and for other purposes.
Vetoed, September 2, 1958.

Passed One House

S. 1474, passed Senate, April 18, 1957, to provide for permanent
certification of air-cargo carriers. Hearings, House, April
17, 1958.

S. 1423, passed Senate, April 4, 1957, to amend Sections 801, 802,
and 1102, Civil Aeronautics Act.

S. 2919, passed Senate, March 6, 1958, to amend Civil Aeronautics
Act to authorize free or reduced transportation for retired
employees of air carriers.

S. 1963, passed Senate, May 21, 1958, to increase penalties for giving false information concerning destruction of aircraft or
motor vehicle.

S. J. Res. 167, passed Senate, May 7, 1958, to direct study by the
commissioner of the District of Columbia of factors involved in construction of a heliport.

S. Con. Res. 72, passed Senate, March 17, 1958, covering congressional recognition of twentieth anniversary of civil aviation
under Civil Aeronautics Act.

S. Res. 87, passed Senate, March 8, 1957, favoring regulation of
aircraft flight over urban areas.

S. Res. 360, passed Senate, August 14, 1958, for postponing the CAB
investigations into air operations between the United States
and Alaska.

Reported

H.R. 4305, House Report No. 2693 on August 22, 1958, to reimburse
Ryan-Hemet (California) Airport for damages.

PART II

Case Narratives

CHAPTER 4

Policy Evolves: Congress, the Executive, and a Trade Association

This chapter tells the story of the background, drafting, and passage of a law of the United States. The law—the Federal Aviation Act of 1958—was an important one: It was a surge forward in the policy on aviation safety.

A law is a response to a situation in which needs or problems are thrust above a line of toleration of imperfections. Accordingly, in this story attention is given to the development of a situation in which the need for safety in the airways impelled men to search for establishment through law of new governmental arrangements for meeting the need. A law is also the result of the action of persons. The story which follows is told primarily in terms of the roles played by several groups of actors. The account shows how persons with different institutional connections, responsibilities, and abilities were drawn into, and contributed to, the flow of events which led to a law.

To meet the need for air safety many problems had to be solved. Some were minute, technical, and peculiar to air transport. Others were illustrative of major problems of government organization. One such problem was that of coordination of civil and military functions. The Federal Aviation Act was a response to the need for welding into a single system the civil and military controls over air traffic. The Act created a Federal Aviation Agency and gave it powers of rule making and management with respect to air navigation. In creating the Agency and defining its position and powers, it was necessary to find solutions for difficult problems of coordination between civil and military functions. These problems related to the

NOTE: Reprinted with minor modifications as published in 1961.

extent of the Agency's controls over military functions, the question of military participation in the Agency, and the extent and means of civilian control over the Agency. They are the same issues and problems which may be faced recurrently in the future.

There were other recurring problems of organization for which solutions had to be found. One was the question of location and responsibility of the Agency. Should it be outside the executive departments and what should be its relation to the President and to the Congress? This was the confusing issue of "independence." In addition, there were questions concerning the location of powers of rule making and investigation of accidents. The latter presented somewhat special issues, but the former raised the familiar question of whether rule-making powers should be vested in a single official responsible to the President or in an independent regulatory board.

Background

Safe and efficient use of airspace was the primary objective in the passage of the Federal Aviation Act. The airspace of the nation had become congested, and an effective system for control of the use of airspace by both civil and military pilots was required if air transportation was to continue to grow.

Air safety had long been a central objective in national policy. The first general national aviation statute was the Air Commerce Act of 1926. It provided for safety regulation by the Secretary of Commerce. At the same time, however, it authorized the Secretary of War to designate military airways, and it gave the President authority to make airspace reservations for national defense or other governmental purposes. Except for the authorities over airspace use vested in the Secretary of War and the President, the Air Commerce Act was superseded in 1938 by the Civil Aeronautics Act. This comprehensive act remained the basic statute on civil aviation until 1958. It provided for both economic and safety regulation. It created a Civil Aeronautics Authority (board of five), an Administrator, and an Air Safety Board, all to be appointed by the President with the advice and consent of the Senate. Congress delegated to the Authority responsibilities in economic regulation, including the power to grant certificates and permits for commercial service, and the duty of regulating domestic rates. The Authority was also delegated the basic safety functions, including safety rule making and the granting, suspension, or revocation of airman, aircraft, airworthiness, and air-carrier operating certificates. The safety rule-making authority included the prescribing of "air traffic rules" for "flights in air commerce." The Administrator, whose position was defined as being "in the Authority," was delegated authority to establish civil airways, to acquire and operate air-navigation facilities, and to train control tower operators. His authority included protection of safety on the civil airways and operation of control towers at major airports. With the passage of the Federal Airport Act of 1946 he received the additional responsibility of administering a system of grants-in-aid to states and municipalities for developing airports. The third agency, the Air Safety Board, was responsible for investigation of air accidents.

Modification of this organization and these allocations of authority were made in subsequent executive, legislative, and administrative actions. In 1940 President Roosevelt, through Reorganization Plans III and IV, (1) changed the name of the Civil Aeronautics Authority to Civil Aeronautics Board (CAB); (2) abolished the Air Safety Board and transferred its functions to the CAB; (3) transferred to the Administrator the authority to grant airman and other safety certificates, leaving in the Board the safety functions of rule making, suspension and revocation of certificates, and accident investigation; and (4) removed the Administrator from the CAB and placed him in the Department of Commerce where, as Civil Aeronautics Administrator, he would operate "under the direction and supervision of the Secretary of Commerce." In 1948 Congress authorized the CAB to delegate to the Administrator safety rule-making functions (subject to such provisions for appeal as the CAB would prescribe) and functions with respect to accident investigation. In 1950, by Reorganization Plan V, President Truman transferred all functions of agencies and persons within the Department of Commerce to the Secretary, who in turn, by Department Order 115, effective May 24, 1950, redelegated to the Administrator the authority theretofore exercised by him. In 1950 the Secretary of Commerce created an Under Secretary for transportation, in effect placing an intermediate layer of supervision between him and the Civil Aeronautics Administratior.

These developments beginning in 1926 resulted in a division of authority with respect to safety and matters affecting it. The Civil

Aeronautics Administrator granted airman, aircraft, airworthiness, and air-carrier operating certificates; these were subject to suspension and revocation, after hearing, by the CAB. The CAB delegated some safety rule-making power to the Administrator and reserved other rule-making powers. The Administrator investigated some civil aviation accidents, and the CAB, others; the military investigated military accidents. Civil airways (that is designated lanes between various points) were designated by the Administrator, while authority to designate military airways remained in the Department of Defense. The President could make reservations of airspace for particular uses. The CAB made air traffic rules for both civil and military aircraft, though the regulations permitted military authorities to authorize deviations; it had delegated to the Administrator of the Civil Aeronautics Administration (CAA) authority to designate restricted areas, but this authority had historically been exercised only by agreement in the Air Coordinating Committee. The military could establish military airports; the Administrator, after consultation with the CAB, could approve or disapprove expenditure of national funds for civil airports. Both civil and military authorities maintained control towers, though flight operations of all planes—civil or military—from civilian airports were managed by ground personnel of the Civil Aeronautics Administration situated in the Department of Commerce.

Coordination was sought through committees. Chief among these was the Air Coordinating Committee (ACC), an interagency body established by executive order September 19, 1946. It included, among others, representatives of the CAB, the Department of Commerce, and the Department of Defense. It served as a forum for discussion and agreement on many matters which were of interest to the several agencies. The committee, like the other coordinating committees, reached decisions only by unanimous consent.

Safety and efficiency in air navigation are dependent upon complex systems of navigation aid and control, built primarily upon a system of electronic communication to and from the pilot but including also elaborate ground facilities and traffic controls. Research and development have been important in the evolution of new and improved systems. These research and development functions have been dispersed among the three armed services, the civilian governmental agencies, and manufacturers and other private organizations. A problem of coordination arose as the separate armed services and government and industry agencies interested in civilian aviation searched for improved navigation systems in a period of rapid development of air use and of technological knowledge.

A number of committees struggled with the problems of coordination. For years a Radio Technical Committee for Aeronautics (RTCA) was the most effective unit for interservice and civil-military coordination. The committee sought to establish a common system. One of the most famous technical committees was "SC 31—Air Traffic Control," established by RTCA upon request of ACC, after a subcommittee of the House Committee on Interstate and Foreign Commerce had recommended the development of a single system. SC 31 submitted a report in 1948 on an all-weather traffic control system. Ultimately the chief of the coordinating committees, other than ACC, was the Air Navigation Development Board (ANDB), which sought to coordinate the research and development functions of the several types of users.

The navigation requirements of civil and military users were different. Thus the military services were concerned with security, that is with coding and other safeguards to prevent disclosure of position to the enemy. Also, the military, particularly the Navy, had to have a system which would meet the requirements of high-density traffic and of shipboard and other mobile installations. In general, such military requirements as these called for a more stringent system and for more expensive, heavy, and complex equipment than was required for civil aviation. The military was concerned that any common system should meet peculiar military requirements, while civilian aviation groups feared that the costs of such a common system, containing more heavy equipment than they would need, would be too great for them to bear.

By 1950 two major systems of electronic navigation had developed sufficiently for informed observers to discern a conflict arising. One was a system called VOR/DME—VOR to give the pilot azimuth guidance, DME to give him distance information. A rival system was TACAN. which performed both services. The two systems were not completely compatible. The CAA was developing VOR/DME and through fiscal year 1957 had invested approximately $54,000,000 on it. The Department of Defense was developing TACAN and had spent or obligated about $277,000,000 for the system by January 1, 1957. To many persons interested in civil aviation, the existence of TACAN, developed under security safeguards, first became known as a result of a press announcement in December, 1953. It was clear that establishment of either system would involve tremendous expenditures by both government and industry. The industry delayed use of the DME element because of uncertainties over whether it would be used permanently or supplanted by TACAN. Not until 1956 did ACC agree on a combination of TACAN and VOR for use by civilian and military aircraft.

The controversy which developed over these systems was aired repeatedly from 1955 in committees of the House of Representatives and led to widespread sentiment in Congress that more coordination was needed than could be achieved through committees. In the meantime, the advent of the jet plane made intolerable the old system of primary dependence on the pilot's vision for air safety (commonly referred to as "see and be seen"). Influential elements in the commercial industry, including the Air Transport Association (ATA) and the Air Line Pilots Association (ALPA) had come to favor "full positive control" over flights in airspace above certain minimum altitudes. This would be a system of air traffic control in which all aircraft operating in controlled airspace would be subject to procedures which caused them to be identified by ground controllers as to location and relationship to other aircraft, so that the controllers could maintain at all times separation between the aircraft. It was plain that such a system would be meaningless unless it could reach all planes in controlled airspace, both civil and military.

ENTER THE EXECUTIVE OFFICE

After his election in 1952 Dwight Eisenhower set up what became the President's Advisory Committee on Government Organization, composed of Nelson Rockefeller, chairman, Dr. Milton Eisenhower, and Dr. Arthur Flemming. The committee worked quietly, informally, and closely with the President and also with the Bureau of the Budget, which supplied staff assistance to the committee and to its staff director, Arthur Kimball. The committee recommended to the President that a study of transportation policy and program should precede a study of organization of government agencies in this field. As a result the President on July 12, 1954, appointed an Advisory

Committee on Transport Policy and Organization. Shortly after starting its work, this group narrowed its study to surface transportation. Seeing that aviation was not being covered, Rockefeller suggested that William B. Harding, an investment underwriter and broker with collateral experience as instructor in aeronautical science and in other aviation activities, be brought in for a conference. In the conference the needs for a study of air transportation were presented to Sherman Adams, assistant to the President. He questioned whether the study proposed was a proper concern of the Rockefeller committee, and it was decided to have a study made under the official sponsorship of the Bureau of the Budget.

The result was a formal request (May 4, 1955) from Rowland Hughes, director of the Bureau of the Budget, to Harding to serve as consultant on aviation problems. The communication set forth the responsibility of the bureau to review the government's programs dealing with aviation and its concern "that today's decisions be based upon an appreciation of the probable aviation requirements for the next decade or two." Harding was asked to provide recommendations on the following:

1. Should a study of long-range needs for aviation facilities and aids be undertaken?

2. What should be the coverage of such a study, if it should be made, including an indication of the special areas and subjects which seem to require particular attention?

3. How can such a study, if made, best be organized and conducted?

Harding formed an Aviation Facilities Study Group, consisting in the main of himself and six consultants on special aspects of aviation. A report for the group was sent to the Director of the Bureau of the Budget on December 31, 1955. It gave an affirmative answer to Hughes' first question, noting the absence of a "top-level systems study and master plan" for aviation facilities development. In reply to the second question it noted the need for study on "how to make more use of airspace by allocation and traffic control, . . . how to integrate civil and military expenditures, . . . how the cost should be financed from public and private sources," and "what kind of government organization is required to control use of the airspace" and protect federal interests in government-financed military and civil facilities. On the third question, it said that the study should be conducted "under direction of an individual of national reputation, with a broad understanding of civil and military aviation" backed by presidential authority and operating independently of existing organization.

On February 10, 1956, Edward P. Curtis was appointed special assistant to the President for aviation facilities planning. Curtis was an experienced executive in the Eastman Kodak Company. He had been a pilot in World War I and had risen to the rank of major general in the Air Force in World War II. The President ordered Curtis to direct and coordinate a long-range study of the nation's requirements for aviation facilities, to develop a comprehensive plan for meeting the needs disclosed by the study, and to formulate legislative, organizational, administrative, and budgetary recommendations to implement the comprehensive plan.

ENTER SENATOR MONRONEY

In the meantime Senator Mike Monroney of Oklahoma, motivated by different immediate considerations, had moved toward the center of the aviation stage. Monroney had served six terms in the House of Representatives, and while there had achieved distinction as vice-chairman of the Joint Committee on Organization of the Congress and coauthor of the Congressional Reorganization Act of 1946. In 1956 he was completing his first term in the Senate and had moved into a strategic position for influence on aviation matters.

Monroney saw great potentialities for the development of civil aviation and believed that the national government should take the lead in seeing that the facilities needed for this development were provided without delay. His first intervention in aviation matters as chairman of the Subcommittee on Aviation was to introduce and obtain the passage of a bill in 1955 which extended and broadened the Federal Airport Act.

At the time of the introduction of the airport bill Frederick B. Lee was Civil Aeronautics Administrator. Lee had been appointed to this position from the career service by President Eisenhower. During consideration of his 1955 bill Monroney had many telephone conversations with Lee, and Lee testified in the Senate hearings on the bill. Although the Eisenhower Administration had been unsympathetic to requests for federal grants for assistance to states and municipalities for airport construction, Monroney considered that Lee had been quite cooperative in supplying the subcommittee with facts and figures and in revealing needs for airport construction. Accordingly, when the Secretary of Commerce asked Lee to resign in the fall of 1955, Monroney was convinced that his cooperation on the airport bill was the reason for the "firing." Other members of the Committee on Interstate and Foreign Commerce held Lee in high regard, and on December 9, 1955, the day after Lee's resignation, Democratic Senator Warren Magnuson, chairman of the committee, sent a telegram to Monroney requesting that the Subcommittee on Aviation investigate the basis for the resignation.

In the meantime Monroney had become convinced that development of aviation facilities was being impeded by the supervisory structure in the Department of Commerce. To Monroney CAA was a "satellite" held under a Department of Commerce "umbrella." He considered that the effects of the creation of the Under Secretary for Transportation in 1950 were to degrade aviation one level in the departmental hierarchy and to increase the difficulties of presenting its requirements to departmental offices and to the Bureau of the Budget. He thought that, except for the brief period when Delos Rentzel served as Under Secretary, and beginning with a new incumbent late in the Truman Administration, the requirements of CAA for appropriations were treated unsympathetically by the Under Secretary. The only way that aviation could get attention to its needs, it seemed to Monroney, was to give CAA direct access to the Bureau of the Budget and the President. Accordingly, on January 5, 1956, he introduced his "spin-off" bill (S. 2818), which provided for removal of CAA from the Department of Commerce, CAA "to constitute an independent agency in the executive branch of the Government."

On January 4 Monroney had opened hearings before the Subcommittee on Aviation with the announcement that there was a dual purpose: investigation of the causes of the "firing" of Fred Lee and consideration of the bill for an independent CAA.[1] Several days of hearings were devoted to the "firing" of Lee, and Lee himself was the first witness. Monroney got from Lee statements that he

[1] "Study of Operation of CAA," *Hearings before a Subcommittee of the Committee on Interstate and Foreign Commerce, U.S. Senate on S. 2818*, 84th Cong., 2d Sess. (January 4, 5, 9, 10, 12, 24; February 3, 20, 21; March 5, 17; and May 28, 1956).

had told the Committee on Interstate and Foreign Commerce the previous year about the bottleneck existing on airport construction, and that the reason given for his resignation was lack of teamwork. Monroney focused the blame for the resignation on Louis S. Rothschild, Commerce Department Under Secretary for Transportation, and sought to show that it was the work of subordinate officials in the Department of Commerce and the "palace guard" in the President's office. Monroney next questioned Carlton Hayward, Commerce Department director of personnel, about clearances of appointments; he sought to show that political influence had affected appointments to the CAA and other posts in the Department of Commerce.

In the opinion of at least one major participant in the events of this period, the attack on Rothschild and the effort to discredit the methods of the Eisenhower Administration in these hearings damaged the chances for serious consideration of the Monroney bill. During the hearings the President appointed Edward P. Curtis special assistant for aviation facilities planning, and Monroney felt that this also helped to lessen the feelings of urgency for passage of his bill. Actually, however, there was at this time little enthusiasm —inside or outside Congress—for a separate aviation agency. The only support for the bill in the hearings came from Clarence Sayen, president of the Air Line Pilots Association, and Charles A. Parker, executive director of the National Aviation Trades Association. Stuart Tipton, president of the influential Air Transport Association (ATA), thought that the removal of CAA was not the answer, that the blame for budget limitations could not be placed at any one door, and that cabinet representation for CAA (through the Secretary of Commerce) was helpful. Simply achieving independence for CAA was acceptable to few in 1956 as a reason for organizational change.

Collisions Bring Action

On June 30, 1956, a TWA Super Constellation and a United Air Lines DC-7 collided over the Grand Canyon at 21,000 feet. A subcommittee of the House Committee on Interstate and Foreign Commerce quickly initiated hearings for the primary purpose of establishing the relationship of the tragedy to the problem of airspace use and air traffic control. During the hearings some witnesses, including Sayen and ATA's vice-president of operations and engineering, Milton W. Arnold, expressed strong dissatisfaction with the government's program of air traffic control, and Sayen complained of the inadequacy of CAA appropriations and the salaries of personnel for air traffic control.[2]

Simultaneously, fifteen days of hearings were held by a subcommittee of the House Committee on Government Operations.[3] This subcommittee's interest had been stirred by the Harding report of December, 1955. The chairman stated that the subcommittee was interested in the adequacy of the airport-aid program; in problems of air traffic control and air navigation aids generally (particularly the TACAN-VOR/DME controversy); in the effect of the introduction of jets; in the organizational structure within the executive branch on aviation matters; and in the operating efficiency of CAA. In these hearings Sayen argued that an independent CAA should be given statutory authority over airspace use for both civil and military aviation. This seemed to startle Arnold of ATA who did not see how this could be done, because it would run into security problems and get the Administrator of CAA into war plans.

These hearings revealed congressional impatience with delay in meeting airspace use and traffic problems. One member of the committee, Congressman George Meader (R) of Michigan, had introduced a bill (H.R. 11065) for a study of aviation facilities by a commission representing the Congress, the President, and private industry. Sayen saw no need for further studies, and Arnold thought that a three- or four-year delay for a study by a commission should be avoided. He was for doing something immediately to replace the Air Navigation Development Board (the coordinating group), which was, in his opinion, already dead.

THE EXECUTIVE OFFICE MOVES THROUGH NEW STAGES

Monroney's original effort was abortive; both it and the two

[2] "Airspace Use Study," *Hearings before a Subcommittee of the Committee on Interstate and Foreign Commerce, House of Representatives*, 84th Cong., 2d Sess. (July 7, 18; September 11, 12, 13, 1956).

[3] "Federal Role in Aviation," *Hearings before a Subcommittee of the Committee on Government Operations, House of Representatives*, 84th Cong., 2d Sess. (June 25, 26, 27; July 2, 3, 9, 10, 11, 12, 13, 16, 17, 18, 19, 20, 1956).

House committee hearings were only exploratory and educative. These were merely side shows. The big tent at this time was the Executive Office.

It will be recalled that the eight-month study of the Harding group turned out for the Budget Director in 1955 had stated only some broad subjects on which study should be pursued. In accordance with its recommendations, as we have seen, President Eisenhower had appointed Curtis as special assistant to the President for aviation facilities planning and had instructed him to direct and coordinate a long-range study and to bring in recommendations to meet the needs disclosed.

Fourteen months later, on April 11, 1957, Curtis presented an interim report. He found that the basic cause of the airways problem was that the military and civilian agencies which controlled air traffic were not provided with systems which were acceptable to them. Acceptance would depend on joint testing and evaluation by civil and military pilots and ground controllers. He found that there was "no lack of scientific ideas" but that the key to the difficulty lay in the lack of organization in the executive branch "to set the goals, to develop, and to select the systems and methods which will meet these goals." He noted that "the problem of modernizing the airways was clearly recognized in 1948 as one which required urgent action" but that the "actions taken had not been effective." To meet the problem of modernization which had developed by 1957, he recommended substitution of an Airways Modernization Board for the ANDB.

To implement this recommendation the Bureau of the Budget sent a bill to Congress which was introduced in both houses on April 12. The bill provided for an interim organization, called the Airways Modernization Board (AMB), to be composed of the Secretaries of Commerce and Defense and a chairman. The Board was to be a research and development organization. Until its termination on June 30, 1960, it would have responsibility to:

. . . develop, modify, test, and evaluate systems, procedures, facilities, and devices, as well as define the performance characteristics thereof, to meet the needs for safe and efficient navigation and traffic control of all civil and military aviation except for those needs of military agencies which are peculiar to air warfare and primarily of military concern, and select such systems, procedures, and devices as will best serve such needs and will promote maximum coordination of air traffic control and air defense systems.

It would have no responsibility for installing the systems selected or for joint management of civilian and military air traffic.

On May 10, 1957, Curtis transmitted to the President his final report on aviation facilities planning, and the report was released and became available to Congress on May 14. The report declared that there was a "crisis now in the making" which derived "from the inseparable mixture of civil and military interest in the same limited resource." It said that with the exception of the radar system the method for control was essentially the same as it had been two decades earlier, when air speed had been only 160 miles per hour. It recommended development of a plan which would include controlled separation of all aircraft above designated altitudes where visibility and speeds made see-and-be-seen flight unsafe; that funnels and cylinders of space be reserved for controlled separation of aircraft traveling from these highways of the air to airports; that airspace outside these highways, funnels, and cylinders be reserved for aircraft capable of visual collision avoidance; that aircraft be controlled by a central ground authority; that airspace be further divided into blocks of airspace defined electronically as a navigation system; that the controllers be guided by a mechanized operation of processing, storing, communicating, and displaying data.

Selection of systems would be the task of the temporary Airways Modernization Board. In addition, Curtis' final report recommended a special assistant to the President to develop plans for a permanent organization. It recommended that "an independent Federal aviation agency should be established into which are consolidated all the essential management functions necessary to support the common needs of the military and civilian aviation in the United States." The agency would be responsible for airspace planning and assignment; for "air operations, modernization of the airways, safety rule-making and enforcement;" for investigation of air accidents, including military accidents involving civil-military aviation or civilian property. The agency would absorb CAA, and the special assistant would take "prompt steps" to examine the feasibility of consolidating civil and military operations for air traffic control and for safety communications. The agency would be staffed jointly by civil and military personnel and should be headed by an outstanding civilian.

The Curtis report contained the foundation pieces for a new aviation agency. In effect the report recommended an independent aviation agency as part of a plan for modernization of the system of air traffic and airspace control. Included with this recommendation were features which would be central in the subsequent development of an aviation bill: (1) a single system of air management control for both civil and military aviation; (2) civilian control of the new agency; (3) staffing by civil and military personnel; (4) integration in one agency of rule-making, investigative, and administrative functions related to air safety.

Curtis' recommendation for an independent agency was not cleared with and approved by all parts of the Executive Office. It was not difficult for those familiar with the traditions of the Bureau of the Budget to predict its reactions to a proposal for another independent agency. A long concern of the Bureau had been to keep the executive branch as manageable as possible and to this end to reduce the number of independent agencies. Moreover, the establishment of a unified transportation agency had been envisaged in Bureau studies for more than a decade.

The framework for such a department had been partially developed by creating the post of Under Secretary for Transportation in the Department of Commerce and by placing under his jurisdiction such agencies as the CAA, Maritime Administration, Bureau of Public Roads, Coast and Geodetic Survey, and the Weather Bureau. Some officials in the Bureau of the Budget believed the next step would be to transfer to Commerce, under the new Under Secretary, the Coast Guard and certain executive functions of the Interstate Commerce Commission. One complication in plans for establishment of a transportation department was the opposition of some people in the Department of Commerce to a step which would reduce it from one of the largest to one of the smallest executive departments. Hence sporadic suggestions had been made for creation of a Department of Commerce and Transportation.

The Bureau of the Budget kept in close touch with the development of Curtis' proposals. Curtis often visited the offices of the organization and management staff of the Bureau, and discussed informally the things he was considering. The Bureau worked closely with him in the preparation of the proposals for an Airways Modernization Board. When he was putting the finishing touches on his final report, some officials of the Bureau tried to convince him that unified control of air navigation could be achieved within the Department of Commerce and that he would not be doing the President a service by recommending something that did not take into consideration the needs of all means of transportation. Curtis insisted that he had been made responsible only for aviation matters and that an independent agency would be best for aviation. The issue was not at this time pinned down and brought into focus for formal Executive Office consideration. Curtis had been brought in as a special consultant, and the report, which went to the President and to the Congress, was a Curtis recommendation.

CONGRESS PRODS THE EXECUTIVE

Monroney had been in frequent contact with Curtis and had repeatedly urged that a recommendation for an independent aviation agency be included in his final report. The recommendation in the report did not, however, fully satisfy the desires of some within and outside the Congress. These persons felt that there was unnecessary delay in the planning in the Executive Office. This dissatisfaction was expressed in the 1957 committee hearings on the airways modernization bill. Thus, for example, Magnuson, presiding, asked Curtis how long before a federal aviation agency could be established. When Curtis said a year or more, Magnuson commented, "By that time we will probably have a bureau of outer space established" [laughter]. Later, Monroney, while presiding, prompted witnesses into statements on need for prompt action. Thus he led Sayen of the Air Line Pilots Association into an elaboration of his view that there was need for immediate creation of a new agency which could put into effect any plans developed for modernized systems of air travel control. He also elicited from Sayen a statement that he felt the Senate should confirm the appointment of the Airways Modernization Board head, as this would reinforce civilian control.

Monroney decided to try to get a speed-up provision in the airways modernization bill. As a result, the Senate Committee on Interstate and Foreign Commerce amended the bill to include a new section:

Section 7. It is the sense of the Congress that on or before January 15, 1959, a program of reorganization establishing an independent aviation authority, following the objectives and conclusions of the Curtis report of May 14, 1957, entitled "Aviation Facilities Planning" be submitted to the Congress.

CAB MAKES A MOVE

It will be recalled that although the CAB had delegated to the Civil Aeronautics Administrator the authority to designate restricted areas of airspace, this authority was exercised by agreement in the interagency body, the Air Coordinating Committee, which included a representative of the Defense Department. The military had not admitted the jurisdiction of the CAB over airspace uses, and conflict was avoided by the unanimous-consent procedure of the ACC. The differences between the interpretation of powers by the civil and military agencies were brought to a head in 1957 when the CAB decided that designation of restricted air areas was rule-making rather than executive action. Hence, the CAB maintained, the procedure under which decisions on such designations were cleared by the Civil Aeronautics Administrator with the ACC violated the procedural requirements for rule making set down in the Administrative Procedure Act. Accordingly, on July 29, 1957, the CAB gave notice of a proposal to amend the Civil Air Regulations to state that designation of restricted areas was rule making and that the CAA Administrator would make his decisions without limitation of unanimous consent in the ACC. This assertion of unqualified authority over airspace use by the CAB, excepting only airspace reservations made by the President, gave rise to a controversy with the military. By the end of the controversy three things had been achieved: (1) the Secretary of Defense had acknowledged the authority of the CAA Administrator, under delegation from the CAB, to designate restricted areas; (2) the right of the military to authorize deviation from the Administrator's designations had been confirmed; and (3) the CAB and the Administrator had agreed that a reconstituted Airspace Division of the ACC should be the forum through which the Administrator would collect information and conduct hearings in proceedings for designation of restricted areas.

ATA TAKES A POSITION

On November 26, 1957, the Board of Directors of the Air Transport Association passed a resolution favoring the establishment of an independent agency to develop a common system of control over use of airspace by civil and military aviation, to make air safety rules, and to control airspace. Thereafter Tipton, president of ATA, telephoned Monroney and asked for a conference on legislative matters. At a conference in Monroney's office in December, attended by Tipton, Leo Seybold and Ed Rogers of ATA, and Monroney and his administrative assistant, Tipton reported the action of the ATA board. Tipton said that ATA officials had come to the conclusion that it was now necessary and legislatively feasible to move toward an independent CAA with the more comprehensive changes recommended in the Curtis report.

A BILL IS DRAFTED AND INTRODUCED

Notification of ATA's new position was the first of the events which led Monroney to a position of leadership in the passage of the Federal Aviation Act of 1958. Following the December, 1957, conference with ATA officials, Monroney contacted a number of persons in the aviation industry. He then called for a second meeting with ATA officials. At this meeting, held in January, 1958, with Tipton, Seybold, and Rogers again attending, Monroney reported that he had found consensus that the time was ripe for preparation of a bill. He then asked ATA to prepare a bill and laid down guidelines on its substance.

To draft a bill three kinds of specialized competence had to be synchronized. One was competence in understanding subject-matter needs—in this case the basic requirements for an adequate system of air traffic management. A second was competence in government organization planning, since the essential problem was to devise a plan of organization which would meet the requirements in aviation and fit into the organizational pattern of the government. A third was competence in draftsmanship—a task of phrasing and organizing the desired changes in conformity with legal standards.

Monroney had no technical specialists, either on air navigation requirements or organization planning, to assign to the drafting of a bill. Neither within his own office nor within the Committee on Interstate and Foreign Commerce were there persons who had the time and the knowledge to move quickly toward the framing of a bill.

One person who has observed Monroney's activities for years has remarked that even though Monroney had a leading part in the passage of the Legislative Reorganization Act he was slow to take advantage of the opportunities that act had provided to obtain adequate staff assistance, even in his own office. This, however, would be an incomplete explanation of the lack of staff assistance for the task of quickly framing an aviation act. Monroney's aviation subcommittee was new, and in the spring of 1958 had a number of items before it for consideration. Congressional subcommittees are not staffed to handle more than a limited number of projects at one time, and even on these they often need a considerable amount of outside aid.

Monroney was to have the part-time assistance of two men in the drafting of a bill. Both were attorneys and, though neither began with great experience in aviation and organizational problems, both had quick grasp, were capable of working long hours, and were sensitive to Monroney's objectives. One of the two men was Administrative Assistant Thomas Finney, a young attorney from Oklahoma City. Finney had come to Monroney's office in February, 1956, during the hearings on the "firing" of Fred Lee. He returned to Washington in August, 1957, and began to be aware of the problems of airspace use and air traffic control in the fall of 1957. The other man was Robert Murphy, an attorney on the staff of the Senate Committee on Interstate and Foreign Commerce, who had first worked on aviation matters in the summer of 1957.

Beginning in 1958 another man began to work for the subcommittee. This was John Black, who was at the time a law school student. He worked continuously on the bill from the time of introduction until it passed.

Although these men were to be available to Monroney at a later stage, his only recourse for immediate and adequate assistance in January, 1958, was the Air Transport Association. The ATA had knowledge and technical competence for the task. Its organization included experts on every phase of civil aviation. Because government administration of aviation was splintered, the ATA was the most complete repository of knowledge on civil aviation problems in or out of government. Although its knowledge of military needs and its perspective on government-wide organizational problems were limited, the ATA team which worked on the aviation bill included experts in airline operations and legal experts. Three members of the team—Seybold, Robert H. Doyle, and William B. Becker—were also to be in frequent contact with Monroney's office during the later process of perfecting and passing a bill.

Monroney had two major objectives in mind. The first was to free the prospective agency from the dominion of the Department of Commerce, which he regarded as a ground-minded organization; the second was to establish a clear grant of authority to control the use of airspace by any users, civil or military. He told the ATA that he was anxious to confine the bill to these objectives, on which he hoped there would be consensus. His guidelines to the bill drafters included specific direction that the economic regulatory jurisdiction of CAB should not be disturbed, and Tipton, recalling the failure of omnibus bills for changes in economic regulation in the preceding term of Congress, directed his staff to stick closely to the central objective. It was agreed also at this time that the bill should be in the form of amendments to the 1938 Civil Aeronautics Act, supposedly an easier way to get a bill passed.

As the team started to put a draft bill together, Monroney informed Congressman Oren Harris, chairman of the House Committee on Interstate and Foreign Commerce, of the steps being taken.

Following conclusion in March of work on certain other legislation before Congress related to aviation, the ATA staff worked under special pressure to get a draft bill prepared for Monroney. After a succession of drafts had been prepared and dismissed inside ATA, one was sent to Monroney in April. His administrative assistant, Finney, then called Murphy to his office and advised him that Monroney wanted him to study the Curtis report and the ATA bill.

Until this time Monroney's objective had been merely to take steps which would speed the pace of the creation of an independent airspace and safety agency as envisaged in the time schedule of the Airways Modernization Act. But on April 21 a United Air Lines plane and a military jet fighter collided over Las Vegas. The two were flying under instructions issued from two sources, one military, the other a CAA control center.

This disaster led Monroney to feel the need for quick, positive action. Beginning a few days after the collision his calendar of appointments showed a succession of conferences with leaders of the airline industry and with public officials who had responsibilities relating to aviation. The decisive event in this series of conferences was a luncheon on May 1 with W. A. (Pat) Patterson, president of United Air Lines.

Patterson had been in airline work since 1929 and had been president of United since 1934. He had a paternal interest in the employees of the company and was proud that he knew personally the pilots and other personnel who had served for some period with it. He was deeply distressed that two collisions—Grand Canyon and Las Vegas—had occurred to United flights, killing the pilots and leaving their eight children fatherless. Patterson flew to Washington and first urged Tipton to get a draft completed promptly. He then lunched with Monroney and said in effect: "Look here, you must insist on this being done now. . . . And the day that you tell me you are ready to go, I'll work on this thing full time. I'll get out in the country, talk to aviation people, send out letters, contact editors, and build up support for it."

Monroney went directly from this luncheon to the Senate chamber and made a statement on the problem of unified control of airspace. He announced that he had "asked the staff of our committee, with the help of the aviation industry, to draft suggested legislation creating an overall modern aviation agency."

Another man who volunteered his services after the Las Vegas collision was Delos (Del) Rentzel, who after seventeen years in the aviation industry had been, successively, Administrator of CAA, chairman of CAB, Under Secretary of Commerce for Transportation, chairman of ANDB and ACC, and by 1958 president of Slick Airlines, a resident of Oklahoma City, and a friend of Monroney. Rentzel, like Patterson, was to give practically his whole time during the next three months to the aviation bill. While Patterson mobilized public support, Rentzel worked with Monroney's staff. He worked at any level—from pasting amendment drafts to breaking log jams. He became Monroney's expert consultant and confidential adviser. His prestige in the aviation community enabled him to take soundings in the industry and to link Monroney with Tipton, General E. R. Quesada (who by now had been appointed special assistant to the President for aviation matters), and others whose cooperation was needed. He also made available for typing and other services the facilities of the Washington law office which represented his firm.

The immediate aim after Monroney's announcement in the Senate was to get a bill ready for introduction. On Saturday, May 10, an all-day conference was held which was attended by Finney, Murphy, and Black for the congressional staff; Seybold, Becker, and Doyle for ATA; Del Rentzel; and Pat Boyle, general counsel of CAA. Finney had requested Boyle to attend, and Boyle had said he couldn't unless he got authorization from his agency. This permission was granted Boyle by William B. Davis, Deputy Administrator of CAA, the Administrator being absent from the city. Boyle had been invited because, as he was told, the Senate needed technical aid from someone who had had experience with the old legislation and knew what sections were obsolete or inadequate. Such technical aid to committees by administrators, after appropriate clearance, was not unusual. In this instance Finney, Murphy, and Black were getting their first intensive experience with the problems of airspace and air traffic control, and their dependence on the technical aid of the CAA general counsel was considerable.

At the May 10 meeting the group went over the ATA draft section by section and made many changes. It was decided that a revised draft should be circulated but that a draft of amendments alone would be confusing. So Rentzel volunteered to take it to his legal representative's office and with Black's aid prepare a comparative print (or Ramseyer, as it is called in the House of Representatives) of the amendments and the provisions of existing law.

While the comparative print was being prepared, conferences went on concerning particular sections. Participants report that literally hundreds of telephone calls and conferences were held with industry people and with officials of the CAB and other agencies. Rentzel was in the middle of these negotiations—contact man between Monroney and Finney on the one hand, and Quesada and industry people on the other.

A draft and a Ramseyer were completed by about May 20, the date of a new tragedy—a collision of a military jet and a commercial plane at Brunswick, Maryland. This tragedy set off speeches in the Senate and House, committee hearings, and action in executive departments and in the Executive Office. In Monroney's office the pressure for a bill was increased. The night of the tragedy the staff worked at three tasks: (1) with the cooperation of Peter LeRoux, assistant legislative counsel in the Senate, the draft of a bill was perfected; (2) a comparative print was readied for the printer; and (3) contacts were made to obtain additional sponsors for the bill.

As an article in *American Aviation* reported later:

It was well past midnight and the lights were burning brightly a few weeks ago in a small room high up in the Senate Office Building. Acrid cigarette smoke filled the high-ceilinged room as aides hurried in and out, legislative assistants pored over carefully wrought legislative phrases and a small coterie of professional volunteer advisors argued policies.

The article attributed the earlier "placid legislative situation" to an attitude of "Let's see what the White House comes up with first."[4] It stated that the decision for an all-out effort came only a few hours after the Brunswick collision on May 20 and that one reason for the haste was the fear of Monroney and Harris, with whom Monroney was in contact, that hastily prepared legislation would be introduced by angry legislators.

On the following day, May 21, S. 3880, the Monroney bill for an aviation agency with unified control over civil and military flight, was introduced in the Senate, and by the next day thirty-three senators were listed as cosponsors with Monroney. All members of the Subcommittee on Aviation were included, except Schoeppel. Also on May 21 the same bill was introduced as H.R. 12616 by

[4] "The Inside Story of the Aviation Act," *American Aviation*, XXII, No. 2 (June 16, 1958), 41.

Representative Oren Harris, chairman of the House Committee on Interstate and Foreign Commerce.[5]

ACTION IN THE EXECUTIVE OFFICE

To understand White House reaction to Monroney's bill it is necessary to review what had been happening in the Executive Office of the President since the passage of the Airways Modernization Act in August, 1957.

On August 17, 1957, in line with the recommendations of the Curtis report, President Eisenhower had appointed E. R. Quesada, retired Air Force lieutenant general, aviation expert, and Lockheed Corporation executive, as special assistant to the President for aviation matters, and "charged him with the leadership in securing the implementation of the Curtis plan of action."[6] Subsequently, Quesada was also made chairman of the new Airways Modernization Board and chairman of ACC. Thus he wore three hats. In the fall of 1957 he was absorbed in the work of setting up the Airways Modernization Board. He also had before him the problem of the location of a second airport for Washington, D.C., on which he reached a decision in December. Nevertheless, he had the responsibility for initiating the organization study needed to meet the requirement Congress had inserted in the Airways Modernization Act: namely, that a program establishing a federal aviation agency be submitted by January 15, 1959. To help him meet this deadline, Quesada brought in Ford Luikart to serve as staff director of a federal aviation organization study. Luikart began work on December 21, 1957, and was directed to complete his phase of the planning for an aviation agency not later than July 1, 1958.

After graduating in 1939 from Syracuse University's Maxwell School of Citizenship and Public Affairs, Luikart had served sixteen years in management activities in the national government. Thereafter, he had worked as a management consultant with a private

---

[5] Congressman Harris in an address to the House had pointed out on May 19, one day before the Brunswick collision, that the CAA had issued a report showing 971 reported near misses of planes in flight for the year 1957. That the CAA report would show an alarming number of near misses had been known months before by leaders in the industry and by government officials.

[6] Message of the President to the Congress, June 13, 1958.

firm. He was, therefore, a specialist in organization and management, not a specialist in aviation matters. In order to familiarize
himself more completely with the problems at hand, he decided to
make a study of all the functions dealing with the management of
air traffic in the national government, including civil and military
sides. He had substantially completed his analysis when the air
collisions occurred in April and May.

The immediate effect of the receipt of the Monroney bill in the
Executive Office on May 22 was to focus the issue on whether support should be given to an independent aviation agency.

At this time the President's Advisory Committee on Government
Organization and the Bureau of the Budget were moving forward
with plans for a department of transportation. Clearance had been
obtained for staff work looking toward preparation of a bill and a
reorganization plan, and it was hoped that by January, 1959—the
date set by Congress for a report on an independent aviation agency
—a way could be found to accommodate the idea of an aviation
agency with the broader plans for a department of transportation.
When the Monroney bill came to the Executive Office, spokesmen
for the Bureau of the Budget promptly noted that the establishment
of an independent aviation agency would delay, perhaps for years,
the establishment of a unified transportation agency. In the background, also, was the Bureau's reluctance to approve the establishment of yet another independent agency.

After the Maryland collision there was discussion in the Executive Office for about six days (May 23 to 29, 1958) on whether
support would be given to the proposal for an independent aviation
agency. Division of opinion in the office led to several conferences
with the President. The principals in these meetings with the President were Quesada and representatives of the Advisory Committee
on Government Organization, the Bureau of the Budget, and the
White House group working with the Congress.

Quesada was convinced that an independent agency (that is, one
located outside an existing executive department) was essential,
because the Department of Defense would never go along with a
proposal which subjected it to decisions by another department.
There was also realization in the Executive Office of the President
that, because of the collisions, so much momentum was behind the
idea of a prompt establishment of an independent agency that it

was questionable whether it would be possible to withstand the movement. Moreover, since the advocates of a department of transportation had no concrete proposal ready to submit, there was really no immediate alternative.

An amazing lack of opposition was displayed by two departments affected by the proposal. The Department of Commerce had already come to accept the idea of losing the civil aviation function, for this would be the result of the creation of either a department of transportation or an independent aviation agency. The Department of Defense recognized the need for common control over civil and military aviation. As a retired general, Quesada had good relations with the Department of Defense; he knew its people well and had their confidence. Throughout the deliberations of the succeeding weeks Quesada and Malcolm A. MacIntyre, who as Under Secretary of the Air Force represented the Department of Defense, worked in close cooperation and with mutual understanding.

The decision of President Eisenhower to support an independent aviation agency brought complete consensus on a main objective: the establishment of unified control over airspace and air traffic through the medium of an agency located outside the Department of Commerce. This consensus set the boundaries within which all remaining issues and problems would be considered.

By this time also there was consensus on another point: that action should be taken promptly. Shortly after he introduced his bill—the day after the Maryland collision— Monroney had asked the executive agencies to appear at hearings on June 6, but the Executive Office asked for an extension of time to permit consideration of the problems presented by the bill. It was under pressure to move quickly to the consideration of the detailed provisions of the bill.

Quesada did move quickly. After the Executive Office had decided its position, near the end of May, he went to Monroney's office and said in effect: "I am all for this; there are sections of the bill on which you shouldn't be expected to be expert, and there are sections we cannot be expert on. We'll prepare a draft with suggested amendments." He then directed his aides to get Kenneth McClure, expert draftsman in the Department of Commerce, someone from the Bureau of the Budget, Pat Boyle from the CAA, and an attorney from the Air Force and from the Navy to serve with Luikart as a task force to prepare proposed administrative amendments to the

Monroney bill. McClure, the legal expert, and Luikart, the organization expert, became the coordinators of this effort. Starting early in June, Quesada kept the members of the task force together for about ten days in an office adjoining his. When the group first got together it had the benefit of a working agenda prepared on May 31 by a task committee composed of Quesada; MacIntyre; Gerry Norton, Assistant Secretary of the Navy for Air; James T. Pyle, Administrator of the CAA; Luikart; and McClure.

While the drafting committee was at work, a meeting of the principals in the Executive Office was held to determine the content of the President's message to Congress. It was decided that the presidential message should refer to the background of developments on the problem in the Executive Office and should then set forth the main suggestions for content of a bill creating an agency for unified control of air-space use. The message was drafted under Quesada's direction and sent to Congress on June 13. It did not, of course, carry any reference to the issue which had arisen within the Executive Office. Nor did it contain any reference to the fact that Monroney had introduced a bill, an omission of which Monroney took no note in Senate committee hearings.

A draft called Executive Amendment No. 1 was completed by about June 6. This was in the form of suggested amendments to the Monroney bill. The draft was transmitted to Finney. A conference was held at the Executive Office the following day between Monroney's aides and the team which had worked under Quesada. This conference, called the Executive Office conference, will be described in the next section of this study after a review of the contents of the three drafts (ATA, Monroney, and Executive Office) which contributed to the version that would ultimately become law.

Bill Preparation: Three Versions

Having described the activities on Senator Monroney's side and on the Executive Office side, our story now pauses. On June 4, Monroney's subcommittee was to begin hearings on the bill he introduced just after the Maryland collision.

A perfected draft, generally satisfactory to the many interests and parties and similar in form and content to the final legislation, would not be attained until committee redrafts of the Monroney bill were completed. These redrafts would culminate in a much-amended version of S. 3880, which would be reported to the Senate by the full Committee on Interstate and Foreign Commerce on July 9. The many revisions to be made in the bill were a composite of suggestions and prints coming from many sources. This section of our study describes the versions of the bill that had been prepared by the three major sources.

The main contributors of drafts and suggestions were (1) the persons working around Monroney's office in the Senate office building, (2) those persons working around Quesada's office in the Executive Office of the President, and (3) the ATA team located in the ATA offices some four blocks away.

There was close liaison and friendly cooperation, in spite of some differences, between the ATA and Monroney groups. These shared an interest in the development of civil aviation. Monroney reached, however, beyond the groups represented in ATA, maintaining close contact with Sayen of the Air Line Pilots Association and with some people representing general aviation.

Prior to the Senate committee hearings Monroney flew to Houston to speak at the Aviation Writers banquet (May 28). At this meeting Monroney learned that there was considerable uncertainty among some general aviation groups as to whether they should support his bill. These groups feared that safety requirements to meet military and commercial airline needs would be too burdensome for the many other users of airspace, particularly private pilots and business aircraft. Monroney and Rentzel discussed the bill with these groups until early morning; they apparently succeeded in assuaging major fears concerning its effects on general aviation. That these fears were never fully dispelled was revealed in a critical editorial in *Business and Commercial Aviation* in July[7] and in a letter from the author of the editorial to Monroney on August 5, suggesting an advisory council to the Administrator as a means of providing access to him from all aviation groups.[8] Monroney approved this suggestion in his presentation to the Senate of the conference committee report.

Between Monroney's office and Quesada's, both the principals and the draftsmen came to share a strong mutual respect and co-

[7] "Does Federal Aviation Act Snub Civil Aviation," *Business and Commercial Aviation* (July, 1958), 7.

[8] 104 *Cong. Rec.* 15498–15499 (August 11, 1958).

operative personal relations. Monroney often talked by telephone with Quesada about major problems, and Finney and Murphy of Monroney's staff and Luikart and McClure of Quesada's staff were regularly in communication by telephone. There was, nevertheless, some strain between the Senate and the Executive Office groups. This can be attributed in part to institutional rivalry, accentuated by the fact that the two branches of government were controlled by different political parties, and in part to the fact that events had catapulted Monroney into an all-out drive for legislation at an earlier date than had been contemplated in Executive Office planning. The strain was due also to some fundamental differences arising out of the role of the Executive Office in representing the needs of the military arm of the government. In the background and frequently protruding into the discussion was a basic disagreement over the extent to which an agency of the kind being established should be "in the Executive Branch" or an "arm of Congress."

Each of the three main working centers was a focal point from which contacts radiated in and out from other centers. ATA sought to keep airline attorneys informed on developments. The task force at the Executive Office was formed in such a way as to keep contact with the groups and persons in the Department of Defense, the Department of Commerce, and the Bureau of the Budget who were concerned with the legislation. Also, this task force maintained contact with Senator Schoeppel, ranking minority member of the Subcommittee on Aviation.

The CAA participated in the drafting effort through the Executive Office, with Pat Boyle, its general counsel, serving as a member of Quesada's task force. The CAA's position was defined by that of the Executive Office, which had accepted a plan under which the CAA would in effect be expanded into a larger and more powerful organization with a new name, no longer under the Department of Commerce. The CAB, on the other hand, was not—under its view of its status as an independent regulatory agency—bound by the Executive Office position. It was unhappy over proposals which would take away its safety rule-making powers. It had presented its views to Monroney prior to introduction of his bill and would do so again at committee hearings, but the trend in events and ideas had pushed it to a side position, and an ineffectual one, in the discussions over safety functions.

There was substantial agreement on the fundamental purposes and on the primary means of achievement: a common system of control for civil and military aviation, extending to use of airspace and air traffic management; a single-headed agency located outside executive departments; civilian control and military participation; and initial decisions on safety rules to be made in the new agency (there was agreement on this at the three main working centers with some disagreement outside). The extent of agreement on these things and the accompanying sense of urgency brought about by air accidents set the stage for cooperative effort in solving problems of implementation.

To effect the major purposes hundreds of changes had to be made in the Civil Aeronautics Act, as amended. These included substitution of the words "Board" and "Administrator" for the many uses of the word "Authority" in the original act, change of many definitions, incorporation of changes made in reorganization orders, inclusion of many provisions with respect to housekeeping or administrative phases of the new agency's operation, and many substantive changes to define the powers of the agency with respect to airspace use and traffic control. It was decided early to take out obsolete provisions of the Civil Aeronautics Act, such as the grandfather clauses, and to incorporate changes effected through reorganization orders or statute since the Act was passed in 1938. Many of these matters caused considerable discussion. For example, ATA was so concerned over obtaining a definition of "navigable airspace" which with absolute clarity included all space involved in takeoff and landing, that its attorneys argued for its wording through an entire afternoon session with Finney and Murphy and pushed for a statement in the House committee report interpreting the intent of the language.

The final ATA draft which had come to Monroney in April had covered more than fifty legal-size sheets. The all-day Saturday session in Monroney's office on May 10, attended by ATA's and Monroney's working staffs and by the general counsel of CAA, had resulted in a revised draft. A section containing a definition of "United States" had been referred to the general counsel of CAA with the understanding that he would rewrite it in conformity with international aviation agreements. There had been discussion also on several matters on which no decision had been reached. Thereafter,

Finney and Monroney had penciled in many changes and had put together the draft which had been hurriedly introduced as S.3880 the day following the Brunswick crash.

During the consideration of revisions of S. 3880, Finney convinced Monroney that since it consisted of amendments to existing legislation it would be intelligible only to the few who studied it closely. Finney proposed that the bill should be changed to take the form of a complete rewrite of the Civil Aeronautics Act, as amended. A new Federal Aviation Act of 1958 would replace the old act. When Monroney accepted this suggestion, it was necessary for Finney and Murphy to begin with the Act of 1938 and incorporate the amendments which had been drafted and the amendments passed in previous years and eliminate many obsolete provisions. The result was to be a new basic aviation statute.

Although the bulk of the changes were only implementation of purpose or clarifications or minor adjustments to meet objections, there were others which were elevated to a different status either because they involved major issues of policy or because they became major points of contention. Consideration of these formed the main substance of the process of legislation as it unfolded from the presentation of a draft to Monroney by the ATA staff to the enactment of a law. It will be helpful to outline first the major provisions of the ATA, Monroney, and Executive Office drafts, and then to trace the consideration of differences through the successive stages in the legislative process.

THE ATA DRAFT

The ATA draftsmen began on the basis of the resolution of ATA's directors and Monroney's general suggestions. They also were familiar with the recommendations of the Curtis report on organization and functions of a federal aviation agency. The draft which was developed contained only a limited number of basic policy provisions:

1. It began with a foreword which stated the purpose:

To create an independent Federal Aviation Agency, to provide for the safe and efficient use of the airspace by both civil and military operations, and to provide for the regulation of civil aviation in such manner as to best permit its development and safety.

2. It defined the word "Administrator" to mean the Administrator of the Federal Aviation Agency, and provided throughout for transfer to the Administrator of the Agency the powers vested in the Administrator of CAA.

3. It gave a six-point declaration of policy for the Administrator and amended the declaration of policy for the "Authority" in the Act of 1938 to become, with some deletions, a declaration of policy for the "Board."

4. It provided with respect to the Administrator:

    a. For appointment without tenure by the President with the advice and consent of the Senate.

    b. "At the time of his nomination he shall be a civilian."

    c. "The Administrator shall make an annual report to the Congress."

5. It contained two provisions with respect to military participation:

    a. The declaration of policy included "The use of both civil and military personnel in carrying out objectives common to both civil and military utilization of airspace."

    b. Section 209(a) said:

The Administrator shall recognize that, while the Agency is a civil agency, his actions will affect and control both civil and military operations. He shall provide for participation by military personnel in carrying out these functions to such an extent and in such a manner as may be necessary to make certain that to the maximum extent practicable, both the interests of national defense and the national interest in safe and efficient civil aircraft operations are met. To this end, and with the approval of the President, members of the Army, the Navy, the Air Force or the Marine Corps may be detailed by the appropriate Secretary, pursuant to cooperative agreements with the Administrator, for service in the Agency to the same extent to which they may lawfully be assigned to such service in the Department of Defense.

6. It vested in the Administrator several functions not possessed by the Administrator of CAA:

    a. To establish "federal airways." This was a broadening of the authority of the Administrator of CAA to establish "civil airways." The Administrator of the new agency could establish both military and civil airways. The section on definitions also included substitution of a definition of "federal airways" for "civil airways."

b. To "develop long-range navigable airspace plans, formulate navigable airspace policy, and assign the use of all such airspace under such terms, conditions and limitations as he may deem necessary."

c. To "develop, modify, test, and evaluate systems, procedures, facilities, and devices" and select those best suited to coordination of air traffic control and air defense systems. This was the authority exercised on an interim basis by the AMB. The grant was comprehensive "except for those needs of military agencies which are peculiar to air warfare and primarily of military concern."

d. To "have authority to disapprove the location of military, civil and joint civil-military airports, or runway layouts therefor, so that aircraft operating from such airports and runways will not interfere unduly with the efficient utilization of the navigable airspace or with the present or planned air traffic control and navigation system. In exercising the authority granted in this section, the Administrator shall give full consideration to the requirements of the National Defense." [Existing law required approval by CAA only for expenditure of federal funds for non-military landing areas.]

e. To make air safety rules and regulations. This power, it may be recalled, had been in the CAB, except insofar as it delegated the power to the CAA.

7. It left substantially intact the division of duties between an Administrator and the Board on grant, suspension, and revocation of airman, production, air worthiness, and other safety certificates. The grant was determined by an Administrator and suspension (except for sixty days by the Administrator) and revocation were determined, after hearing, by the Board. Only the jurisdiction to alter or modify certificates was affected, this being transferred from the Administrator to the Board.

THE MONRONEY BILL

The Monroney bill, as introduced on May 21, had followed the general outlines of the ATA draft. But, in addition to a multitude of technical and minor substantive changes, it included a number of major additions or alterations relating to public policy:

1. The provision for military participation, which was to be a troublesome problem in the succession of drafts, was substantially changed. Consideration of military needs and problems by the Administrator and detailing of military personnel to his staff were still specified, but a key element in military participation was now to be a military adviser to the Administrator.

In order to insure that . . . the Administrator shall be properly advised as to the needs and special problems of the military services, the Secretary of Defense shall appoint a special military adviser to the Administrator, and shall detail such military personnel to such adviser as may be required for the proper discharge of his responsibility.

2. A provision was added accepting military administration in time of war.

The Administrator shall develop in consultation with the Department of Defense and other affected Government agencies, plans for the transfer of the Agency intact to the Department of Defense in the event of war, and shall propose to Congress on or before January 1, 1960, legislation providing for such transfer: Provided, that the President may effect such transfer by Executive order in the event of war prior to enactment of legislation for this purpose.

3. Additional clarification of the Administrator's control over airspace was added, especially in the declaration of policy for the Administrator and through addition of "use of airspace" in the planning responsibilities of the Administrator (Sec. 307) and of "efficient use of airspace" in the objects of air traffic rule making (Sec. 601[a][7]).

4. The proposal in the ATA draft for approval by the Administrator of *all* airport and runway locations was changed so as to require his approval only for military airports and for civil airports on which federal funds were expended, and to authorize his advice to any person, upon request, on the effects on airspace use of plans for other civil airports.

5. An effort was made to compromise rival contentions over rule making by a single officer or by the Board by providing for appeal from the Administrator's rule-making decisions, on the ground that

his rules "will impose substantial economic hardship on persons affected without sufficient cause."

6. The provisions in the Civil Aeronautics Act for suspension or revocation of aircraft, airman, and other types of safety certificates were changed to allow for suspension or revocation by the Administrator with appeal to the Board. Procedural safeguards at both Administrator and Board stages of consideration were included.

7. Provision was added for special boards of inquiry on major accidents:

In any accident which involves substantial questions of public safety in air transportation the Board may establish a Board of Public Inquiry consisting of three members; one member of the Civil Aeronautics Board shall act as Chairman of the Board of Public Inquiry; and two members representing the public who shall be appointed by the President upon notification of the creation of such Board of Public Inquiry by the Civil Aeronautics Board.

8. The Senate had passed bills for extension of civil penalty provisions of the Civil Aeronautics Act to all types of violations of safety regulations and to violations of security regulations relating to air traffic. The content of these bills was incorporated with the Monroney amendments.

9. In line with Monroney's belief in the high level of responsibility required by traffic management personnel, particularly tower operators at congested air traffic centers, provision was included for 175 supergrade positions (grades in the classified civil service at levels 16, 17, and 18) in addition to those authorized to be placed in such grades by the Classification Act of 1949.

EXECUTIVE OFFICE PROPOSALS

In the Executive Office the Monroney bill was regarded as highly unsatisfactory in many particulars. The most numerous of the objections to the bill related to the protection of the military function, but there were also strong objections to other features. The objections and the proposed remedies can best be summarized by reference to the seven sets of directives contained in a "Working Agenda for Legislative Drafting" and the amendments which were proposed in line with these directives.

1. The first directive was "Clarification of Executive Branch

status of FAA" through "Elimination of word 'independent' in title paragraph of bill" and "Provision for reporting to the President and through him to the Congress."

The Executive Office drafting committee left in the word "independent" but it inserted the words "in the Executive Branch" in the provision for establishment of the FAA (Federal Aviation Agency). It changed the provision for an annual report to Congress to provide for an annual report "to the President for transmittal to the Congress."

2. A heading on "Safety" began: "The general intent being to remove all safety functions from the CAB."

The drafting committee eliminated the provision for appeals to CAB in cases of economic hardship and the provisions for special boards of inquiry on accidents. Whereas the Monroney bill had left the power to investigate accidents in the Board and had added authorization for special boards of inquiry, the executive draft provided for investigation by the Administrator, with review of the record by the Board "to determine the probable cause or causes" of accidents. It added a section for joint civil-military investigations of accidents affecting both civil and military aircraft or involving a function of the Administrator and for supply of information by the military to the Administrator on accidents involving solely military aircraft.

3. On "Airspace Control," the primary directive was for "recognition of military exceptions."

In all of the discussions in the Executive Office the military raised no objection to control of airspace by a federal aviation agency. It did want a broad authorization for deviation from air traffic rules and wanted this to be in the statute. There was difference of opinion in the Executive Office both on the form of the authorization and on whether it should be by regulation or statutory provision. After much discussion a provision was added which followed closely the amendment to Part 60 of the Civil Air Regulations, effective April 1, 1958, which had been issued after settlement of a prolonged controversy between the CAB and the Department of Defense. The provision allowed appropriate military authority to "authorize deviation by military aircraft of the national defense forces" from air traffic rules in case of "military emergency or urgent military necessity." Prior notice was to be given to the Administrator, and "every reasonable effort" was to be made to consult with him in advance of such authorization.

In addition to this provision for "deviation," there was added a provision for the Administrator to grant "exemptions" from the requirements of any rule or regulation. This provision was not, however, considered to have any significant relation to the military problem. Boyle wanted it placed in the statute to meet a situation with which CAB and CAA had had experience: While CAB had statutory authority to make exemptions to economic rules and regulations, no statutory authority had existed for exemption from safety rules. Waivers to safety rules had been issued on the assumption that the authority to make a rule included the lesser authority to issue waivers. The exemption provision was added solely to clarify the authority previously exercised through waivers.

4. On "Military participation," the directives required "provision to be made for either Administrator or Deputy to be an active military person of flag or general rank" and "other language to be inserted to provide that the Administrator of FAA in staffing the agency shall give adequate recognition to military participation in positions of responsibility."

In line with these directives the drafting committee:

    a. Substituted a Deputy Administrator for the military adviser proposed by the Monroney bill.

    b. Dropped the provision in the ATA draft and the Monroney bill that the Administrator should at the time of appointment be a civilian and substituted a provision that appointment to either the office of Administrator or that of Deputy Administrator should not affect status in the Armed Services or pay and allowances payable to a commissioned officer of his grade and length of service.

    c. Reinserted in slightly amended form the ATA draft proposal [Section 209(a)] for military participation through detail of personnel.

5. With respect to "Transfer of functions," there was direction that the President should have discretion to transfer military functions to the agency, with gradual transfer allowed as far as was feasible, particularly with respect to operations outside the continental United States; also that plans for the wartime status of FAA should guarantee support and priority for defense requirements

and stability of personnel of the agency "so that it could perform in support of the military."

The drafting committee accepted a provision in the Monroney bill for transfer of military functions. It took out an amendment of the Civil Aeronautics Act in the Monroney bill which (through definition of "United States") would have given the agency jurisdiction over areas to which United States laws applied by international agreement, and substituted a provision allowing geographical extension of the agency's jurisdiction by presidential order. With respect to the agency's functions in time of war, the executive amendments did not provide for mandatory transfer to the military, as in the Monroney bill, but did add provision for a career service:

The Administrator shall develop in consultation with the Department of Defense and other affected Government agencies plans for effective discharge of responsibilities of the Agency in the event of war or other emergency, including establishment of a career service to assure the availability, responsiveness, and security status of essential personnel in such event, and shall propose to Congress on or before January 1, 1960, legislation for such purpose.

6. On "Airport construction," the direction stated that some control should be lodged in the Administrator over development of civil airports but that the Administrator's function with respect to military airports should be that of receiving reasonable notice of intent on the part of the military.

The draftsmen proposed that "no airport, civil or military, or missile site shall be established, or constructed, or any runway layout substantially altered unless reasonable prior notice thereof is given the Administrator so that he may advise as to the effects of such construction on the use of airspace by aircraft." This meant two changes in the Monroney bill: (1) notice to, instead of approval by, the Administrator of construction of military airports and (2) extension of the provision to include missile sites.

7. On "Civil penalties," the directives asked that these should not be applicable to military personnel, such personnel to be disciplined by the military establishments. The draftsmen met this directive by amendment of the provisions of the Monroney bill with respect to inspections, enforcement, and complaints.

The Executive Office drafting committee made some other

changes not set forth in the seven sets of directives. Among these were two which will be discussed subsequently, namely, addition of the words "by aircraft" in several places and substitution of "national interest" for "public interest" in many places where the latter term had been used. In addition to retaining the 175 super-grade positions, it also allowed the Administrator to fill 15 positions of a scientific or professional nature without regard to the Classification Act of 1949 but in accord with special laws governing such positions, and also to fill 10 positions at salaries up to twenty thousand dollars per year.

The Senate Committee Evolves a Perfected Draft

Monroney desired to hold hearings on S. 3880 promptly. Ordinarily executive agencies are heard first, but since these had asked for delay, hearings began with industry representatives on June 4. (Representatives of the following associations appeared at the hearings and in every case offered amendments: Airport Operations Council, Air Traffic Control Association, Aircraft Owners and Pilots Association, National Business Aircraft Association, National Association of State Aviation Officials, National Aviation Trades Association, Airline Stewards and Stewardesses Association, Air Line Pilots Association, and ATA. A pilot, an aircraft manufacturer, and presidents of airlines also appeared.) Executive agencies were heard by the committee starting on June 16. In the meantime the Executive Office had sent over the first draft of the executive amendments, and the President had transmitted his message to Congress.

Between June 4, when hearings began, and July 9, when the Committee on Interstate and Foreign Commerce sent to the Senate a report accompanied by its amended version of S. 3880, most of the outstanding substantive issues were settled. Many of the differences between the executive amendments and the Monroney bill were gone over in committee hearings, and others were considered without entering that forum. The decisions on the issues were made by Monroney. When these had been incorporated into a revised draft it was presented to the subcommittee and then to the committee for acceptance. Only two provisions were changed by the subcommittee and none by the full committee. The bill that the full committee was to report to the Senate would be essentially a Monroney bill, and the report which would accompany it would be a report written by his staff aides.

The clearest way to summarize this phase in the development of what was to become the Federal Aviation Act is to take each of the main issues or sets of issues presented and show the arguments, insofar as these can be reproduced from written records or memory of participants, and the decisions made as these were revealed in the bill finally reported by the committee.

Position of the Agency. Questions relating to the position of the aviation agency with respect to Congress and the President were vigorously argued in an all-day meeting on June 7 between the Monroney and the Executive Office staffs. This was the Executive Office conference, the meeting which dealt with differences between the Monroney bill and Executive Amendment No. 1, which Quesada's staff had sent to Monroney's office one day earlier. Present at the meeting were Finney, Murphy, Luikart, McClure, and representatives of the Department of Defense, the Department of Commerce, the CAA, and the Airways Modernization Board, with Quesada in and out as questions were presented for his reaction. (After this meeting two more drafts would be prepared in the Executive Office, culminating in Executive Amendment No. 2). The title paragraph of the Monroney bill had declared the purpose to be "to create an independent Federal Aviation Agency . . ." but the bill provided for appointment of the Administrator by the President, by and with the advice and consent of the Senate, and placed no limitations on the power of removal. To Monroney this word "independent" meant outside the Department of Commerce, not independence from the President. Finney and Murphy had spent an evening in the Library of Congress studying the literature on independent commissions, including the Myers and Humphrey decisions of the United States Supreme Court, and had reached the conclusion that the keystone of independence from presidential control was tenure. The question of whether tenure for a stated number of years should be given to the Administrator was discussed in the conference on the ATA draft in Monroney's office, and judgment on the issue was reserved. Some of the industry witnesses appearing in the subcommittee hearings wanted tenure of four to six years for the Administrator. But Finney and Murphy talked to Monroney, and he didn't like the idea of tenure. He was afraid that some Administrator might be a "lemon."

It is reported that "hours on end" were spent in the Executive Office in discussion of the problem. One result was the proposal for amendment of the Monroney bill to read: "There is hereby created in the Executive Branch of the Government the Federal Aviation Agency. . ." The words "in the Executive Branch" had been in the Monroney spin-off bill of 1956, but several committees of Congress had become increasingly assertive in recent years with respect to responsibility of regulatory agencies to Congress. The aviation agency was to receive the safety rule-making powers which had been vested in the CAB, a transfer of power which had not been included in the Monroney spin-off bill. Rule making was a function congressional committees had thought should be vested in "arms of Congress." It is not surprising, therefore, that the amendment proposed in the executive amendments set off an argument in the Executive Office conference. Finney objected to the words "in the Executive Branch." McClure insisted that they must stay. They argued over the applicability of the Myers and Humphrey decisions, and Finney warned that Congress would not accept the proposed change. Quesada was called in. He wanted the words included, and Finney told him of the anticipated opposition in Congress, particularly in the House of Representatives, where Finney predicted feeling on the issue would be strong.

Finney argued that there was no point in raising the issue, since tenure was not granted. This came to be the view of the working group in the Executive Office. Quesada, however, felt strongly on the issue, and the disputed words remained in the second draft of amendments sent from the Executive Office.

There was little discussion of the disputed words in the Senate committee hearings. Malcolm A. MacIntyre, Under Secretary of the Air Force, added the argument that serious constitutional questions would be raised if the power to set aside airspace reservations for national defense purposes (transferred by the Monroney bill to the FAA from the President, who had received it in the Air Commerce Act of 1926) were not placed in an agency subject to the direction and control of the President.

The words appeared in no congressional draft. Moreover, the word "independent" was left in the title paragraph in the drafts submitted from the Executive Office and was in all congressional drafts.

The same issue of agency position and responsibility was presented by differences over the reporting requirement. Finney and Murphy convinced Monroney that the change proposed on this in the executive amendments was meaningless, and it was adopted in the reported bill.

The President's power of appointment, without limitation by tenure provisions, confirmed his control over the agency. Nevertheless, in commenting on the transfer of safety rule-making authority from the CAB to the FAA, the Senate Committee on Interstate and Foreign Commerce, in its report to accompany S. 3880, affirmed: "It is distinctly not the intention of the present measure to make the Administrator of the Federal Aviation Agency in any way less responsive to Congress than is the present Board."[9]

One special safeguard for independence from control by any administrative or executive agency or officer other than the President was added in Monroney's office. It provided:

In the exercise of his duties and the discharge of his responsibilities under this Act, the Administrator shall not submit his decisions for the approval of, nor be bound by the decisions or recommendations of, any committee, board, or other organization created by Executive order.

This provision was designed to prevent subordination of the Agency to coordinating committees and further reflected the Monroney view of the meaning of independence.

Public vs. National. Another controversy over words in the Executive Office conference was over the choice between "public" and "national." Regulatory statutes have conventionally set forth the standard of the "public interest," and the Monroney bill followed the traditional pattern. The military think in terms of "national security," and in a number of places the executive amendments substituted "national" for "public." The argument in the conference did not change either side's position, for the second draft of executive amendments stuck with "national," but all congressional drafts and the Act used "public." However, a proposal in the executive amendments adding to the objectives of policy to be considered by the Administrator went into all subsequent congressional drafts,

[9] Senate Report No. 1811, 85th Cong., 2d Sess. 12 (July 9, 1958).

and into the Act itself, as "fulfill the requirements of national defense."

Safety Rule Making. The issues concerning administrative rule-making powers were argued extensively in the committee hearings. On these there was no opportunity for consensus among all industry and government parties.

The proposal of S. 3880 for transfer of safety rule making from the CAB to a federal aviation agency was vigorously opposed by the CAB. James R. Durfee, chairman of the CAB, presented arguments against the transfer. The chief argument was that "the formulation of basic regulatory policy involves a delicate balancing of rights and interests which is best accomplished by an independent tribunal responsible to the Congress." In answer Monroney sought to establish that there would be no substantial difference between the Board and the FAA. He queried:

. . . can you demonstrate any unusual degree of competence that would make removal of these powers detrimental to air safety when your entire Board has been appointed by the same President who would appoint the Administrator of this Agency, and where your entire staff is taken from the same type of Civil Service Register as is the staff of this new Agency we are creating?

Durfee thought there was superiority in a "multi-member agency" where "there would be a diversity of opinion, so that there would be removed the possibility of undue prejudice, undue predilection on the part of any single person in any of the areas under regulation." He referred to the fact that members of the Board could be removed by the President only "for inefficiency, neglect of duty, or malfeasance in office." Monroney thought that "aside from the tenure of office that the Board members have . . . there is very little degree of independent status that you can establish beyond that which the Administrator would have under this bill," and he minimized the independence of the Board by noting that the President could fail to reappoint. Durfee replied that for this "a very quick remedy would be to provide in the law that members of the Board be appointed for life."

Durfee argued that operational responsibilities should be separated from rule-making responsibilities "in order to be certain that the convenience of the operating agency did not become the principal objective of regulatory policy." He argued also that military participation in the agency would give the military a voice in rule making, if done by the agency, which other interested parties would not have; that rule making should be placed in an agency which could balance safety and other considerations; and that there had been no real division of authority in the past with respect to safety rule making. The right of appeal on economic considerations allowed by S. 3880 would not be a real solution; the Board would have lost its technical staff on safety rule making to the agency, and the agency would not have the competence to weigh the economic effects of rules.

No one supported the Board in its claim for retention of original jurisdiction in rule making. Administration witnesses thought that it was time to put an end to divided responsibility. Tipton thought experience had shown that separation of the making of rules and their administration had been a mistake. It had resulted in duplication of staff, confusion, and delay. Patterson gave support to the transfer proposal by assailing CAB. He cited rapid turnover of Board members—alleging that this made for incompetence—and proclaimed the competence of the technicians in CAA who would be absorbed in the agency. He was irritated by claims made in a speech by Durfee the preceding day and openly dared the CAB to oppose S. 3880.

There was difference of opinion on the provision in S. 3880 for Board review of the Administrator's safety rules on the ground of substantial economic hardship. The provision—not included in the ATA draft—grew out of a conference of Finney, Rentzel, and Sayen and had been sold to Monroney in lieu of a more comprehensive appeal contemplated by him.

Tipton disapproved of the provision. He feared "that because of the controversial character of the regulations almost all regulations of any consequence would be appealed." Monroney and Senator Smathers reminded him that deletion of the provision would leave an appeal on legal points only to courts, but Tipton insisted that ATA was willing to sacrifice appeal on wisdom of regulations.

In contrast to Tipton, Sayen wanted a right of appeal to CAB on safety regulations and did not want the right to be confined to economic hardship. His position reflected the strong personal interest of the pilots in protective safety regulations. He believed that if the Administrator's decision was final he would shrink from the heavy responsibilities forced on him by the conflict of interests and would procrastinate rather than put his head on the block on every rule he made. Some of the representatives of general aviation (that is, non-commercial, civil aviation) also wanted appeal, either on economic grounds or on this and additional bases. These positions reflected a fear that rules for air safety might be primarily adapted to the demands of the military and the large commercial companies and impose requirements which those in general aviation could not meet. Appeal to a second agency would provide another opportunity to avoid such deterrence to the development of general aviation.

The Administration's arguments against the provision for appeal were stated by James T. Pyle, administrator of CAA: (1) Congress had provided adequate safeguards against "arbitrary or capricious actions" in the Administrative Procedure Act; (2) the Board had been making safety rules without an additional level of review, except as provided in the courts; (3) there were many examples of delegation of regulatory authority to officials in the executive branch; and (4) the new agency could be expected to give consideration to the economic impact of proposed rules.

In the bill reported by the committee to the Senate the provision for safety rules to be made by the Administrator was retained, that for appeal to the Board was dropped, and a new provision was added to allow Board appearance and participation as an interested party in rule-making hearings by the agency. Mindful of Congress' many past delegations of rule-making power to commissions, the committee report explained:

The theory that rulemaking is to be done only by a body of judicially minded, disinterested laymen applies well in the field of economic regulation. There the problem is one of balancing competing business interests; technical problems, if existent, are largely incidental. The theory tends to break down, however, when applied to the promulgation of minimum aviation safety standards.

The report continued that such standards were determined principally by technical considerations and that there had been no area in which the Board had been "more completely dependent upon its staff of experts than in the field of safety rule-making." The committee thought also that "aviation safety was essentially indivisible." With reference to deletion of the provision allowing appeal, the committee stated that "in practical effect it would have allowed virtually all rules to be appealed."

Accident Investigations. Only during the appearance of Quesada at the hearings was there any considerable discussion of the allocation of responsibilities for accident investigation. Monroney sought to minimize the differences between his bill and the executive amendments on responsibilities of the Board and the Administrator in accident investigations. He thought that the Board would be freer than the Administrator to call in outside participants, and he and Quesada agreed that it should be "crystal clear" that there was a right to do this. Monroney thought that an investigation by the agency might sometimes be an investigation of itself and that this was reason for vesting the authority in the Board; Quesada thought this was a good point but that the accident-investigation powers could be placed in personnel separated from other personnel on the Administrator's staff. Monroney thought that the Board would be more impartial now that it would not be making safety rules. Quesada agreed but thought, nevertheless, that there were two functions in accident investigation—one technical and the other judicial. He felt that the Administrator's staff would be well qualified to accumulate the technical facts but that, to eliminate any appearance of whitewash, the determination of the cause of the accidents (called a judicial function) should be in the Board. Also, he would add to the Monroney bill a positive obligation on the part of the Board to determine cause.

Quesada's argument for the changes proposed in the executive amendment—accumulation of data by the Administrator rather than the Board and a positive obligation of the Board to determine cause—was rejected by the committee in its reported bill.

Quesada argued for deletion of the provision for appointment of special boards of review. He said the Executive Office had considered a permanent board but had decided against creation of another agency. He was concerned that authorization of special boards would create demands for their use "on an inappropriate number of occasions."

Monroney explained that he anticipated use of the special boards only in case of unusual accidents involving loss of many lives. The committee retained the provisions of the Monroney bill.

One set of suggested additions in the executive amendment was accepted by the committee. These were the provisions for joint participation of the Administrator and the military in investigation of accidents involving both civilian and military aircraft or of military accidents involving some function of the Administrator. The Monroney bill had included provisions only with respect to accidents "involving civil aviation." But in the committee hearings Monroney stated that he regarded the executive proposal for joint participation and free flow of information as a "very important amendment" that deserved "great emphasis."

Thus, on the two problems of rule making and accident investigation the committee, in its reported bill, accepted the ATA-Monroney-Executive Office position for transfer of original jurisdiction on safety rule making from the CAB to the FAA, over the objections of the CAB; accepted the ATA-Executive Office position against any appeals to the CAB instead of the position of ALPA, some representatives of general aviation, and the original Monroney bill, favorable to appeal, at least on some grounds; accepted the provisions of the Monroney bill on accident investigations, opposed by the Executive Office; and accepted the additions on investigation of accidents involving military planes proposed in the executive amendments.

Exceptions. There appears to have been no extensive discussion of the proposals in the executive amendments for exceptions to air traffic rules. MacIntyre stated in the hearings that the two proposals for "exemption" and "deviation" were essential to provide flexibility and merely gave statutory sanction to existing administrative practice. Pyle noted the need for exemptions on such things as "crop-dusting operations"—crop dusting being a small but significant activity for which Representative P. H. Preston (D) of Georgia desired authorization for exceptions.

Civilian Control and Military Participation. From the time the Curtis report set forth the dual objectives of civilian control and military participation, the problem of how to realize these objectives and how to accommodate one to the other confronted every planning and drafting group and was discussed or argued in one forum after another.

The necessity for military participation was admitted by all, but the vital reasons for it were emphasized, nevertheless, by Quesada and MacIntyre in the Senate committee hearings. The head of the FAA would have the duty of providing for airspace needs for national defense. Moreover, the two systems of air traffic control were to be welded together. This meant that at least a considerable part of the 18,500 officials and of the control towers, radar approach facilities, and instrument landing systems which had formed part of the traffic control system of the military would be phased into the FAA. Finally, the maintenance of this system in a state of readiness for war or other emergency affecting national defense was a basic defense need.

Outside the military there was concern over what Senator Schoeppel said was the sixty-four–dollar question: "What assurance do we have the military will not dominate this new Agency if joint participation is authorized?" At the same time the civilian groups saw a special advantage for civilian aviation in military participation. As Tipton stated it, they wanted the military to be "stuck" with decisions made by the FAA. This seemed to require, as Patterson said, that the military be on the inside looking out rather than on the outside looking in.

On the first day of the hearings Tipton stated that the problem was "by all odds the hardest organization problem in the bill." He said that he did not regard the answer of Section 208(a) in the Monroney bill as fully satisfactory. This was, it will be recalled, merely the ATA proposal for assignment of armed services personnel plus the addition of a special military adviser. Monroney, in turn, explained to Senator Schoeppel that he did not consider the bill as the final answer, that there would be much discussion on the problem with the military users, and that he hoped a common ground would be found during the hearings.

With one major exception, the common ground was found insofar as provisions of a bill were concerned. There was agreement that the military personnel should not be counterpart to the civilian personnel in the agency, that the military should be in the agency as participants rather than as advisers or representatives, that such

participation should be provided at the highest level of policy decision, and that the loyalty of the assigned military personnel should
be to the head of the agency. The means of providing the military
participation were those embodied in the executive amendments.
There was to be a deputy director appointed by the President with
the advice and consent of the Senate, instead of a military adviser
assigned by the Secretary of Defense. In words substantially similar
to the original ATA draft, it was provided that military personnel
should be used and that to this end the military departments,
pursuant to cooperative agreements with the Administrator, would
detail personnel to the agency. Appointment to the position of
deputy director or detail to the agency would not affect military
rank, emoluments, and the like. Finally, "No person so detailed or
appointed shall be subject to direction by or control by the department from which detailed or appointed or by any agency or officer
thereof directly or indirectly with respect to his responsibilities
under this Act or within the Federal Aviation Agency."

Monroney was concerned at the hearings over some special problems. He wondered whether a large number of military persons
would need to be transferred to the FAA. He wondered whether the
military participation would not be at the policy-making level.
MacIntyre replied that important policy decisions on local airspace
use would be made at regional offices, and General Curtis E. LeMay,
Air Force Deputy Chief of Staff, went further in insisting that
military personnel would be needed at field stations to operate some
of the transferred equipment.

Monroney had a great interest in the training of personnel for air
traffic control work, intensified perhaps by the location of the training center for civilian aviation personnel in Oklahoma City. He
feared that army personnel would be inadequately trained for traffic
control work and would be detailed for such brief periods that they
would be inefficient and lack loyalty to the agency. Executive witnesses replied that the Administrator could set standards, but Monroney wondered whether his control would be sufficient to prevent
much irregularity in qualifications. Executive witnesses also
thought there was no reason why details should not be for longer
than normal military assignments.

Where the hearings did not produce common ground was on the
means of providing for civilian control. To the executive group,

control by the President appeared to be sufficient; to Monroney, civilian status for the Administrator was essential. There was no discussion of the issue in the committee hearings, but the differences appeared in the drafts. The second draft of amendments sent by the Executive Office to Monroney dropped the provision of the earlier draft that appointment to the position of Administrator should not affect the status a man might have as a military officer. But the amended executive draft did not contain the Monroney bill provision that the Administrator should at the time of nomination be a civilian, while the bill as finally reported by the committee did retain this provision.

Transfer of Functions. Very troublesome was the problem of transfer of functions in case of war or other urgent emergency. The Monroney bill had added to the ATA draft a provision looking to mandatory transfer to the Department of Defense. Plans for this were to be submitted to Congress by January 1, 1960. Tipton, a witness from the Airport Operations Council, and other representatives of the civilian industry objected in the committee hearings to a mandatory requirement for transfer. The Monroney draftsmen were surprised to find that the executive amendments asked only that a plan for emergency administration be submitted to Congress and that nothing was said about transfer to military administration. This change was acceptable to Monroney.

But the omission of a requirement in the executive amendments for mandatory transfer to the military was based on the assumption that a special career service would be established for the FAA. This was to be included in plans to be submitted to Congress for emergency administration. This idea gave rise to a sharp exchange between Monroney and military representatives at the hearings. General LeMay pointed out that the personnel managing the air traffic system would have to report for duty if there was an alert. He insisted that civil servants could not be counted on in a danger situation. He thought, therefore, that the FAA personnel would have to be in uniform. This nettled Monroney, and MacIntyre explained that there was no magic in the uniform but that what was important was sanctions—some system of discipline which would ensure report to duty stations. Monroney wanted to know if the military was making a uniformed service and military discipline a condition for its support of the bill. MacIntyre said, "No." Monroney declared that rather than accept a uniformed and militarized career service, he would compromise on the objectives of the bill and take an integration of systems without an integration of personnel. The military would, under such a compromise, retain its control tower operators. Monroney summarized one attitude behind this position: "But the feeling of the committee, the members who co-sponsored this in the Senate, is that this would be a civilian agency and not a uniformed agency, and not subject to stratification by officers and enlisted men and all the noncommissioned ranks and things of that kind." On the other hand, Schoeppel had expressed his concern over the disciplinary and operations problems facing the military in a military emergency.

S. 3880, as reported by the committee, deferred resolution of the problem. It provided that the Administrator should, after consultation with the Department of Defense and other agencies, submit a plan for emergency operations to Congress by January 1, 1960. The provision said nothing about a mandatory transfer or a career service. The committee bill also provided for the Administrator to make a study of special personnel problems and make recommendations for legislation thereon to Congress on or before January 1, 1960. Among other things, he was to give "due consideration to the need for . . . special provisions to assure availability, responsiveness, and security status of essential personnel in fulfilling national defense requirements." The committee's report stated the belief that "appropriate protection for military needs can be accomplished without the militarizing of this essential core [air traffic control service] of the Agency personnel."

Airport Construction. An equally wide gulf separated Monroney and the military on the Administrator's power over airport construction, and on this matter decision could not be deferred to a later session of Congress. The difference in positions was pointed up in the committee hearings. Monroney believed that the system of unified control would be endangered if the consent of the Administrator was not required for use of public funds in construction or alteration of airports or runways, either civil or military. He had been impressed by Tipton's testimony on how the military had constructed an airfield in Louisiana with one runway leading immediately into the landing pattern of a nearby community airport. He thought the requirement for approval by the Administrator ought to be the same for a city and for the military. MacIntyre argued that there could be no control over private airfield construction or over the building of airports or runways by an agency like the Port of New York Authority without aid of federal funds. Monroney replied that the Administrator could not prevent them from building land facilities but could prevent them from using them, and MacIntyre questioned whether the latter authority was granted. MacIntyre sought to emphasize the constructive nature of the military proposal for notice to be given to the Administrator on construction of missile sites as well as airports and runways. He argued, however, that these were matters which went to the nerve center of national defense and that power to veto could not be granted to one having no responsibility for defense. He put forward a theory of administrative relationship: "Our position is that two heads of the agencies are coequal within the executive branch," that the one with primary responsibility could not be subjected to control by the other, and that differences between the two should go to the President. Monroney inquired whether in case of disapproval by the Administrator the issue might go to the Congress. This led to the following exchange:

Mr. MacIntyre: "Congress never gets into details."

Mr. Monroney: "Sir?"

Schoeppel showed interest in the issue which had developed. He asked LeMay whether the requirement for approval would "be an undue restriction or not?" The General was emphatic in his reply that it would, and Schoeppel stated that he appreciated those views and that this was a matter requiring consideration.

The matter was considered in conferences between Monroney and the executive group. At one time word reached Monroney's office that the military representatives had said they would oppose the bill if there was a requirement for approval. Calls from Monroney's office to the executive group led to a denial that this was true. But no compromise had been found by the time the bill was considered in subcommittee meeting.

The committee draft on S. 3880 still included a provision for approval or disapproval by the Administrator in all cases where federal funds were expended. In the committee, what amounted to two opposed theories on control of administrative action were advanced. Schoeppel argued that if the Administrator, having received notice of military plans for construction of airport, missile, or rocket sites, objected to these, he could appeal to the President. Finney, on the other hand, had come up with the suggestion that the issues be determined in the armed services committees of Congress.

The majority of the subcommittee sought an answer in two long provisions which incorporated the Finney suggestion. The first contemplated that instead of the Administrator approving or disapproving military plans he should assist the Congress in its determinations on carrying out authorized military projects. The provision was Section 308(b) and read:

The Administrator shall be informed by the requesting department or agency of requests to Congress for authorization of an appropriation, or for an appropriation, for the acquisition, establishment, construction, or substantial alteration of any specific military airport, landing area, rocket site, or missile site, and shall advise the appropriate committee of Congress as to the effect of such proposed acquisition, establishment, construction, or alteration upon the safe and efficient use of airspace by aircraft.

The meaning and intent of this provision was explained in the committee report:

Subsection (b) of section 308 is basically an adaptation of a standing rule adopted by the Congress which requires that acquisition of land by the military service, in amounts in excess of $25,000, must receive the approval of the Committee on Armed Services of the Senate and of the House of Representatives on a parcel-by-parcel basis (40 U.S.C. 551 *et seq.*). The general plans for a project for which the land is proposed to be acquired must be disclosed to those committees, together with an estimate of the total costs before authorization for such acquisition, either by purchase or lease, is given. Thus, subsection (b) provides that the appropriate committees of Congress be given the benefit of the Administrator's views and advice before acting upon a request for authorization or appropriation. Once the appropriate committees of Congress have given such authorization or made such appropriation for a specific project, the duty of the Administrator would be discharged.

The second provision was designed, according to the committee report, "to apply in those instances where the appropriate committees of Congress have not authorized or made appropriations for a specific project and incorporates the standing practice now followed by the Armed Services committees of both Houses with respect to real property transactions by the military departments." The second provision provided that no federal funds should be expended for any military airport, landing area, rocket site, or missile site (1) unless an appropriation had been made or authorized as provided in subsection (b), or (2) unless the Administrator approved. If, however, the Administrator disapproved or failed to act, the department or agency concerned could appeal to the armed services committees which could determine the question by concurrent action.[10]

In effect, these amendments provided that military plans could be disapproved by the appropriate committees of Congress or, if they had not acted, by the Administrator, subject to appeal to the armed services committees of the houses. The President was delegated no function with respect to the conflict between the Administrator and the department making the proposal.

Penalties. The committee revisions of S. 3880 accepted the proposals for exemption of military personnel and facilities from reinspection authority of the Administrator and for exemption of military personnel from the penalties and complaint procedures included in the bill.

"By Aircraft." The proposal in the executive amendments to restrict the application of the bill to control of use of airspace "by aircraft" was rejected. In the committee report it was noted that consideration had been given to redefinition of the word "aircraft" as contained in the Civil Aeronautics Act but that it had been concluded that the broad definition stated there should be retained so that the new jurisdiction of the agency, particularly over airspace, "should extend not only to vehicles commonly considered as aircraft, but also, during their flight through airspace, other vehicles such as rockets, missiles and other airborne objects."

Personnel. The executive amendments proposed establishment of 10 positions "without regard to the civil service laws" at compensation not to exceed $20,000. Monroney called the Executive Office and objected to creation of 10 political positions. The subsequent draft of executive amendments proposed 5, subject to civil service and classification laws except with respect to rate of pay. This draft was accepted by Monroney with change of the 5 to 10 and the

---

[10] An exception was made for completion of projects on which substantial work had been done.

$20,000 to $19,500. The proposal in the executive amendments for 15 special scientific and professional positions was also included. In accord with later drafts, both of the executive amendments and of committee prints on S. 3880, 100 rather than 175 additional supergrade positions were recommended.

Monroney was a member of the Senate Committee on Post Office and Civil Service, which had jurisdiction on salary classifications. Informally, he cleared the committee recommendations on salaries and supergrades with that committee.

The Senate committee report stated that the substantive changes made in S. 3880 by the committee were "principally those" recommended by the executive branch. It said the bill as reported differed from the executive proposals in only two important respects: on the Administrator's control over location of future military airfields and missile sites and on the primary responsibility for accident investigations.

If exception is made for the personnel problem, on which decision was deferred, this statement on the degree of consensus reached in approximately one month is supported by the analysis of committee consideration and choice on the preceding pages.

The committee submitted its report to the Senate on July 9. The report recommended enactment of the bill with the amendments reviewed above. The committee had held hearings from June 4 to 18. It had completed its study and recommendations for a basic revision of aviation law in a remarkably short time, judged by prevailing practice on Capitol Hill. One monument of the thorough consideration that the committee had compressed into one month was three large volumes consisting solely of the successive committee prints of the bill and amendments—and these volumes did not include either the hearings or the comparative prints. The sheer weight of the volumes offered some indication of the amount of committee study involved, not to mention clerical and printing work.

One reason the bill progressed so speedily was the sense of urgency felt by senators and representatives as a result of the two collisions and the subsequent press publicity given to the report the CAA had issued on the number of near misses. The fact that one of the collisions occurred near Washington added to the feeling of urgency. Also, there was a heavy and plainly spontaneous volume of mail from constituents who were concerned about air safety.

Many of these letters reflected the alarms expressed in newspaper reports and editorials.

Another reason for the bill's rapid progress through the committee stage was the fact that for six weeks members of Monroney's office staff had worked daily until long past midnight. They would have to maintain the pace for two to three weeks longer when the bill came up for one-day debate in the Senate and for committee consideration in the House of Representatives.

Senate Debate

On July 11, two days after the committee report had been approved, the majority leader of the Senate gave notice that the bill would be considered on Monday, July 14. The Senate disposed of the bill on July 14 with less than one day of debate. Monroney was the first to speak in the Senate discussion of the bill. He noted that the bill was "a complete codification of all the aviation law."[11] For this task, running to some 250 pages he said, he commended Murphy and Finney. He gave a "Big 4" outline of the purpose of the bill:

First. A Single Federal Aviation Agency, headed by a civilian administrator, who has the authority to allocate all airspace and provide for uniform air traffic rules.
Second. Within this agency the equivalent of the Air Modernization Board, operating to bring into being without undue delay the electronic and other devices to increase the safety and capacity of our airports.
Third. Accident investigation to remain in the Civil Aeronautics Board to insure an unbiased search for the cause of [air] tragedies.
Fourth. Adequate participation in our military authorities to insure that national defense needs will be properly safeguarded in the new civilian agency.

Monroney again repeated his criticisms of the organizational arrangements under which responsibility was diffused and the aviation agency subordinated within the Department of Commerce. He noted the general agreement on the bill except, as he said, for one matter, which was shortly to arise in debate.

Monroney was followed by Senator Edward J. Thye (R) of

[11] It should be said that no attempt was made to incorporate judicial interpretations of aviation law. The Senate committee report stated that there was no intention to disturb these interpretations, but that they had not been incorporated.

Minnesota, who expressed concern over the delegation of rule-making authority to the Administrator. He feared a "virtual dictator." Lake Central—an airline operating in his district—had by this time objected to this delegation in the House committee hearings, which had just begun. Thye had also a letter from the Air Line Pilots Association. Thye had an amendment prepared, but after a full explanation by Monroney of the extent of support given to the complete vesting of power in the Administrator, the amendment was not presented.

Senator John W. Bricker (R) of Ohio presented amendments to avoid conflict with a law passed a few days before on training of employees, and these were accepted by Monroney. Monroney offered a few technical amendments to the committee bill. Senator Frank J. Lausche (D) of Ohio got in some remarks about the need for private air carriers to contribute to building of airports and to payment for services rendered in aircraft direction and control. Senator Payne, Republican member of the aviation subcommittee, filed a statement of support of the bill without reservations. Senator Schoeppel declared his support except for one provision—that concerning location of airports. He had submitted an amendment which set off the only issue presented for Senate decision.

The Schoeppel amendment, as submitted originally, read:

In order to assure conformity to plans and policies for allocations of airspace by the Administrator under Section 807 of this Act, no airport or landing area, civil or military, or missile or rocket site shall be acquired, established, or constructed, or any runway layout substantially altered, unless reasonable prior notice is given the Administrator so that he may advise as to the effects of such acquisition, establishment, construction, or alteration on the use of airspace by aircraft.

In opening the discussion of the amendment, Schoeppel added to it the following: "In case of a disagreement between the Administrator and the Department of Defense, the Administrator may appeal to the President for final determination."

With the Executive Office group in the galleries and the Monroney aides on the floor, the Senators themselves now took the issue which had produced deadlock among the participants. In the debate they hammered out an answer.

Lausche, cosponsor of the Schoeppel amendment, and Thye supported the amendment. Senator Thomas H. Kuchel (R) of California wondered why the controls in Congress were not sufficient. He thought the Schoeppel amendment would in effect say to the military that it had to get, first, the consent of the armed services committees; second, that of the appropriations committees; third, that of the Administrator; and fourth, if the Administrator did not approve, then the approval of the President. Senator W. Stuart Symington (D) of Missouri declared in words that were to be repeated by others that "this is an administrative matter." He argued:

If the President, as Commander in Chief, could not decide on a question of this sort, after the Administrator of the new Agency had been raised practically to the level of the Secretary of Defense, then I would be worried about the future security of our country in the air-atomic age.

He and Schoeppel thought that Congress would still have opportunities to express its disapproval of proposed bases.

At this point Senator Joseph Clark (D) of Pennsylvania sought to reconcile the rival claims for presidential and congressional control, as these had been presented by Schoeppel and Symington on one side and Monroney on the other. Clark summarized the problem: "As a former executive, I am inclined to believe that this is an administrative function, not a legislative function. On the other hand, I am concerned that an attempt might be made to bypass the appropriate congressional committees."

He offered an amendment for the Schoeppel amendment which would add after the words "notice is given to the Administrator so that he may advise," the following: "with the appropriate committees of the Congress and all other interested agencies." Schoeppel was willing to accept the amendment. Then Senator Jacob K. Javits (R) of New York offered an amendment to the last sentence of the Schoeppel amendment. His amendment would allow the appeal to be taken to the President by either party, instead of only by the Administrator, as in the Schoeppel draft. He thought that one party should not be a plaintiff and the other the defendant, but that both should stand on a parity. Schoeppel accepted the amendment. Monroney then offered an amendment which would have the effect of removing appeal from the Administrator's decision on civil airports or landing areas supported by public funds.

Schoeppel then asked Monroney whether "if these changes are

made in the amendment will the Senator accept it?" And Senator
Monroney answered:

The amendment offered by the distinguished Senator has been changed
to provide an appeal, which up until yesterday the military was un-
willing to have, since it would be possible to override their wishes or
look at something they wished to place elsewhere. Secondly, there was
originally no reference to any right to come to Congress or any right of
the Administrator to make his views known to Congress.

He expressed his willingness to accept the Schoeppel amendment
with the changes offered by Clark, Javits, and himself.

The Schoeppel amendment, as amended and as ready for vote,
read:

In order to assure conformity to plans and policies for allocations of
airspace by the Administrator under section 307 of this act, no military
airport or landing area, or missile or rocket site shall be acquired, established, or constructed, or any runway layout substantially altered, unless reasonable prior notice thereof is given the Administrator so that
he may advise with the appropriate committees of the Congress and
other interested agencies as to the effects of such acquisition, establishment, construction, or alteration on the use of airspace by aircraft. In
case of a disagreement between the Administrator and the Department
of Defense the matter may be appealed to the President for final
determination.

Without objection, the Schoeppel amendment, as modified, was
accepted. This was the final round of the fight on this issue, for
except for the addition of the words "or the National Aeronautics
and Space Administration" after the words "Department of Defense" in the closing sentence, this was the solution to the problems
of conflict between agencies on airport and other locations and of
conflict between claims for presidential and congressional control
which went into the Federal Aviation Act. Language had been found
which accommodated rival claims and which preserved the positions
of all parties—the military, the Administrator, the President, and
the congressional committees. The merit of the compromise on the
day of its adoption was that it left all parties free to play a card each
time there was an issue on a military location. And when the impasse was broken by Clark's "all things to all contenders" solution,
both sides in the controversy thought that victory had been won.

The Bill in the House of Representatives

Consideration and action in the House was based at every stage on
Senate documents. A copy of the Monroney bill was introduced in
the House by Chairman Oren Harris of the Committee on Interstate and Foreign Commerce on the same day the bill was introduced in the Senate. Senate committee hearings were completed on
June 18, and on June 23 Senate Committee Print No. 1 was run off.
This contained the rewrite of the Civil Aeronautics Act and most of
the changes of the original Monroney bill made as a result of executive recommendations and committee hearings. House hearings
began on June 24. The aviation bill was passed in the Senate on
July 14, House hearings were completed on July 24, and the first
House committee print was dated July 29.

Yet House consideration of the bill was thorough. Congressman
Harris referred the bill to Allen H. Perley, House Legislative Counsel, for analysis. Perley studied the bill section by section and held
many conferences with those who had worked on it. After the
Senate had passed the bill, Perley and a law assistant and Tipton
and Doyle of ATA spent an entire Saturday going over the provisions of the bill—in the same basement room of the House office
building in which Tipton, as a government official, had assisted in
drafting the Civil Aeronautics Act of 1938.

House hearings were at least equally as exhaustive as those in the
Senate. Hearings were held on nine days during the period from
June 24 to July 24 and were conducted by the Subcommittee on
Transportation and Communications under the chairmanship of
Harris. Many of the same persons appeared, and they duplicated
arguments given before the Senate subcommittee.

The position of the new agency was repeatedly brought up in the
questions. Quesada and other representatives of the Administration
made it clear that they thought the Agency would be in the executive branch and under the direction of the President but that it
would be independent in the sense that it would not be within an
executive department. Harris said that it was not his intention at
all that the Agency be set up under the direction of the President;
Representative Kenneth A. Roberts (D) of Alabama thought it
should be out of the "realm of politics"; and Representative John J.
Flynt, Jr. (D) of Georgia thought that the head of the Agency
should be protected so that he could exercise his best judgment with-

out being dictated to by anyone. Flynt regarded the wide grant of rule-making power, subject only to appeal under standards of the Administrative Procedure Act, as quite exceptional. But in spite of these statements and apparent misgivings by some other committee members, the committee did not add any amendments limiting the President's power of removal or providing for appeal on rule making to the CAB.

The committee report said nothing with respect to independence, but Harris, in presenting the bill to the House, said the Agency would be "responsible both to the President and to the Congress." The committee made a change in the reporting requirements to emphasize this double responsibility. Whereas the bill as passed by the Senate provided for an annual report by the Administrator "to the President for transmittal to the Congress," the committee provided for such a report "to the President and to the Congress." In floor discussion Flynt explained that this was to ensure that the Administrator would not be restrained by the executive branch from reporting forthrightly to Congress. He said the committee thought this was very important in view of the delegation of powers of the legislative branch to the Agency. He concluded, "It is the legislative intent of your committee that the Federal Aviation Agency is now and shall be an independent agency of the Government, and not a part of the executive branch."

Another change made by the committee related to the qualifications of the Deputy Administrator. The committee, as Flynt said to the House, desired "to make certain that civilian aviation is not subordinated to the requirements of the military except in time of war." The Senate bill had provided that the Administrator at the time of his appointment should be a civilian. The House provision added that "if the Administrator is a former regular officer of any one of the armed services, the Deputy Administrator shall not be an officer on active duty with one of the armed services or a retired or resigned regular officer of one of the armed services." In using the terms "former regular officer" and "retired regular officer," this provision seemed to imply that a "retired regular officer" is not a "former regular officer." In doing so, it appeared to limit eligibility to the Administrator's position, making ineligible for that position a "retired regular officer" who had not by resignation become a "former regular officer." In other words, to be Administrator a retired officer would have to sacrifice his retirement benefits by resigning his commission.

A third change by the House committee was to strike out at three places in the bill the provisions for supergrades. Flynt explained to the House that it was the committee's sense that such positions should be justified as need arose. Representative H. R. Gross (R) of Iowa noted that such positions should be justified before the House Post Office and Civil Service Committee.

Certain minor changes were made, such as the inclusion, under certain conditions, of parachute jumpers in the definition of "airman" and the alteration of wording with respect to appeals on safety certificates from the Administrator to the CAB and to the courts.

The discussion on the floor was brief, and the committee bill was adopted without amendment on August 4.

Conference Committee Report and Passage of the Bill

The Senate approved a motion on August 5 to disagree with the House amendments and to request conference with the House. The conference committee met several times and took the following actions after varying amounts of discussion of the several House amendments:

1. *Accepted the House amendment on annual reports.*

2. *Accepted with slight clarifying language the House amendment on the qualifications of the Deputy Administrator.* There was much discussion of this provision in and out of the conference committee. The discussion centered on the effect of the provision in making Quesada ineligible for the position of Administrator unless he resigned his commission as a "retired regular officer." Finney suggested to Luikart and to Republican committee staff members that if the President intended to appoint Quesada to the position, an amendment should be offered which would save his eligibility without sacrifice of his military retirement benefits. Schoeppel, who was in a position to represent the Administration's viewpoint on the conference committee, did not like the provision but did not offer a substitute. The statement of the House managers in the conference committee report pointed out that the effect of the provisions was to ensure that the Administrator should be "a civilian in the strictest sense of the word" and that specifically he could not at the time of nomination "be on the active or retired list of any regular com-

ponent of the armed services or be on extended active duty in or with the armed services."[12]

3. *Compromised on the three provisions with respect to supergrades and special positions—providing, beyond those allowed under existing law, for 8 in a provision where the Senate had specified 15; for 50 in a provision where the Senate had specified 100; and for 10 positions at not more than $19,500, as had been provided in the Senate bill.* There was extended discussion on supergrades in the conference committee, with Harris expressing fear of the opposition of the chairman of the House Committee on Post Office and Civil Service to authorization of a large number of supergrade positions.

4. *Rejected the House amendment on parachute jumpers.*

5. *Modified still further the details of the appellate provision.* This provision had been the subject of discussion and amendment at earlier stages. The pilots were deeply concerned that adequate protection be given against unfair cancellation of their certificates. The original Monroney bill had transferred the jurisdiction for amendment, suspension, and revocation of all types of safety certificates from the CAB to the Administrator, but had provided that any person affected by an order of the Administrator could appeal to the CAB, and that the Administrator or any person affected by a decision of the CAB could appeal to an appellate court. A later draft dropped the right of appeal by the Administrator. The provision was rewritten in the aviation subcommittee which added some technical changes to the advantage of the person whose certificate was under consideration. The House put back a provision for appeal to a court by the Administrator from a CAB decision, but it restricted this appeal to "matters of law." The conference committee gave added protection to the pilot or other person affected by an order when it took out this provision for appeal by the Administrator and added the following: "In the conduct of its hearings the Board shall not be bound by findings of fact of the Administrator." The total effect of the several changes in the bill as it left the conference committee was to strengthen somewhat the protections for the person whose certificate was being considered.

The Senate approved the conference report on August 11, the

[12] After the passage of the Federal Aviation Act, Quesada was appointed to the position of Administrator and resigned his commission as a retired officer of the armed forces.

House on August 13, and the President signed the Federal Aviation Act on August 23.

Concluding Comments

1. Each story of the enactment of a law will reveal distinctive aspects of the process of legislation. Much has been written about the dependence of the Congress upon executive leadership. There was substantial executive contribution to the enactment of the Federal Aviation Act, but there was also a seizure of initiative and leadership by a person occupying a strategic position within the Congress. The Congress was dependent upon the executive branch in many ways, but resourcefulness and energy within the Congress were also significant. Much attention has been given also to decision making as a process of choice from among alternatives, and to the making of choices in a setting of conflict in which warriors are struggling for contending interests and viewpoints. There was necessity for choice and there was conflict among parties in the instance of the Federal Aviation Act, but there were also unity of purpose and congruences of interests which led to cooperation in the search for solutions and to accommodation of rival needs in order to achieve the consensus necessary to enact a law. Conflict and cooperation were intermingled, but the reach for consensus moderated the former and accentuated the latter. Much has been said also about the pressure of special groups for particular advantage. There was in this instance strong presentation of special need, but there was also a core of common interest which bound the parties and which seemed to accord with the general needs of the public and the nation.

Much study has been given to hierarchical arrangements for making decisions. There was in this instance authority within the Congress and the President acting together, but the Congress and the President in action were each a plurality of forces sharing influences with each other and with strategic centers outside the government. At this level of policy making and with the accompanying distribution of influence the search for answers to problems was essentially one of finding what other centers of influence would accept, that is, it was explicit or implicit bargaining.

Finally, much attention is ordinarily given to the activity of the principal actors in the legislative drama. This is true in this story also, for their activity was important; but the story reveals the great part which may be played in the process of legislation by staff aides and task forces composed of groups of specialists of various sorts, including specialists drawn from private organizations and interest groups.

All in all, this story illustrates the many-sidedness of the process of lawmaking and the possibilities of variation in the balances between executive and legislative leadership, between struggle and striving for consensus, between special interest and general purpose, and between staff aid and leadership of principals.

2. Some who participated in the work on the Federal Aviation Act referred to its passage in a summer span as a "legislative miracle." One may, without adopting such extravagant terms, recognize that it was a remarkable achievement. In three months and two days a bill was born, adapted into a revision of a major act, refined, and passed. Safety regulation was strengthened through uniting powers of control in an agency with high status; the CAB had lost its rule-making function with respect to safety to the new organization, and the military had yielded to an outside agency what Quesada had said could be an independent command position in time of war and what, short of war, might prove to be a very substantial restriction of its independence.

Nevertheless, the special circumstances accounting for the quick passage of the Act should not be overlooked. Safety was an objective on which there was common interest among travelers, pilots, companies, and the military. The overriding interest in the adequacy and the safety of airspace led to willingness to subordinate and compromise most other interests. There were dramatic accidents, in close succession, which spotlighted danger and need. Prior to these, congressional impatience over existing conditions had been growing, and the Curtis report had laid out the course for a new development. Among participants in the events, pettiness and striving for recognition were notably absent. Finally, the crucial points of difference were postponed. "Independence" was resolved by resort to ambiguities which permitted the President to regard the FAA as being "in the Executive Branch," allowed the Congress to regard the agency as owing special attention to it, and required the FAA Administrator to meet both tests of loyalty. Conflicts arising over military airport and missile locations were to be resolved by presidential or congressional committee action. More significant, the phasing of military facilities into those of the Federal Aviation Agency would be delayed pending resolution of the issue of the kind of personnel system which would suffice for national security. The passage of the Federal Aviation Act demonstrates the flexibility and resilience of the legislative system, but it also demonstrates that a law results from a special concurrence of setting, need, leadership, and common purpose, among other factors.

CHAPTER 5

An Administrative Center at Work: The CAB's General Passenger Fare Investigation

For over eighty years there has been government regulation of the rates of transportation and utility companies in the United States. The regulation has been based on the assumption that rates resulting from unregulated private enterprise would not always be in the public interest.

A twofold pattern of public regulation has evolved. First, the substance of regulation generally extends to setting maximum or minimum rates or both. The issues may relate to the level of rates, that is, to how high rates may go without being unfair to the public or how low they may go without endangering the solvency of regulated industries. Rate regulation may also extend to the structure of rates, that is, to determining what portion of total revenue shall be obtained from users of different types or quantities of service. Although public regulatory power may be exercised over both level and structure, the most difficult and persistent issues have related to the level of rates and chiefly to how high rates should be. This issue of level has, in fact, so absorbed the attention of regulators that issues of structure are frequently not given much attention.

Second, regulation is embedded in procedural rules and practices. Fixing rates for the future is normally referred to as a legislative function and is defined in the Administrative Procedure Act of 1946 as rule making rather than adjudication.[1] But rate making after "full hearing," says the Supreme Court, has "a quality re-

NOTE: Reprinted with minor modifications as published in 1965.

[1] 60 Stat. 234, Sec. 2(c) (1946).

sembling that of a judicial proceeding."[2] Legislatures generally require that rates be set after "hearing," and this is interpreted to mean a judicial type of hearing. This may not mean that all the procedural rules applicable to adjudication generally must be applied, but it does mean that the hearing must meet basic standards applicable to judicial proceedings.

The Civil Aeronautics Board (CAB) was created in 1938 to regulate commercial aviation, including rates for domestic transportation. In 1960, twenty-two years after the passage of the Civil Aeronautics Act, the CAB concluded its first comprehensive proceeding on the question of what level of domestic passenger rates would be reasonable.

This proceeding, the General Passenger Fare Investigation (GPFI), Docket No. 8008, dealt with the level of rates of trunkline carriers (the dozen companies supplying scheduled domestic service between major traffic centers). The story of the investigation reveals many features and problems that attend government regulation.

First, it reveals problems with respect to standards of behavior of members of regulatory boards, congressional committees, and parties affected by regulation.

Law requires that a decision such as that in the GPFI be made on the basis of facts in the record. The CAB is expected to avoid scrupulously any suspicion that its decision on that record has been affected by any outside influence. Procedure and practice insulate the examiner who has conducted the hearing against external influence. In the CAB's "Principles of Practice" is a provision that proscribes efforts by outside persons to influence decisions in quasi-judicial proceedings. Moreover, it is the usual practice of congressional committees to avoid questioning Board members as to their opinions on issues in such proceedings.

But should these same principles also apply to CAB decisions to institute or drop proceedings? Should Board members avoid unrecorded discussions with representatives of the regulated industry on matters of this kind? Should congressmen or congressional committees seek to influence such decisions? The GPFI presents a further question: whether a difference should be recognized between a de-

[2] Morgan v. U.S., 298 U.S. 468, 480 (1936).

cision to initiate or to drop a prosecution against an individual or corporation and a decision to institute or to refrain from instituting a general investigation? A federal court has drawn a distinction between a rule-making proceeding involving "resolution of conflicting private claims to a valuable privilege" and a matter in which "the Commission was seeking all sorts of advice and information preparatory to setting up a general nationwide rule-making proceeding . . ."[3]

These questions on proper conduct are related to another problem —that of congressional oversight. A number of regulatory boards have been established, and Congress has sought to make them independent of policy direction by the President. They are repeatedly referred to in Congress as "arms of Congress." What oversight, then, is appropriate for the Congress to exercise over regulatory boards like the Federal Communications Commission, the Securities and Exchange Commission, and others? Was the failure of the CAB to conduct a general passenger fare investigation over a period of years a proper concern for Congress, even though the level of rates to be set after investigation would be determined in a quasi-judicial proceeding? Is it appropriate for congressional committees to inquire into the reasons for conducting, or not conducting, such an investigation? If the answers are in the affirmative, then is it appropriate for members of congressional committees, to try to persuade an agency to take a particular course of action? What is the route to public responsibility? Complete independence? Congressional inquiry? Resolutions of Congress? Suggestions or pressure by committees or members of Congress?

Second, the GPFI illustrates the procedures of a regulatory agency. It reveals basic patterns and intricacies of procedure and some of the means developed for regulating, simplifying, and expediting proceedings. It also serves to focus attention on a difficult procedural problem in regulation: What should be the procedure for determining standards to guide the Board in rate making? Can

---

[3] Sangaman Valley Television Corp. v. U.S., 269 F.2d 221 (May 8, 1959), involving transfer of a television station, distinguished from Van Curler Broadcasting Corp. v. U.S., 236 F.2d 727 (1956), which held that ex parte calls and conversations in a general nationwide intermixture proceeding did not vitiate an assignment of a particular channel.

staff studies provide guides for the Board that will be useful in rate cases? Or is presentation of facts and arguments by interested parties essential for fairness and efficiency? If the latter method is used, should it be a shortened procedure, without some of the usual requirements of a judicial process, such as cross-examination of witnesses? Is there need for fashioning a type of process that meets more precise requirements than those for legislative hearings in general and yet is less meticulous and time consuming than a full judicial proceeding?

Third, the GPFI illustrates the complexities of the substantive problems faced by government in rate regulation. It shows some of the many difficult issues that arise in determining standards for setting the level of rates.

The GPFI had a double purpose—determination of standards and determination of whether rates should be immediately increased or decreased. The interest of members of Congress and of the CAB led to emphasis on standards for setting rate levels.

Finally, the GPFI story suggests broader problems of public policy than those mentioned above. Such problems include choosing a method of controlling an industry. One method is unregulated competition. Under this system the impersonal forces of the market are assumed to govern, except insofar as government may intervene to maintain competitive conditions or perhaps to cleanse the market of force and fraud. Another method is regulated competition, under which government may seek, through such means as control of entry, consolidations and agreements, and service rights, to determine the amount and conditions of competition. A third method is government rate regulation, under which some measure of government control is exercised over charges to be exacted for service. One or a combination of these methods may be selected or allowed to continue.

One question raised by the GPFI is whether the involvements of procedure and the complexities of rate making seriously impair the utility of rate making as a regulatory tool. If this be true, then two further problems appear: What means are available to make the tool more effective? Are the imperfections so serious that the tool should be used cautiously and even sparingly?

If rate making is selected as a regulatory tool, then there arises the need to find the appropriate balance between public and private responsibility. What degree of accuracy, and therefore of tightness, should characterize government rate making? Can dependence on rate regulation be reduced by encouragement of competition? How much discretion in rate setting should be left to private management in the interest of managerial flexibility and adaptiveness? What balances are feasible in a pattern of regulation designed to meet the rival objectives of (1) promotion of service and (2) safeguarding this service to the public at fair and reasonable rates?

In addition, the GPFI draws attention to the question of whether it is possible to establish standards that will have any lasting effect on rate making. As conditions in the economy and in an industry change, the special problems for which solutions must be sought change also, and the solutions of yesterday may become unacceptable. Parties may shift positions or insist on reargument on the standards that were established. Are regulators driven inevitably to seek simplification of their task by the setting of standards? Are they nevertheless forced recurrently to reanalyze standards as new conditions come into being and as the regulated firms accordingly find it in their interest to change their positions on how rates should be determined?

The reader should be told three things. First, the story of the GPFI is inherently complex. I have tried to simplify the account by explanations and summaries but not by omitting vital detail. Second, to simplify the account the discussion of substantive issues has been limited to standards for rate making. Analysis of figures on costs, revenues, and earnings is included only as these figures throw light on arguments about standards. No purpose would be served by analysis of the arguments of parties about the specific level of rates that should be set at the end of the investigation. Third, the objective is to challenge the reader with the issues, not to offer him the answers. He may be his own judge of these, and, indeed, of the possibilities for ever achieving conclusive answers.

Economic Regulation of Domestic Air Carriers

Promotion of service and stability of the industry have been the dominant objectives of government economic regulation of commercial airlines. The two objectives, conceived to be complementary but potentially in conflict, were embodied in the Civil Aeronautics Act of 1938, which as amended has now become the Federal Aviation Act of 1958.

In general, the act of 1938 provided for conventional public utility regulation. Yet its provisions and rationale were in part distinctive. One such feature was the emphasis on promotion. The act's "Declaration of Policy" defined "the public interest" and "the public convenience and necessity" as including, "among other things":

(a) *The encouragement and development* of an air-transportation system properly adapted to the *present and future needs of the foreign and domestic commerce of the United States, of the Postal Service, and of the national defense;*

(b) The regulation of air transportation in such a manner as to *recognize and preserve the inherent advantages of,* assure the highest degree of safety in, and foster sound economic conditions in, such transportation, and to improve the relations between, and coordinate transportation by, air carriers;

(c) *The promotion of adequate, economical, and efficient service* by air carriers at reasonable charges, without unjust discriminations, undue preferences or advantages, or unfair or destructive practices;

(d) Competition to the extent necessary *to assure the sound development* of an air-transportation system *properly adapted to the needs of the foreign and domestic commerce of the United States, of the Postal Service, and of the national defense;*

(e) The regulation of air commerce in such manner as to *best promote its development* and safety; and

(f) *The encouragement and development of civil aeronautics* [Italics supplied]

The policy of promotion was to be carried into effect, in part, by subsidy payments for carriage of mail. The payments for mail were to be determined by:

. . . the need of each such air carrier for compensation for the transportation of mail sufficient to insure the performance of such service, and, together with all other revenue of the air carrier, to enable such air carrier under honest, economical, and efficient management, to maintain and continue the development of air transportation to the extent and of the character and quality required for the commerce of the United States, the Postal Service, and the national defense.

The act provided a second instrument for effecting regulatory policy. This was the certificate of public convenience and necessity that airline companies had to secure from the CAB before they could operate any commercial route. Restriction of entry was thus the means for achieving objectives stated in the "Declaration of Policy": "foster sound economic conditions in" air transportation; prevent "unfair or destructive competitive practices"; and allow competition only "to the extent necessary to assure the sound development of an air transportation system . . ."

Economic regulation of air carriers was vested in a board composed of five members appointed by the President with the consent of the Senate. No more than three members could be appointed from the same political party, and board members could be removed from office by the President only for inefficiency, neglect of duty, or malfeasance in office. The President designated one of the members as chairman.

CERTIFICATION POLICY

"Sound development" of the air transport industry, protected against "uneconomic, destructive competition," has been a constant concern of the CAB, perhaps even with some sacrifice of promotion of service. The CAB has regarded economic soundness as a requisite for safety, as an essential for reducing and ultimately eliminating subsidy, and as a necessity for expanding service. Its tool has been the management of the certificate system, through which it could establish categories of service to be certificated (international, territorial and overseas, domestic trunkline, local service, all-cargo, helicopter), grant or deny certificates for service in these categories, define the routes to be served and the conditions of service, and set up categories of service to be exempt from the requirements for certification.

Domestic trunkline service (that is, scheduled service between major traffic centers) has been restricted to the grandfather carriers. Although the CAB has never ruled out the possibility of a new company obtaining a certificate for trunkline service, it has never shown disagreement with its statement in the Delta case in 1941:

The number of air carriers now operating appears sufficient to insure against monopoly in respect to the average new route case, and we believe that the present domestic air-transportation system can by proper supervision be integrated and expanded in a manner that will in general afford the competition necessary for the development of that system in the manner contemplated by the act. In the absence of particular circumstances presenting an affirmative reason for a new carrier there appears to be no inherent desirability of increasing the present number of carriers merely for the purpose of numerically enlarging the industry.[4]

All new certifications for domestic trunkline service have gone to the existing carriers. There were nineteen domestic grandfather carriers in 1938. Twelve of these formed the trunkline system during the GPFI. These twelve did approximately 97 percent of the certificated, domestic airline passenger business; and of these twelve, the Big Four (American, Eastern, TWA, and United) had about 70 percent of trunkline revenues.

Certificates for scheduled domestic service have been issued to a second group of companies, called local-service or feeder carriers. The general authorization of scheduled carriage of persons, property, and mail between smaller cities began in 1946. Initially there were over four hundred applications for local routes; there were for a time twenty-two local-service companies, but the number now is thirteen. Their certificates were for short periods, normally three years, and each had obtained one or more renewals prior to an act of Congress providing for their permanent certification in 1955.[5]

At that time Board member Josh Lee explained the CAB's concept of these carriers. He said that they were "a secondary type of air transportation," that they differed from trunklines in that they were confined to a trade area and normally operated without air competition; he also recalled that the CAB had said it did "not propose to allow these carriers to metamorphose into trunklines." He stated further that they were designed to release the twelve trunklines from local-service duties.[6]

[4] Delta Air Lines et al., Service to Atlanta and Birmingham, 2 *CAB Reports* 447, 480 (1941).

[5] 69 Stat. 49 (May 19, 1955). The CAB could still give limited-duration certificates for not over one-half the intermediate points served. Intermediate points are cities certificated for service between origination and destination cities.

[6] "Permanent Certification for Local Service Air Carriers," *Hearings before a Subcommittee of the Committee on Interstate and Foreign Commerce on S. 651,*

The CAB has usually rejected applications from trunklines wanting to provide local service and has favored trunkline withdrawal from local-service competition. In this it has generally had the cooperation of the trunklines. The division of service rights under which, in the words of Lee, the local-service carriers "live on crumbs" (and on subsidy) is apparently acceptable to the trunkline carriers.

The chief threat to the position of the trunklines came after World War II with the increase in service by carriers offering nonscheduled (nonsked) and irregular service. Carriers of this type existed in 1938, but their economic significance at that time was not great. The CAB exempted them substantially from economic regulation. It required only that they obtain letters of registration, for which no proof of public convenience and necessity was required. Following the war, surplus planes and trained pilots were available in large numbers. Many companies or persons—oftentimes as a result of other activities, such as sale or service of aircraft, flight instruction, or operation of airports—inaugurated call-and-demand service without fixed schedule. Some of these pioneered in the development of coach service, which the certificated carriers had until 1948 failed to institute. They were, therefore, a major influence in the transition from luxury to mass air transportation service.

From 1944 to 1955 the Board struggled under rival pressures for a policy for the expanded nonsked airline service. It regarded the nonskeds as cream skimmers, operating between the best traffic-generating cities without providing adequate service to intermediary cities or on less profitable routes. In general it sought to prevent these carriers from setting up regular or scheduled service, but it found its task complicated by numerous violations of its restrictions. The CAB prosecuted violators, and its decision revoking the operating authority of North American Airlines in 1957 was sustained

U.S. Senate, 84th Cong., 1st Sess. 205–214 (1955). In a speech at Norman, Oklahoma, May 25, 1950, which was printed and widely distributed, Lee had presented a full and carefully reasoned statement in favor of the proposition that local service should be a distinct category. A main point in his argument was that "feeder carriers" would supply better local service than the trunks, but he also argued that separation would be the means of making the trunks self-sufficient.

by the courts.[7] At the time of the GPFI the CAB allowed ten flights a month between any two points by these carriers, once called "large irregulars," later "supplemental" carriers. Though to the scheduled carriers, this seemed too generous, the threat of the nonskeds to the established industry was apparently ended by CAB policy.

The CAB uses its certification powers today to apportion opportunities among existing carriers. This it does by a continuous process of granting or denying applications for new routes or extensions of routes, and by attaching conditions to route grants to balance the opportunities of trunklines. The Federal Aviation Act denies the CAB the power to prescribe schedules, though it does have power to determine that service is inadequate.

The major significance of the CAB's use of the certification powers is now, as it has always been, to determine the amount of competition that will be allowed in the airline industry. A drastic change in CAB policy was reflected in a series of decisions dating from September 1, 1955. The decisions, reached in a number of large cases affecting service over a major part of the country, authorized one or more additional airlines to serve over many routes that had previously been served by only one carrier, and authorized additional companies to compete on many routes that already had some competition. The effect was to augment substantially the amount of competition in the trunkline industry.

POWERS OVER RATE CHANGES

The revenues of certificated carriers have been derived from two kinds of carriage recognized as distinct by the Civil Aeronautics Act. The first is carriage of mail. For this carriage the airlines may receive only a service rate, as compensation for service rendered, or also an additional subsidy payment, determined on the basis of need. Since 1953 the distinction between the two has been emphasized by payment of the service cost by the Post Office Department and pay-

[7] North American Airlines v. Civil Aeronautics Board, 240 F.2d 867 (C.A.D.C., 1956), *certiorari denied*, 353 U.S. 941 (1957). For a detailed study of CAB procedure in a large route certification case, see Winston M. Fisk, *Administrative Procedure in a Regulatory Agency: The CAB and the New York-Chicago Route Case*, Inter-University Case Program Study No. 85.

ment of the subsidy increment by the CAB.[8] The rates of payment for both are determined by the CAB. The second kind of carriage is of passengers and nonmail cargo. For the trunkline carriers the main source of revenue is the passenger traffic.

With respect to domestic, nonmail cargo, and passenger traffic the Federal Aviation Act (in provisions carried from the Civil Aeronautics Act) provides:

1. Carriers shall file all rates with the CAB and post and publish these in accordance with regulations of the CAB.
2. No change shall be made in any rate without notice to the CAB of the proposed change. The notice must be given 30 days in advance of the change, unless the Board consents to a shorter notice period.
3. It shall be the duty of every carrier to establish and observe "just and reasonable" rates.
4. The Board may, upon complaint or its own initiative, "enter upon a hearing concerning the lawfulness" of any proposed rate, and may suspend a proposed change for a period of 180 days. It may after the hearing issue an order determining the rate of charge, but if it does not conclude its proceeding and issue an order within 180 days the proposed rate will be effective at the end of such period.
5. The Board may, upon complaint or upon its own initiative, and "after notice and hearing," find rates to be "unjust or unreasonable, or unjustly discriminatory, or unduly preferential, or unduly prejudicial" and determine and prescribe the lawful rate (or the maximum or minimum, or maximum and minimum).

It is clear from the above provisions that the Board cannot substitute its judgment on rates for that of carriers without formal proceedings, that is, without "hearing." It can, however, allow carrier proposals to go into effect without hearing. It can also under the governing act approve or disapprove agreements, including agreements relating to rates. In addition, the CAB may use extralegal means to obtain rate changes. It may offer advice or exert pressure for rate changes. Particularly significant is its opportunity to suggest

[8] Reorganization Plan No. 10 of 1953, 67 Stat. 644.

what rates will be accepted, in lieu of those proposed by carriers. Although these extralegal means are exceptional rather than customary in the practice of regulatory agencies, they have been important in CAB procedure.

How High Should Rates Be?

The Federal Aviation Act gives the CAB a set of guides for its rate decisions. It "shall take into consideration," among other factors:

(1) The effect of such rates upon the movement of traffic;
(2) The need in the public interest of adequate and efficient transportation of persons and property by air carriers at the lowest cost consistent with the furnishing of such service;
(3) Such standards respecting the character and quality of service to be rendered by air carriers as may be prescribed by or pursuant to law;
(4) The inherent advantages of transportation by aircraft;
(5) The need of each carrier for revenue sufficient to enable such carrier, under honest, economical, and efficient management, to provide adequate and efficient air carrier service.

This set of guides offers no definite standards. How high should rates be in view of the first and the fifth of these guides—effect upon movement of traffic and "revenue sufficient . . . to provide adequate and efficient air carrier service"? Low rates will move traffic, high rates may possibly yield more net revenues. How should one determine the "lowest cost consistent with the furnishing" of "adequate and efficient transportation"? What return to the airlines should be allowed as part of the "lowest cost"? These and many other issues were left for the Board to resolve.

Earnings for the trunkline industry were relatively low for several years after 1938. During the war, with heavy utilization of airline capacity, earnings were good. After the war the trunks suffered losses for three years: 1946—1.5 percent of total investment; 1947—2.9 percent; 1948—1.7 percent. But in the years that followed, earnings were far above the standards of reasonableness established for utilities by state and national commissions: 1949—6.1 percent; 1950—11.2 percent; 1951—14.6 percent; 1952—14.2 percent; 1953—11.3 percent; 1954—10.4 percent; 1955—11.8 percent. Though there was wide disparity in the rate of earnings of different companies, every trunkline was on the plus side every year beginning with 1950, except Northeast in 1951 and Colonial for four years.[9] By late 1958 it appeared that all the trunks might be free of subsidy need.[10]

The Board has denied many proposals for fare increases. Up to 1960, however, it had never concluded a general investigation of passenger rate levels. It initiated such an investigation in 1943 but dropped it when compromise reductions of approximately 10 percent were made for most carriers. Nearly two years later it again initiated and subsequently dropped a general investigation, again after achieving certain reductions. In 1947 the Board was so concerned with the serious financial conditions of the airlines that its chairman called the presidents of the lines to his office and proposed that they file with the CAB a formal agreement for a 10-percent increase. This was done. In 1948 a similar conference resulted in no agreement and quite diverse actions by the carriers, even including discounts of various types. In 1948 the CAB also set minimum freight rates. With earnings again high, the Board instituted a general passenger fare investigation in 1952 but dropped it in 1953. In sum, the CAB's rate activity, though heavy, has been related largely to subsidy payments.

THE INDUSTRY AND THE CAB

The industry has in general regarded the administration of economic controls by the CAB as satisfactory. Writing in 1955, Stuart G. Tipton, then general counsel of the Air Transport Association (ATA), and Stanley Gewirtz, executive assistant to the president of ATA, concluded: "Regulation has benefited air transportation. It has benefited the country."

The industry had not been fully satisfied with all CAB policies. It did not think the protection against the noncertificated carriers

---

[9] Figures are taken from Board opinion, Order No. E-10279 (May 10, 1956). Colonial has now merged with Eastern. Figures are after subsidy payments and after income tax deductions.

[10] Northeast has been in a marginal position. Order No. E-13208 (November 28, 1958), granted it temporary subsidy for the period from February 7, 1957, to December 31, 1958. Order No. E-13465 (February 3, 1959), put Northeast on a subsidy-free rate effective January 1, 1959.

was adequate. It was not always pleased with subsidy decisions, nor with Board decisions on applications for passenger fare increases. And inevitably some competing carriers were disappointed over route awards. By 1955, nevertheless, there was satisfaction in general with the regulatory system as such.

A series of events, beginning in mid-1955 appeared to have altered the friendly, though uneasy, relationship between the CAB and the industry. First, in the second half of 1955 the CAB issued its series of decisions tremendously increasing the amount of authorized competition. Trunkline companies thus were forced to compete vigorously with each other. Second, the jet age arrived, and this called for enormous expenditures by the airlines for new equipment. Third, the Board instituted a new General Passenger Fare Investigation in 1956.

The GPFI was initiated by the Board under congressional pressure, and the thrust of the proceeding was toward consideration of a rate decrease. By 1957 the airlines were running into a period of depressed earnings,[11] and were at the same time facing the need for new capital for jet equipment. In 1957 they began a series of requests for rate increases and found the CAB reluctant to grant increases while the GPFI was being conducted. Some in the industry thought that this reluctance arose from the CAB's sensitivity to congressional opinion. At any rate, by late 1957 the industry had become highly critical of the CAB.

A gauge of relations may be found in the remarks of Stuart G. Tipton, president of ATA, on May 19, 1958.[12] After painting a picture of profit decline, the success of the Russians in jet advance, and general unhelpfulness of the American government, Tipton attacked "the 'police the monopoly' aspects of rate regulation" as "largely outmoded and archaic, at least so far as air transport is concerned." As for the CAB, he said:

I do not, by any means, suggest that the Civil Aeronautics Board desires to push the domestic trunklines back onto subsidy. However, I sometimes wonder if the shortsighted policies of the Board will not have the actual result.

[11] Average profits for the year 1957 were less than 5 percent.

[12] "The Jet Airliner: Investment for National Security," speech at Eleventh Annual Convention of the National Federation of Financial Analysts Societies, Los Angeles, California.

Unfortunately, the CAB has seemed to forget its promotional responsibilities. . . . I am sure it is difficult to avoid the negative attitude inherent in regulation—and the Board has not avoided it.

The principles of the Act are good ones. It just seems necessary so often to remind the administrators of their existence.

On the other hand, CAB Chairman James R. Durfee maintained in a speech to the Chicago Association of Commerce and Industry on October 23, 1958, that the agency had acted quickly in granting interim passenger fare increases in February and October, 1958. He added:

Unless the airlines tap new markets, there are going to be some dark clouds on the jet age sunrise.

The expansion of capacity—perhaps up to a 200 percent increase—that the airlines plan dwarfs any previous expansion.

. . . .

We are inclined to think that the way ahead lies in experimentation with new, higher density, lower priced services which—coupled with the still greater speeds of today's aircraft—should cut further into private auto travel and attract completely new travelers, particularly vacationers.

How can airline service be promoted? How can sound growth of an industry be ensured? The answer of the "new competition" of modern business, as applied to air transport is speed, comfort, favorable scheduling, dependability of service, courtesy, and fringe appeals, such as good meals and liquor service. Through such means, it is maintained, traffic will be drawn from other means of transportation. But some of this improved service may be self-defeating because of cost, as when luxury service becomes too expensive or when competition among airlines leads to overscheduling and thus to many vacant seats.

Unavoidably, costs, price, and earnings must be considered. In private industry the search for earnings may lead down either of two paths: price above cost to ensure earnings on each unit of sale, or price promotionally to broaden the market and reduce cost per unit. The shrewd merchandiser may build his own compromise path between these two; his price structure may mix promotional pricing with cost-plus pricing.

But airline pricing policies are subject to public control. Company proposals for price change may be suspended and set aside after hearings by the CAB; or the CAB may upon complaint or its own initiative, and after hearing, find rates to be "unjust and unreasonable, or unjustly discriminatory, or unduly preferential, or unduly prejudicial" and determine and prescribe the lawful rate.

A formal investigation with courtlike procedures is the customary method of public determination of just and reasonable rates. Whether this is a fruitful approach for determining standards and what standards shall guide judgment are primary issues raised by the General Passenger Fare Investigation.

Initiating a General Passenger Fare Investigation

Was there to be a general passenger fare investigation? This issue split the Board, aroused industry opposition, and activated congressional interest. The issue had two components: a substantive one— was an investigation of fares needed?—and a procedural one—what was the fair and efficient means of investigation?

The developments leading to the institution of the GPFI in 1956 had their beginning as far back as 1952. In that year the trunkline carriers, excepting Northeast Airlines,[13] filed rate revisions proposing a flat increase of one dollar in all one-way passenger fares, as well as the elimination of round-trip discounts. The carriers claimed rising costs and lowered revenues during recent months. On April 9, 1952,[14] the Board, without opinion, ordered an investigation "to determine whether the fares . . . presently on file or subsequently filed" were lawful; the one-dollar increase was granted "pending the outcome of the investigation of the level and structure of passenger fares"; the proposal to eliminate discounts was suspended "pending such investigation . . . to and including July 14, 1952." The order was headed "In the Matter of a General Investigation of all Passenger Fares . . ."

The order as a whole was approved by only two of the five Board members—Josh Lee and Donald W. Nyrop. Chan Gurney and Oswald Ryan dissented on the suspension portion of the order, and Joseph P. Adams dissented on the grant of the one-dollar in-

[13] Commissioner Joseph P. Adams, in his dissent in this case, said Northeast feared that a further increase would price it out of the market, and that National Airlines' management had made it clear to the Board it did "not actively favor the increase."

[14] Order No. E-6305 (April 9, 1952).

crease without an investigation to supply further factual information. Ryan and Lee were veterans on the Board, Ryan having been an appointee to the original Board in 1938 and Lee having been appointed in 1943. Adams and Gurney had each barely completed two years of service, and Nyrop was near the end of his first year of service.

It is customary in formal proceedings for the chief hearing examiner to appoint a hearing examiner to hear the parties, to make findings at the end of a hearing, and to make an initial decision or certify the record to the Board. The hearing examiner normally holds one or more prehearing conferences to define areas of agreement and clarify issues. In the course of the proceeding he may rule on motions presented or certify or allow appeal on these to the Board. In this proceeding a hearing examiner was appointed, two prehearing conferences were held, and issues on the scope of the investigation were taken to the Board for decision.

A CAB order of October 17, 1952,[15] sought to redefine and clarify the issues in the investigation. The Board noted that the carriers had withdrawn the proposal to eliminate round-trip discounts and "there remains therefore only the investigation into the increase of one dollar." This proposal, said the order, had raised two issues: (1) the level of rates and (2) the structure of rates, namely, the "tapering rate structure based on distance, in contrast to the previous relatively uniform rate structure."[16] It was further noted that, at prehearing conferences, parties had raised other issues. The Board restated the issues to be included: First, "Will the general level of domestic fares prevailing just prior to April 9, 1952, be just and reasonable and what changes upward or downward should be permitted or prescribed therein and how should such changes, if any, be effected?" Also to be included were the questions of whether fares varying with length of trip, the dollar increase specifically, and charging first-class fares on segments of coach flights were discrimi-

[15] Order No. E-6894 (October 17, 1952).

[16] Some carriers with relatively short routes desire a rate structure that allows substantially more per mile for short trips than for long trips. This is called a "tapering rate structure." The one-dollar increase, being applied to all trips, irrespective of distance, was a step toward a tapering rate structure and hence raised the issue of structure of rates.

natory or otherwise unlawful. The carriers were allowed fifteen days to file motions to include additional issues.

United Air Lines filed a motion on November 3, 1952, for clarification and expansion of the issues, and counsel for the Bureau of Air Operations of the CAB filed an answer on November 13. The Board granted[17] those parts of the request on which United Air Lines and the Bureau Counsel were agreed, namely, that the first issue stated in the order of October 17 be amended to relate to fares "now existing" (rather than to those existing prior to April 9), and that the issues be expanded to include the question whether fares that did not vary with length of haul were preferential and unlawful. The Board, though stating that both tourist and first-class fares were included in the investigation, accepted the argument of the Bureau Counsel that the relation between tourist and first-class fares should not be included, this not being necessary to the determination of the general fare level.

On December 16, 1952, the Board again modified the statement of issues.[18] Noting that the one-dollar increase was being charged pending completion of the investigation and also noting the need to avoid a decision on a stale record, the Board expressed a desire that the proceeding be expedited so that a decision could be reached within a year. It, therefore, limited the first issue in the order of October 17 to allow consideration only of a percentage increase or decrease in fares, that is, of level of rates only. The issue was restated as follows: "Is the general fare level of domestic fares (standard and tourist) now existing just and reasonable and, if not, what percentage increases or decreases on an overall basis should be permitted or prescribed?" On the other hand, it clarified its statement of other issues to retain full freedom on any type of rate change (flat percentage or structural) deemed desirable if the one-dollar increase on first-class fares or coach-flight segments was found to be discriminatory.

DECISION ON THE PETITIONS TO DISMISS

It appears that the carriers had precipitated, by their proposal for rate increases, and the Board, through successive clarification of

17 Order No. E-6969 (November 21, 1952).
18 Order No. E-7037 (December 16, 1952).

issues, had slid into a general investigation in which the chief issue was whether rates were too low or too high. This change was not welcomed by the carriers, and in March and April of 1953 all carrier parties to the proceeding filed petitions for dismissal of the investigation.

At first, the Board found itself deadlocked on these petitions. With one vacancy, the Board was split two to two—Gurney and Ryan for dismissal, Adams and Lee against. On April 7, Harmar D. Denny became a member of the Board. In a Board meeting on April 10 he was the third member of a majority in favor of continuing the investigation; on April 23 he reversed his vote to produce a majority in favor of dismissal.[19]

An opinion by Denny, Gurney, and Ryan had significance with respect to procedural and substantive issues:

1. The opinion stressed the procedural issue of whether there should be a formal or an informal investigation. The Board had long since been relieved of any legal obligation to conduct a formal proceeding by the carriers' withdrawal of the petition for elimination of the round-trip discount. Before ruling negatively on a carrier filing, it is necessary to conduct formal proceedings on the issue presented. But no such proceeding would be required to allow the one-dollar increase to stand. The Board could accept this increase and make either a formal or an informal investigation of the level of rates, or make no investigation at all.

The majority favored an informal staff investigation instead of a formal investigation. Its opinion noted that "any formal investigation must of necessity be lengthy, time-consuming, and costly" because of the necessity of presenting evidence on possible alternative orders. On the other hand:

An informal investigation will serve to narrow and define the areas in which corrective action appears necessary and can result in specific changes only if a formal hearing is later held. The parties will have an opportunity before such actions are taken to present evidence for or against them. In proceeding informally it is clear that protective and unnecessary materials need not be advanced and thus much time can be saved. With the extensive amount of data now available to the Board an informal investigation can be very broad without necessarily tak-

[19] Order No. E-7376 (April 23, 1953).

ing up a great amount of time and effort of the carriers. The parties can submit such additional data as the Board's staff deems necessary in addition to the normal reports and then when a prima facie case has been established for a specific tariff change, the Board would institute a specific formal investigation with much more limited issues.

The majority thought that the failure of the Board to conduct a general passenger fare investigation over the first fourteen years of its existence was of "no special significance." The Board had considered hundreds of proposals and had not been uninformed on "airline economics, proper tariff principles, and the relation of fares to other operating factors in the industry."

The majority concluded with a statement that it had instructed the staff to prepare a study, with industry cooperation, on problems of "fare structure and fare level . . . to provide the necessary background for Board consideration of future fare and rate problems."

2. This decision involved more than a procedural issue. It meant confirmation of the one-dollar increase and refusal to consider immediately other rate changes. Moreover, the opinion stated a cyclical theory of rate making. Concerning recent earnings, it was said:

The Board has considered the latest available earnings reported by the domestic trunkline carriers, as well as those reported for recent years, and it believes that, looking at these years alone, such earnings must be considered excessive when measured by any reasonable standard applicable to a regulated industry.

But it was believed that it was "neither possible nor desirable" to "relate fares to returns in the short run."

To do so would require lowering fares in times of prosperity and raising them when traffic conditions were poor. This would not make business sense and it is, therefore, our belief that both the industry and the public will be better served by a level of fares which reflects the cyclical needs rather than the needs of any particular year.

In line with this philosophy, the opinion placed the carriers on notice that in the future they would be expected to absorb losses "without resort to fare or mail rate adjustments unless it can be demonstrated that such earnings are below the level necessary to provide a fair return over a reasonably extended period which includes the good years as well as the bad."

DISSENTS

Board member Lee dissented. He noted that "thousands of man hours and dollars" had been expended in procedure which included two prehearing conferences and preparation of exhibits. He thought the issue was broader than reduction of rates, though the majority's reason for dismissal "appears to stem from an unwillingness to have the Board placed in a position where it could order a rate reduction." He thought the investigation was needed to consider the following:

1. The tapering rate issue. [He stated his purpose in voting for the one-dollar increase was to equalize disadvantages of short-haul operations as compared to long-haul operations.]
2. The question of establishing an equalization reserve—to assure that excess profits would be saved for lean years.
3. The justification for the $1.00 increase.
4. Whether the present method of figuring profit on investment should be changed to an operation ratio concept.

On the procedural question Lee said:

Only after a formal proceeding, where the evidence of record has been tried in the fires of cross-examination, would the Board be in a position to make findings and orders. . . . By dismissing this proceeding and substituting a staff study, the majority is tying the Board's hands so that no matter what facts may be developed by the staff, the Board will be powerless to act without instituting an entirely new passenger fare investigation.

Board member Adams also dissented. Like Lee, he did not consider that fare reduction was "the only or principal" purpose of the investigation. He noted also such issues as tapering fares and the possibility of use of the operating-cost ratio. But primarily the purpose was to "evolve a sound, well-reasoned, passenger fare policy." He argued that for fourteen years the Board had "by-passed . . . its statutory duty" to investigate charges to the public. He thought the Board had been "penny wise and pound foolish" in spending so little time on passenger rates (82.3 percent of airline revenues) in comparison with the man-hours on mail rates (10 percent of revenues) or even with time spent on the worthwhile Air Freight Rate Investigation (relating to about 5 percent of airline revenues). He thought that facts already known required this investigation. A year earlier the staff had prepared data with which the airlines had disagreed. A staff study would produce only a refinement of facts known now by the Board; it could not provide findings that could be activated without a public hearing and investigation. He answered the argument of airlines that there was no public clamor for an investigation: Congress made it the duty of the Board to act on its own initiative.

CONGRESSIONAL PRODDING

Investigation of passenger rates by formal proceedings appeared to be dead. But it was only sleep from which the patient was to be roused by congressional inquiry. The Antitrust Subcommittee of the House Committee on the Judiciary conducted a study in 1956 of "Monopoly Problems in Regulated Industries." It began with "Airlines" and held hearings on the subject on twenty-four days between February and June. Although the primary interest was in competition, the subcommittee's chairman pointed out that rate regulation was related thereto, since it provided "the counterpart to the competitive determination of prices."[20] Subcommittee questions ultimately were directed to the passenger fare investigation and its discontinuation.

One focus of the subcommittee's inquiry was Denny's changed vote. The majority (Democratic) members were interested in a visit by Tipton (of ATA) to Denny's office between the dates of his two votes.

The subcommittee was divided rigidly along party lines. Denny had been the first Eisenhower appointee to the CAB, and the political overtones in this inquiry were clear. Two Democratic members of the subcommittee, Chairman Emanuel Celler (New York) and Representative James M. Quigley (Pennsylvania), led the interrogation, while two Republican members, Representatives Kenneth B. Keating (New York) and Hugh Scott (Pennsylvania), interposed in defense of Denny. The roles of the two sets of inquirers appeared to be comparable to that of prosecutor and defense attorney, respectively. A few quotations reveal the flavor of the proceedings:

[20] "Monopoly Problems in Regulated Industries," *Hearings before the Antitrust Subcommittee, Committee on the Judiciary*, House of Representatives, 84th Cong., 2d Sess., Airlines, I, 3 (1956).

The Chairman: . . . I suggest that hereafter you get down at that table and be at the right or left of Mr. Tipton, who will back you as an excellent counsel.

Mr. Keating: In view of that remark, I will say to the chairman that his bias in these hearings has been pretty evident from the beginning. The Chairman: I deny that . . .[21]

. . . .

The Chairman: Let the record be corrected, if it may, that this is no political inquiry. I want the gentleman from Pennsylvania to understand that, because this whole inquiry takes in a number of administrations, Democratic as well as Republican.

Mr. Keating: We ought to have some Democratic commissioners up here, then.[22]

A QUESTION OF PROPRIETY

Incidental to inquiry about the Tipton-Denny meeting, there was comment on the proper conduct of a commissioner. A section of the "Principles of Practice of the Civil Aeronautics Board" was inserted in the record. The section stated that certain functions of the Board were similar to those of a court and set forth the impropriety of "private communication on the merits" of a case or "any effort by any person interested" in a case "to sway the judgment of the Board by attempting to bring pressure or influence." Commissioner Denny frankly stated that there was generally considerable pressure from airlines and members of Congress on the members of the Board, but he averred that he had followed the customary rule for members of the Board: namely, refusing to discuss ex parte the merits of a pending case. He thought, however, that there was some difference between a proceeding like the Passenger Fare Investigation and a case, such as a route case, where there were airlines facing each other in an adversary position. His questioners were reluctant to admit a difference and pushed the point that it was a "formal proceeding."

In general, Denny took the following position: He had come to the Board meeting a few days after his appointment, and the Passenger Fare Investigation was sprung on him; learning that there had never been one, he had thought "it might be reasonable to have

[21] *Ibid.*, III, 1486.
[22] *Ibid.*, II, 1199.

one"; after the meeting he had obtained "facts and figures" from the staff and had seen that there was "a very sharp closing of the gap between the costs and the fares" from the middle of 1951; he had evolved a substitute plan for a staff study, through which the same information would be obtained more quickly and with less expense; he had not discussed the passenger fare case with Tipton, but Tipton had given him information about the financial status of the airlines, and probably had said to him "what had already been provided to the Board" in the motions to dismiss; Tipton had not influenced him to change his mind; he had reported the conversation to the Board.

If the line between discussion of the rate case and the type of information given by Tipton was not clear, many of Denny's responses further confused the inquirers. On a second appearance he had to correct certain of his statements that appeared to be inconsistent with his line of testimony, including (1) that he had not discussed the fare case with Tipton, and (2) that his report to the Board on the Tipton meeting was made on the day of the Board's vote to dismiss the investigation. He flatly denied the testimony of Jack Anderson, associated with columnist Drew Pearson, that he had told Anderson by telephone that Tipton had caused him to change his mind.[23]

The committee tried to learn what Denny had said in the Board meeting about his conversations with Tipton. But both Commissioners Denny and Adams refused to answer such questions, even though directed to do so, on the ground that the Board had voted two days before that such discussions were privileged. But Josh Lee, now retired from the Board, testified that Denny had told the Board the Tipton conference concerned the general fare investigation.

Tipton's version of the meeting was as follows:

As I recall the conversation, it went like this. As the committee understands, I was calling on Commissioner Denny as a part of getting acquainted with him as a new member of the Board and I referred to the general passenger fare investigation which was pending. I pointed out the position of the airlines, which was that it should be dismissed and said that a number of petitions had been filed by the carriers who were in the case; that I regarded those petitions and the data in them as the

[23] *Ibid.*, II, 1187–1216.

best current studies of the airline financial conditions and prospects that I had seen; and that I hoped he would have an opportunity to read them before the case was decided.

His reply at that point, I believe, was that he was in the process of making a study of those very petitions, as well as the other material that he had available; and the conversation involved also this proposal —and I don't recall how this came up—this proposal that a staff study be made as a preliminary to any continuation of the investigation, and I have a recollection at that point that Commissioner Denny inquired as to whether, in the absence of a formal investigation, it was possible for the Board to get all the information they wanted from the carriers, whether they had the legal power to do that.

I replied that they did have; that he would want to check that question with the general counsel of the Board, but it was my view that they had the power to secure virtually any information that they wanted from the carriers under their powers under the Civil Aeronautics Act.

As far as my recollection is concerned, that ended the conversation on that particular point.[24]

Tipton stated that it was his custom to get acquainted with new members of the Board, and he was "sure" he did not call on Denny because his vote was crucial in the fare case. He was asked whether the conference violated the CAB's "Principles of Practice":

Mr. Tipton: I do not so regard it.

The Chairman: Will you tell us in your way why it was not a violation?

Mr. Tipton: The conversation, it is my recollection, was limited to stating the position of the carriers, and referring him to the argument the carriers were making in formal petitions in support of that position. I did not argue—my recollection—I did not argue the case privately to Denny. It is my conclusion that that is not a violation of those standards.

The Chairman: On your statement now, weren't you presenting the position of the airlines?

Mr. Tipton: I was stating what it was. There is a difference I think, between stating what your position is, you are for or against something, and arguing that position.[25]

The questions about Denny's changed vote were only a part of a broader inquiry concerning the need for a formal investigation of

24 *Ibid.*, III, 1477.
25 *Ibid.*, III, 1485.

the passenger rate level. On March 7, 1956, seven days before Denny was first questioned and nearly three years after his crucial vote, the Antitrust Subcommittee questioned Ross Rizley, new member and chairman of the CAB,[26] Board member Adams, and Irving Roth, chief of the Rates Division of the CAB, on formal investigation of passenger rates. Representative Celler, chairman of the subcommitee, asked most of the questions. He got on the record the substantial earnings of the trunklines from 1950 to 1955 and the story of the dismissal of the passenger fare investigation by a divided Board. He learned from Roth that, though the staff had made "individual studies," including a large statistical study of aspects of rate structure,[27] it had never completed a study of the level of rates. He learned from Rizley, who had been on the Board for one year, that he had never even been told that the Board had, in dismissing the formal investigation, ordered a staff study. And he got from Rizley an admission of Board fault "that this thing has not been brought up to date." When Roth explained the cyclical-earnings philosophy of the Board, as announced in the dismissal order of 1953, Democratic Congressman Quigley questioned whether it had

TABLE 1

Civil Aeronautics Board

Members in 1952	Changes in Membership					
---	1953	1955	1956	1957	1959	1960
Nyrop	Denny				Gilliland	
Ryan		Rizley	Durfee*			Bragdon
Lee			Minetti			
Adams				Hector	Boyd	
Gurney						

* Durfee came on the Board twenty-seven days before, Minetti fourteen days after, institution of the GPFI.

[26] Table 1 shows changes in membership of the Board from 1952, when the first passenger fare investigation was instituted, to 1960.

[27] "Preliminary Report on the Domestic Passenger Fare Structure Based on a Sampling of Individual Fares," from the Rates Division, Bureau of Air Operations, June 7, 1954. It may be found in "Monopoly Problems in Regulated Industries," *Hearings, House* Airlines, I, 221–292.

"any legal basis in the law." He said also, "I think when the chips are down you are not going to say to these airlines, 'you had some good years; we are not going to give you these subsidies'." At one point Celler said to Rizley: "I am just asking for your advice and counsel—would it not be better for the Board itself to conduct an open, formal hearing rather than to have the staff do it, in view of the fact that nothing really has happened?"

Later this interchange occurred:

The Chairman: Of course, I think we agree, Commissioner Rizley and Mr. Adams, that these factors certainly indicate the need for that general inquiry that we spoke about as to the level of fares. I think we agree with that.

Did you nod your head? I did not notice whether you did.

Mr. Rizley: Yes, I think the whole matter needs to have a grade A look and a fresh look. I don't think there is any question about that.

Thus, the Board chairman, who had stated he did not know until that day that the Board had directed an investigation, had committed himself to the need for a new look.

THE COMPTROLLER GENERAL REPORTS

On April 9, Comptroller General Joseph Campbell transmitted to the speaker of the House of Representatives a "Report on Audit of Civil Aeronautics Board," which dealt mainly with mail payments but also included comments on passenger fares. The report noted the procedure in informal disposal of rate cases. It said that proposed tariff revisions had been studied by the Rates Division and "we have found that in practically all instances tested the Board adopts the recommendations of the Rates Division." The report further stated that the Rates Division had not been provided with fixed standards. It then took up recent Board actions on rate increases. As Adams had done in 1953, the report noted the discrepancy in time spent on mail and freight revenues and on passenger fares. As to the one-dollar increase granted in 1952, the report said:

However, we do not understand why the high rates in more recent years should be averaged with earlier loss years so that the resultant overall rate of return could warrant further rate increase. One reason advanced by a member of the Board for his concurrence in permitting

the general $1 fare increase was the desire to attain a "taper" pattern.
. . . On the other hand, if it was felt that a "taper" pattern was desirable, the Board could have attained this pattern by adjusting fares without any increase.

[The report went further:]

We recommend that the Board institute a full-scale investigation of the current level of passenger rates, and accumulate the information necessary for formulating additional sound industry-wide passenger fare policies.

Thus, the Comptroller General's report supported the view expressed by Board member Adams in his earlier dissenting opinion that the Board should "evolve a sound, well-reasoned, passenger fare policy."

On April 12 a subcommittee of the Committee on Appropriations, holding hearings on the CAB's budget requests, took note of the Comptroller General's report and questioned the Board about rates. Congressman Sidney Yates thought it was inconsistent to protect existing carriers from competition with new companies and to fail to determine whether rates were fair to the public. Either competition or Board determination of rates appeared to him to be necessary for public protection. Yates said, "It seems to me that it is essential that the Board should go into the matter of determining whether the rates being charged are exorbitant and that you do it as promptly as possible." Congressman Albert Thomas wanted to know, "Will the Board make an intensive study of this as recommended by the General Accounting Office without any further nudging from the committee?" The question was addressed to Board member Gurney, who proceeded to defend his vote against an investigation in 1953. Thomas replied, "I disagree. You should have done it." Yates questioned Board member Adams on whether he would favor a hearing. Subcommittee members objected to the question; Chairman Preston thought they should not question the "thinking of a quasi-judicial body"; Yates agreed "in principle" but thought the question was related to the amount of funds the Board wanted Congress to appropriate. Adams, however, had already explained that there had been no change in his position since 1953. Rizley too had said, "I am in favor of it."

Rizley, however, left the Board the following day and was replaced immediately as member and chairman by James R. Durfee.

At hearings on Durfee's nomination on April 11, a letter from Senator Alexander Wiley of Wisconsin noted Durfee's five years of experience on the Wisconsin Public Service Commission and referred to his "experience and skill in rate regulation . . ." Durfee, questioned by Senator John Pastore (Rhode Island) about his opinion on the passenger fare investigation, said that all he knew was what he had read in the newspapers, that he had no opinion at that time on whether he would favor it, and that before he committed himself he "would like the privilege of examining the record as to its necessity."

On May 2, the Comptroller General appeared before the Antitrust Subcommittee. In the course of his testimony about the audit report he stated that a draft of the audit report had been sent to the CAB and that on November 10, 1955, the Board had informed him "it will again give consideration to the need for a formal investigation of passenger fares." Campbell added that he had received no further word from the CAB.

The same day certain CAB policies were discussed in the House of Representatives in debate on the appropriation for the Department of Commerce and Related Agencies. Twice Celler directed attention to the Comptroller General's testimony that morning that there had been no general fare investigation since 1938. Celler stated that the "CAB had been most derelict in that regard." With respect to the one-dollar increase, he said, "There was no reason for that increase," and that the airlines got together to propose it and the CAB "rubber-stamped it." Yates also concluded the Board had been "derelict."

Two days later, representatives of ATA were questioned by the Antitrust Subcommittee about a formal investigation. Tipton said that while in 1953 most of the trunklines opposed such an investigation, they did not now "oppose, endorse, or fear" one. However, Donald Markham, assistant general counsel of ATA, saw a practical difficulty:

As you have just pointed out, facts in this business are very transitory and very temporary. They change almost from day to day, certainly as far as economic conditions are concerned. So that you have a very legitimate question as to whether the best way to stay on top of a business is to hold a formal proceeding which will extend over a period of

18 to 36 months in which you are largely bound by a formal record, or whether it is better to proceed partly formally and party informally.[28]

Questioning Markham was Congressman Quigley, who, though not explicit on the method of investigation, considered that the Board had "just waltzed around this question of fares and tariffs and what the rates should be" and in fact had been guilty of "scandalous abdication of responsibility."

Six days later, on May 10, 1956, CAB issued an order instituting a new passenger fare investigation.[29] In doing so the Board took note, in a very brief statement, of reported operating results of the domestic trunkline carriers for 1955, the rates of return from 1950 to 1955, and the relatively stable passenger load factor of 63 to 65 percent (that is, 63 to 65 percent of seat capacity filled). The next day Durfee told a Senate subcommittee "it would require conservatively nine months to a year to conclude the investigation question."

The following year this exchange occurred at House committee hearings on CAB's appropriation requests:

Mr. Thomas: Did the Committee not urge you to do it and tell you if you did not do it we would do it for you?[30]
Mr. Durfee: The Committee never told me that.
Mr. Thomas: You were not here, but if you will get out the record, you will find it there.
Mr. Durfee: I voted for it and I am happy to say that there was a unanimous vote of the Board to support it.
Mr. Rooney: After last year's hearing?
Mr. Durfee: I was not here at last year's hearing.
Mr. Thomas: He came in about two months later.
Mr. Durfee: I can say I came here as Chairman of a Commission which had regulated rates for 5 years, and I was not appalled at the idea of having to face a general fare investigation.[31]

[28] Ibid., III, 1528.
[29] Technically and in a legal sense the Board was ordering a new investigation. Actually, it was, as the preceding recital of events shows, a revival of a rate investigation that had been dropped.
[30] This threat does not appear in the record of the hearings of the preceding year.
[31] "Department of Commerce and Related Agencies Appropriations, 1957," Hearings before the Subcommittee of the Committee on Appropriations, House of Representatives, 84th Cong., 2d Sess., 344 (May 11, 1956).

Procedure in the Investigation

The activity in a formal proceeding involving route certification or rate determination is concentrated within CAB in three organizational centers: the Bureau of Hearing Examiners, the Bureau of Air Operations, and the central Board offices.[32]

The hearing is conducted by an examiner assigned by the chief examiner, who is the administrative head of the Bureau of Hearing Examiners. The bureau includes about sixteen examiners for economic proceedings, all of whom are classified as GS 15. Their independence is safeguarded by Section 11 of the Administrative Procedure Act (APA) of 1946.[33] They are removable "only for good cause established and determined by the Civil Service Commission." They "shall receive compensation prescribed by the [Civil Service] Commission independently of agency recommendations or ratings." To further ensure independence of examiners from Board control, the APA provides that examiners "shall be assigned to cases in rotation so far as practicable."

The APA declares that examiners shall "regulate the course and conduct of the hearing" of cases assigned to them and gives them power to examine witnesses, issue subpoenas, rule on motions, and the like. The CAB's "Rules of Practice in Economic Proceedings" authorizes certification of questions to the Board by the examiner "within his discretion, or upon the direction of the Board." These rules also provide that the examiner shall pass upon all motions properly addressed to him, except that he may refer a motion to the Board for decision "if he finds that a prompt decision of the Board . . . is essential to the proper conduct of the proceeding." Rulings of the examiners on motions shall not be appealed to the Board "prior to its consideration of the entire proceeding except in extraordinary circumstances and with the consent of the examiner."

For a case of this kind (rule making) heard by an examiner, the APA provides [Sec. 8(a)] that (1) the examiner shall make an initial decision, or (2) the agency shall make an initial decision after recommendation from the examiner, or (3) "in lieu thereof

---

[32] All facts regarding organization, procedure, and personnel in this discussion are stated as of the time the GPFI was in progress (1956–1959).

[33] 60 Stat. 237 (1946).

the agency may issue a tentative decision or any of its responsible officers may recommend a decision," or (4) "any such procedure may be omitted in any case in which the agency finds upon the record that due and timely execution of its functions imperatively and unavoidably so requires." The CAB's "Rules of Practice in Economic Proceedings" provides that in cases relating to rates the examiner "shall render an initial decision orally on the record or in writing if, before the close of hearing, any party so requests." In a case as complex as the GPFI a written decision is obviously essential. If no party requests an initial decision by the examiner, he shall, by CAB rules, certify the record to the Board for decision. Ordinarily, the examiner will render an initial decision. Such a decision, under Section 8(a) of the APA, becomes final unless appealed to the Board or reviewed by it upon its own motion.

THE BUREAU OF AIR OPERATIONS

The Bureau of Air Operations (BAO) is the largest unit within the CAB. It carries responsibility for development of all aspects of the program of economic regulation, except compliance and accounting and statistical reporting, including matters related to domestic and international routes, carrier agreements, bilateral agreements with foreign countries,[34] and rates. It has the responsibility for developing and presenting the public's position on routes and on rates before examiners and the Board.

Within the BAO, supervisory responsibilities with respect to the GPFI rested in four officials: the director of the BAO (GS 17); the associate director (GS 16), who advised the director on all matters affecting domestic aviation; the chief of the Rates Division (GS 15); and the assistant chief of the Rates Division (GS 15), who had responsibilities with respect to commercial rates. All of these men had long careers in government service and within the CAB. The director served continuously for fourteen years in the Reconstruction Finance Corporation, except for three years in military service, during which time he attained the rank of lieutenant colonel. From 1946 to 1958 he was secretary and comptroller of the CAB, and in May, 1958, he became director of the BAO. The associate director,

---

[34] Negotiated by the Department of State with collaboration of the CAB.

after obtaining the B.A. degree from Brooklyn College and pursuing graduate studies in business administration at Columbia University and New York University, served three years as financial analyst in the Public Utilities Division of the Securities and Exchange Commission and three years as a statistician on telephone rate investigations in the Federal Communications Commission. Except for three years of military service he had been in the CAB since 1941, serving first on the rates staff, then as chief of the Rates Division. He had occupied the latter position when the GPFI was instituted. The chief of the Rates Division received degrees from Columbia University and Brooklyn College, then went into government service. He had completed twenty years of such service, twelve of which had been spent in rate work in the CAB. The assistant chief was educated at Columbia University, had worked in airline and management consultant service, and had been in rate work for the CAB for about twelve years—as analyst, as chief of the Mail Rates Section, and in the post he then occupied. The ages of these four men varied from fifty (the director) to a low of thirty-nine (the assistant chief). All except the director had had ten years or more of service in rate work in the CAB. One, the chief of the Rates Division, had a legal education.

All policy questions about the GPFI were cleared with the director of the BAO. The other men were consulted often about policy stands. The associate director, the chief of the Rates Division, and the attorney in charge of the case rode together twice daily, with one other CAB official, in a car pool, and the problems presented by the GPFI were a frequent subject of discussion on these trips.

Nevertheless, responsibility was assigned to a large extent to the Commercial Rates Section, headed by the assistant chief of the Rates Division. The active direction of the preparation of the case was assigned to an attorney (GS 14) in the section. He had completed his academic and legal education at the University of Iowa in 1937, had engaged in general practice of law, had entered wartime military service, and had become assistant commerce counsel of Iowa, then director of the Property Tax Division of the Iowa State Tax Commission. He had been supervisory attorney in the Commercial Rates Section for about five years.

At the start of the GPFI the Commercial Rates Section included three attorneys, two senior analysts, and two junior analysts. Five of these seven worked almost continuously on the investigation. Subsequently, additional staff was added, so that by about December 1, 1957, there were three attorneys, four senior analysts, and two junior analysts working on the case. A fourth attorney was added in January, 1958, and a fifth attorney on March 1, 1958. The classifications of the attorneys ranged from GS 7 to GS 14, of the senior analysts from GS 12 to GS 13, and of the junior analysts from GS 5 to GS 11. Such was the staff responsible for preparation of the public's case, and it was substantially the total staff capacity available in the BAO for dealing with domestic commercial rates.

THE BOARD AND THE STAFF

The Board itself gives no direction to the staff from the Commercial Rates Section in the presentation of the public's case, except insofar as direction is provided in the Board's opinions and orders. The staff will generally follow any indicated lines of Board policy, but it may argue for deviations therefrom. In this case substantial guidance lay in the principles of rate making followed by the Board in mail rate proceedings, but the area of judgment on choice and elaboration of arguments was extensive.

Attorneys in the Office of the General Counsel of the Board have no power of direction over attorneys in the BAO. Officials in the BAO sometimes ask for legal or policy advice from the Office of the General Counsel, and there is a rate specialist in the latter office. Yet officials in the BAO and the Office of the General Counsel recall no communications or conversations between those in the two offices on the GPFI.

The Board preserves its judicial role pending the presentation of a case to it for decision.[35] In the meantime, it defines the scope and issues of the proceeding and rules on motions presented to it. Ultimately, it will make a decision, as a bench of judges, on the case.

[35] It should be noted that Section 5 of the Administrative Procedure Act, requiring separation of prosecuting and judicial functions, does not apply to rule making, which includes "prescription for the future of rates." The Board has gone beyond the requirements of the APA and the Civil Aeronautics Act in assuming a "waiting position."

This will occur after the examiner's initial decision, exceptions thereto by parties, and submission of briefs and oral arguments to the Board.[36] Petitions for reconsiderations may follow the Board's decision, but such petitions will not operate as a stay of the Board's order unless the Board specifically so orders.

In making its decision the Board will have the assistance of its Office of the General Counsel, including the Opinion Writing Division. Each Board member also usually has one legal aide. There is no provision in the APA or the Federal Aviation Act to prevent consultation by a Board member with other experts in the agency.

SCOPE

As in 1952 the first procedural problem was to determine the scope of the investigation. This was done by the Board before the case was assigned to an examiner. This time the Board was to limit the investigation strictly to the overall level of fares, denying all petitions that the structure of fares should be included also.

In the order of May 10, 1956, the Board said:

> It is our tentative opinion that an essential to achieving a prompt determination of this important question [overall level] is a limitation of the issues in the investigation to those concerning the general level of the passenger fares of the trunkline carriers, excluding all issues as to the lawfulness of particular fares or classes of fares or the interrelationships between them, and a limitation of the scope of the possible order to be issued herein to flat percentage changes in the fares of particular carriers or groups of carriers.

The Board added that this would leave it free to require changes for some or all carriers or to require uniform or differing changes as between carriers, and would not prejudice consideration of lawfulness of particular rates or fare relationships in other proceedings.

Nevertheless, the Board added that it did not want to decide finally upon limitation of the issues without affording interested parties an opportunity to be heard. Accordingly, it gave notice that oral presentation and submission of written data to the Board on the scope of the investigation were set for June 12, with all parties having an

---

[36] By provision of APA, the examiner's initial decision would become the Board's decision if no exceptions thereto were filed. This could not be expected in a case of this importance.

opportunity to appear who filed written requests by June 1. Subsequently, the chief examiner sent out a notice setting forth the order of appearance and time allowed to each of eight parties and to others to be heard as *amicus curiae*. At the oral argument before the Board the attorney for the Conference of Local Airlines and attorneys for certain carriers suggested inclusion of rate structure in the investigation; requests were made also for inclusion of other issues, namely the relations between various classes of fares, the "no-show" problem (that is, failure of passengers with reservations to appear), and the soundness of certain practices, such as baggage allowances and charges.

The Board, showing anxiety to get a prompt decision, issued an order on July 27[37] refusing to enlarge the scope of the investigation. As to investigation of rate structure, it said the question was "not whether it should be done but when."

PARTIES

The order of May 10 made the thirteen trunkline carriers respondents. Before the end of July the merger of Colonial Airlines and Eastern Airlines reduced the number to twelve. The BAO automatically became a party with the responsibility of presenting the public's case. Petitions to intervene were received from the General Services Administration (GSA), the Department of Defense, ATA, the Conference of Local Airlines, and the Los Angeles Chamber of Commerce. The local service carriers and the GSA were accepted by the Board as parties, with the status of interveners rather than respondents, in its order of July 27. The ATA's request of August 2 for right to intervene was contested by counsel for the BAO (hereafter referred to as Bureau Counsel) in a written answer of August 10, which was in turn met by a rebuttal statement of ATA on August 15 asserting that the industry, "as an industry," was entitled to the status of a party with right to cross-examine witnesses, present oral argument, and the like. The Board on August 22 granted the petition.[38] Subsequently, it granted right to intervene to the Conference of Local Airlines and to the Department of the Air Force on behalf of the Department of Defense.[39]

[37] Order No. E-10488 (July 27, 1956).
[38] Order No. E-10551 (August 28, 1956).
[39] Order No. E-10724 (October 31, 1956).

DESIGNATION OF EXAMINER

For this case the chief examiner selected Ralph Wiser, examiner in CAB for fifteen years. Wiser was born in 1909 and obtained his higher education at George Washington University, where he receieved an A.B. degree with a major in economics, as well as a J.D. degree, and did graduate study in economics. He served fourteen years in the Navy Department in various phases of supply, accounting, and disbursing, two and one-half years in the Navy during World War II, and one year in the Economic Bureau of the CAB. During his service as examiner he had handled cases covering all phases of economic regulation, including the Large Irregular Air Carrier Investigation and the Reopened Transatlantic Final Mail Rate Case. The former was a general investigation pertaining to nonscheduled air carriers, involving over 200 applications for certification and extending to 331 days of hearings, 36,000 pages of testimony, and a total record of more than 60,000 pages. The latter case involved determination of offsetting excess earnings in a large transatlantic subsidy case.

After living with the GPFI for two and one-half years (by December, 1958), Wiser struggled with the issue in a small two-man office, with typewriters clanging from the adjoining room.[40] He was surrounded by the materials in the case, and the observer could see that he worked systematically with an extensive card file system. He, of course, assiduously avoided any reference to the issues or testimony in the case, but he was deeply interested in discussion of the possibilities for procedural simplification in complex general investigations.

PREHEARING CONFERENCE

The "Rules of Practice in Economic Proceedings" stated that "ordinarily" a prehearing conference will be held:

The purpose of such a conference is to define and simplify the issues and the scope of the proceeding, to secure statements of the positions of

---

[40] CAB had been quartered in the Commerce Building and one of the temporary buildings. Examiners were crowded in a wing of the temporary building. Beginning in January, 1959, with a move to a new location, each examiner had a separate office.

the parties with respect thereto and amendments to the pleadings in conformity therewith, to schedule the exchange of exhibits before the date set for hearing, and to arrive at such agreements as will aid in the conduct and disposition of the proceeding. (Sec. 302.23)

Since the Board had already defined the scope of the proceeding in the GPFI, the prehearing conference was limited to the other purposes stated in the "Rules of Practice." By notice to parties on August 2, 1956, the chief examiner set September 9 as the date for the prehearing conference, and on August 7 the hearing examiner requested the parties to submit the following in writing by August 29:

1. Proposed statements of issues,
2. Proposed stipulations,
3. Requests for information,
4. Statements of positions of parties,
5. Proposed procedural dates.

Though statements of position were not filed until November, 1957, the prehearing conference was held on September 5 and 6, 1956. While certain stipulations (that is, matters for agreement between attorneys) were proposed, no agreement was reached on any. The examiner served on the parties on October 15 a "Report of the Prehearing Conference," dealing with issues, information, procedural dates, and "Ground Rules of the Proceeding." After the parties had had opportunity to object by written communication, the examiner issued on November 12 a "Supplemental Report of Prehearing Conference," ruling on objections filed and amending the original report. There were motions by attorneys, examiner's rulings, and Board decisions on matters considered in the prehearing conference; all of this preceded by many months the hearings on the issues in the case but did not prevent the beginning of the process of exchange of written documents.

Issues and Evidence

The examiner defined the "primary issues" as:

1. Whether fares and charges received, individually or jointly by carriers, for transportation of passengers within continental United

States, excluding Alaska, are or will be[41] generally unjust and unreasonable, and

2. If found to be unjust or unreasonable, what overall percentage changes of fares or charges of the respondents, collectively or individually, are required.

He noted that the rate-making factors were set forth in Section 1002(e),[42] that reasonable rates in past periods were not in issue, and that parties could submit evidence on other issues listed in their written submittals to the prehearing conference.

Bureau Counsel objected at the prehearing conference to consideration of (1) value of service,[43] (2) valuation of assets at other than original cost less depreciation, (3) effects of changes on surface carriers, or (4) effects of changes on the National Transportation Policy defined in the Interstate Commerce Act. In the "Report" on the conference the examiner ruled that the first two were appropriate subjects for evidence; that evidence could be submitted on whether, and if so to what extent, the third should be considered; and that since no one had contended that the National Transportation Policy applied to air carriers, this question would not be considered unless there was further showing of its relevance. Bureau Counsel objected to the rulings on 1, 2, and 3, and in the "Supplemental Report" the examiner reaffirmed his rulings. Bureau Counsel subsequently asked for permission to appeal to the Board on these rulings [under Sec. 302.18(f) of "Rules of Practice"]; the examiner granted the request, even though he thought it had been "unduly delayed," and directed parties to file briefs with the Board by December 3. The Board denied the BAO's request, saying the relevance of specific evidence should be determined by the examiner, and that the CAB was not ready to determine that only one type of evidence was relevant.[44]

[41] The words *or will be* were added in the "Supplemental Report" as the result of an exception from Eastern Airlines.

[42] Quoted above, page 149.

[43] "Value of service" is a vague phrase meaning, in general, the utility of the service to the public. The airlines were to argue that the public was getting a real bargain in airline service and that this should be considered in setting rates; Bureau Counsel were to argue that rates should be set on the basis of the cost of rendering the service, with no allowance added for the intrinsic value to the user of airline service.

[44] Order No. E-11009 (February 6, 1957).

REQUESTS FOR INFORMATION

At the prehearing conference there were, of course, many requests by parties for filing of information by opposing parties, that is, BAO and the carriers. One request by Bureau Counsel was particularly significant. It asked for the carriers to submit financial data for the twelve months ending June 30, 1956, for four previous years on a calendar basis, and for forecasts for 1957. The carriers accepted the main part of Bureau Counsel's request, but most carriers preferred to submit forecasts for 1958 instead of 1957. In view of the delays which were to occur, it is interesting to note that the examiner thought the briefs would not reach him "before well into the year 1957" and hence decided in favor of submission of forecasts for 1958. Bureau Counsel objected, but the examiner reaffirmed his decision in the "Supplemental Report."

Since it could be foreseen that capital requirements for jet-age expansion and the reaction of financial markets to carrier financing would be involved in the arguments of the parties, Bureau Counsel requested certain information from the carriers on loan commitments and on cost of jet aircraft. The carriers objected to the requests. The BAO reserved the right of subpoena. Subsequently (December 6), Western Air Lines moved to quash a subpoena issued at request of Bureau Counsel for copies of data submitted by Western to financial institutions. The examiner on December 19 denied the motion, noting the relevance of "what the carriers have said to their bankers in support of requests for funds." On December 26, Western by telegram to the examiner asserted his lack of power to act on the motion, and the examiner by return wire on December 27 answered that this claim was without merit. The following day Western appealed to the Board, which took jurisdiction and ruled against Western's motion to quash, citing relevance of the information and the CAB's policy of giving protection on confidential information where need was shown.[45]

The airlines, on the other hand, wanted to get a look at information from the CAB's files. Some of the airlines asked at the prehear-

---

[45] Order No. E-11008 (February 7, 1957). There was, as is usual practice, no hearing on the motion to quash the subpoena. At the time of Western's appeal, but not at present, CAB rules allowed an appeal without the examiner's consent on a motion with respect to a subpoena.

ing conference for information on complaints about their charges that had been sent to the CAB. Bureau Counsel objected, but the examiner indicated approval of the request and asked Bureau Counsel to report on their willingness to supply the information. Subsequently, Eastern Airlines and United Airlines requested certain information, and Bureau Counsel objected. The information related to staff studies on effects of new cumulative competition, working papers and studies presented to the Board in connection with this investigation, and the like, and included also an Item 7, which revived the request for "all complaints received by the Board about the level of domestic passenger rates." The examiner denied the motions on all except Item 7. In answer to carriers' arguments that airlines should have the same rights to examine the CAB's studies as it had to examine theirs, he said that while no precedent was shown that carriers' studies were private, Board staff studies, internal memos, and recommendations of Board experts ordinarily are not subject to discovery. Eastern filed motion for permission to appeal for a subpoena, and the examiner, noting the uncertainty of the CAB's governing rule of practice, allowed appeal. By order on September 27, 1957, the Board overruled the examiner's decision on Item 7, saying that although there is "general relevance in a theoretical sense, as a practical matter they [complaints received by Board] are neither relevant nor material."[46] The Board stated that the other requests should not have been referred to it by the examiner, but decided against Eastern, adopting the examiner's opinion as its own. To the carriers' assertion of right under Section 12 of APA (that all requirements relating to evidence "shall apply equally to agencies and persons"), the Board noted that the section began, "Except as otherwise required by law," and that the courts had recognized the privilege against disclosure of matters in agency files.

GROUND RULES

The examiner may most effectively regulate the proceedings, limit their length, and ensure clarification of party positions through

---

[46] There is some belief that there might be included in such files considerable congressional correspondence.

his prescription of ground rules. The examiner in this case laid down the following "Ground Rules":

1. Cross-examination, except by Bureau Counsel, will be limited to witnesses whose testimony is adverse to the party desiring to cross-examine.

2. Second rounds of cross-examination will not be permitted except upon a showing of good cause.

3. Cross-examination of any particular witness, or oral presentation on any motion of objection, will be limited to one attorney for a party, except on a showing of good cause.

4. Oral presentation on any motion or objection will be limited to the party making the motion or objection and the party or parties against which the motion or objection is directed.

5. All evidence (except that brought out on cross-examination) shall be in written exhibit form insofar as practicable, and all statistical and analytical material shall be so presented, with witnesses cognizant of the exhibits to be made available for cross-examination. Witnesses will not be permitted to read prepared testimony.

6. The authenticity of all documents submitted as proposed exhibits in advance of the hearing will be deemed admitted unless written objection thereto is filed prior to the hearing, except that a party will be permitted to challenge such authenticity at a later time upon a clear showing of good cause for failure to have filed such written objection . . .

7. Exhibits shall be exchanged on prescribed dates prior to the hearing, i.e., one copy of each exhibit shall be served on the Examiner and on each party . . .

8. Each party, except Bureau Counsel, shall obtain the necessary information to prepare its case prior to the hearing, and shall be prepared to go forward at the hearing on the basis of a position which it indicates prior to commencement of the hearing, and which it supports by its evidence, such presentation to include the specific rate change or changes which the party contends should be required or permitted. Bureau Counsel shall indicate his position at the time his written testimony is exchanged after hearing on the other parties' evidence.

9. A trial brief shall be presented by each party to the Examiner prior to the beginning of the hearing, which should include a showing of the party's theory of the case and an explanation of

the points involved in that theory which each exhibit is designed to prove.[47]

PROGRESS OF THE PROCEEDINGS

The prehearing conference and the "Ground Rules" had the aim of simplifying and expediting the proceedings. To further regulate the proceedings the examiner set forth in the "Report" and again in the "Supplemental Report" the procedural steps and the date for each. These dates were to be extended several times.

The chief procedural steps set forth by the examiner were exchange (among parties) of requested information, exchange of direct exhibits, exchange of rebuttal exhibits, exchange of written testimony presented by carriers and carrier associations, hearing on carrier and carrier-association presentations, distribution of Bureau Counsel's written testimony, hearing on Bureau Counsel's case, and rebuttal to Bureau Counsel's case. The statements of position and trial briefs required by the "Ground Rules" were to be submitted at the commencement of hearings on their cases by carriers and Bureau Counsel, respectively.

The information and direct exhibit exchanges occurred near the original schedule dates, on September 3, 1956, and February 27, 1957, respectively, and hearings were scheduled to commence on May 6. At this point new tariff filings were made on behalf of seven trunkline carriers seeking, generally, increases of approximately 6 percent. The carriers, now in a period of declining earnings, were seeking an emergency increase, pending completion of the GPFI. The CAB was not required to complete its own investigation in the GPFI within a time period, but the Civil Aeronautics Act precluded suspension of carrier petitions for more than 180 days. The Board suspended the proposed increases on March 15, 1957, and ordered an investigation in what came to be known alternately as the Suspended Passenger Fare case or the Six Percent case. The new proceeding placed a new burden on Bureau Counsel and expert witnesses. Hence, Bureau Counsel requested postponement of further steps in the GPFI until the hearings on the suspension case were

[47] In "Report of the Prehearing Conference." As a result of exceptions some minor changes were made in the "Supplemental Report of Prehearing Conference."

concluded.[48] The Board granted the petition. The effect of the Six Percent case and granted postponements by the Board was a delay of approximately six months in the GPFI.

The Board announced its decision in the Six Percent case on August 6, 1957,[49] denying the petitions for increased rates. One Board member made it clear that he was only passing on the need for interim relief pending completion of the GPFI, and the majority opinion stated that most of the issues were decided subject to further consideration in that proceeding.

The Board on August 8 consolidated the record in the Six Percent case with the GPFI docket "to avoid needless duplication of time and effort."[50] Nevertheless, the Six Percent case led to additional procedural and evidentiary requirements in the GPFI. The examiner asked the parties to bring their exhibits up to date. Revised direct exhibits were exchanged by parties (September 13) and rebuttal exhibits followed one month later (October 11). But more than revision of exhibits was necessary. The Board said in its consolidation order of August 8: "Most of the carriers contend that the nub of their case for a fare increase is the requirement that earnings be kept at a reasonable level in order to maintain investor confidence and thereby permit financing of their jet programs." But the Board thought that the carriers had not shown that higher earnings were necessary for new financing. Accordingly, the Board in its consolidation order decreed that the carriers should submit five-year forecasts. Specifically, they were to submit evidence with respect to:

[48] "We do not have enough staff to carry on both investigations at the same time. We are using the staff at the moment on the expedited hearing that has to be completed in 180 days," stated Board member Gurney (*Hearings on the Department of Commerce and Related Appropriations for 1958, before a Subcommittee of the Committee on Appropriations*, House of Representatives, 85th Cong., 1st Sess., 941 (1957). The Six Percent case was assigned to the same examiner who was serving in the GPFI.

[49] By press release. The opinion of the Board was issued on September 25, 1957. In 1956 there was a leak of information on a Board decision on an important route case between the date of decision and the framing of an order and opinion. Subsequently, the Board followed the policy of announcing its decisions immediately by press release. Board member Hector always disagreed with the policy.

[50] Order No. E-11669 (August 8, 1957).

a. Plans for purchase of new equipment for at least each of the five years 1958 through 1962;
b. Traffic forecasts for at least five years based upon such planning;
c. Plans for financing the purchase of such equipment;
d. Plans for the retirement of existing equipment; and
e. The effect of future equipment plans and financing programs upon the general rate level and passenger fares in the long run.

Thereafter, on August 13, the examiner notified parties that the evidence would be received in three phases:

1. Rate-of-return evidence,
2. The five-year forecasts,
3. All other evidence.

Also, the examiner amended the "Ground Rules" to require that each party, including Bureau Counsel, should in its statement of position "include the special rate of return and rate change or changes contended for."

All of the many procedural steps prior to hearing, including exchange of revised exhibits and rebuttals thereto, exhibits on five-year forecasts and rebuttals thereto, surrebuttal exhibits, written testimony, statements of positions, and trial briefs, were completed in slightly more than two months after the Board had consolidated the record of the Six Percent case.

The hearings began on November 18, 1957, took a total of 142 days, and were concluded on August 1, 1958. Since the "Ground Rules" required in general the exchange of evidence prior to the hearings and prohibited reading of written testimony, the hearings were devoted in the main to cross-examination of witnesses. The hearings are replete, therefore, with objections and arguments on relevance and with the examiner's rulings thereon. At times attorneys were contentious, and arguments over minutiae were persistently pushed and reraised in new lines of questioning. Note may be taken of the large number of parties and attorneys in the case; even with the limitations of the "Ground Rules" the meticulous and time-consuming process of cross-examination made exceedingly lengthy hearings inevitable.

Demands for Faster Action

The airline industry, experiencing profit decline in the recession period of 1957–1958, was impatient over the length of the proceeding and the failure to obtain interim rate increases. This impatience is revealed in statement and action. In 1958, Tipton, after noting that decision by the Board in the GPFI would probably not be rendered until the first quarter of 1959 [too sanguine a hope!] and that the chairman of the Board had informed Congress there would follow another investigation "of equal size" of fare structure, concluded flatly, "Unfortunately, the jet age will not wait upon this schedule."

Not deterred by the refusal of the Board to grant an increase in the Six Percent case, the airlines sought other fare increases prior to the completion of the fare investigation. On January 15, 1958, Continental Airlines filed with the CAB a tariff reflecting a 15-percent increase in the fares over its system. Also, TWA filed a tariff modifying existing fare structure and providing a fare increase. The Board voted to suspend these tariffs. But a general economic recession had taken place in 1957, and by early 1958 the Board was impressed with its effects on airline revenues. By press release it informed the airlines that it would approve an interim fare increase of 4 percent plus one dollar per ticket, to net an average increase of 6.6 percent in domestic trunkline rates, if the carriers came forth with such a proposal. The carriers did so and the increases were granted.[51]

The policy of announcing in advance what will be approved is an informal procedure not provided for in the governing act. It provides a short cut by which encumbrances are avoided.

Certain trunkline carriers proposed further increases for the fall of 1958. The Board suspended the increases and ordered investigation, and again announced by press release (October 14) what it would accept. The carriers were told that the Board would approve an immediate increase, to be effective to July 31, 1959, with expectation, however, that the carriers would propose new promotional fares (that is, special rates for some kinds of service aimed at increasing traffic) by that date. The carriers agreed to the increases, which were not across-the-board raises but rather elimination of round-trip discounts, reduction of the family-fare discount from 50

[51] Press release of January 24, 1958, confirmed in Order No. E-12203, In the Matter of Passenger Fares Proposed by Trans-World Airlines, Inc. ("Interim Fare Increases") (February 25, 1958).

percent to 33⅓ percent, and elimination of free stopover privileges.

In the meantime, further procedural motions also indicated dissatisfaction with the pace of the GPFI. The usual procedure after completion of hearings and the filing of briefs is an initial examiner's decision and opinion, followed by written exceptions, briefs and oral arguments before the Board, and finally Board decision. On January 20, 1958, American, supported by letters from three other airlines, filed a motion asking that the Board order the skipping of the examiner's decision, or the alternate procedure of a tentative Board decision, and require the certification of the record directly to the Board for "final" decision. Three airlines and Bureau Counsel objected. The Board denied American's motion on March 13, noting that it had recognized the financial needs of the carriers by an emergency increase. It stated that it would not sacrifice the objective of the GPFI by "hasty, superficial consideration." The Board, moreover, could not under the Administrative Procedure Act dispense with an initial (examiner's) or a tentative (Board's) decision without a finding that the "due and timely execution" of its "functions imperatively and unavoidably so requires. . . . Equally important," the conclusions of the examiner on the voluminous evidence would be denied to the Board.[52]

On the day of this order William Kloepfer, Jr., chief of the Office of Information of the CAB, issued a press release answering the charge of "more than fifty of the nation's largest daily newspapers, plus many commentators, trade journals and general circulation magazines . . . that the CAB is dragging its bureaucratic feet while the financial structure of the country's airlines is going to pot." On March 20 the Board issued a statement disassociating itself from this press release. Later in the year the Board commented as follows on the situation that led to these unusual releases:

An example of indirect pressure can be found in connection with the Board's current General Passenger Fare Investigation. This proceeding has not been the subject of wide news coverage but at the same time it has been the subject of a considerable editorial comment. Particularly during the winter of 1957–58, editorials appeared in a large segment of

[52] Order No. E-12247 (March 13, 1958). American also requested that the hearings be completed in one month after end of Phase I of the hearings. This was denied. It would have limited Bureau Counsel's time on the companies' five-year forecasts.

the daily press containing a similarity of statistical references, urging the Board to provide financial relief to the air transport industry through higher passenger fares. While the Board made no official judgment as to the source of this editorial campaign, it did make clear that it would not be influenced by or accept the validity of the published material. On March 20, 1958, the Board stated publicly:

We have, of course, regretted the statements in the press and in trade publications which to us seemed to give an inaccurate picture of the general passenger fare investigation and of the Board's attitude toward passenger fare increases. However, we believe as a basic principle of democracy that the right of the press to comment freely on all public affairs is one of the surest and strongest forces for good government.[53]

Further delay in the GPFI resulted from a motion of Bureau Counsel on March 21, 1958, for a four-week recess to give them time to prepare their Phase III ("All other evidence") presentation. Bureau Counsel argued that they needed to make a "posthearing evaluation of the evidence." The examiner indicated this was his function and that he would approve only a one–and–one–half–week recess. Bureau Counsel with the examiner's consent appealed, five carriers objected, and the Board granted the petition. It noted that it "must be assured that the 'public's case' is adequately presented"; that over four hundred new or revised exhibits, some very substantial, had gone on the record since commencement of Phase

[53] In unpublished answer to 138 questions from the Legislative Oversight Committee of the House Interstate and Foreign Commerce Committee (Fall, 1958).

As is frequently true today of cases of vast import—for example, antitrust and desegregation—this issue of higher earnings was being "tried" also in the forum of public opinion. The ATA, through its public relations program, presents airline needs to the public. It also presents these to congressional committees. See, for example, "Operating the Jet," *A Symposium Presented to the Subcommittee on Aviation of the Committee on Interstate and Foreign Commerce*, U.S. Senate, 85th Cong., 2d Sess. particularly 53–66 and 100 (May 9, 1958). As to the Board's decision granting a fare increase in February, 1958, Mr. Tipton in a letter to the Honorable A. S. Mike Monroney, chairman, said, "While the CAB's decision is a step in the right direction, it is a very short step. What is needed now is a long step" (p. 100).

Board member Hector said, in reporting rate petitions and decisions in 1957 and 1958: "In such times of tension, of course, tempers become frayed and the air for a while was filled with violent charges and counter-charges" (address to the New York Society of Security Analysts on November 28, 1958).

II of the hearing; and that the transcript of hearing since that date was already over four thousand pages.

After the conclusion of hearings the examiner decided various motions concerning corrections, substitutions, and the like, of exhibits and other matters in the record. He also issued two statements of directions for attorneys' briefs. The first, on September 22, included the following:

The examiner indicated, from time to time during the hearing, subjects which he would expect the parties to cover on briefs. These included, among others, the method of regulation that should be followed, including the question of whether a price should be fixed that would result in opportunity for proper profit (measured by return on investment, operating ratio, or other yardstick) for the average carrier, for the most poorly situated carrier, or for carriers determined on some other basis . . . [and] reference to any decisions of courts or regulatory bodies passing upon proposals similar or analogous to Bureau Counsel's proposals with respect to load factor and representative costs.

The second direction came on October 1:

The examiner requests coverage on brief of the legal and economic feasibility of a method of regulation encompassing automatic adjustment of the general level of passenger fares with changes in the carriers' or groups of carriers' costs (including break-even load factor as a cost indicator), rate of return on investment, operating ratio, or other measurement standard. Consideration should not be limited to current year's results but should include periods of other duration. The frequency of adjustment should be covered. Among other things, discussion is requested of a regulation requiring inclusion of such an automatic adjustment clause in all passenger rate tariffs.

On October 29, 1958, briefs to the examiner were exchanged among the parties. More than two years after his assignment to the case, the issue of what the airline industry should earn on its domestic business was before him for decision. We must turn now to the issues that were presented to him and then to decisions of the Board relating to these issues in other cases prior to his decision.

Substantive Issues in the GPFI

All airlines except National asked for higher rates in their statements of position and trial briefs filed in November, 1957. The requests for increase ranged from 12.5 to 20 percent, as follows: American, 15 percent; Braniff, 12.5 percent; Capital, 20 percent; Continental, 15 percent; Northwest, 13 percent; TWA, at least 15 percent; United, 17 percent; and Western, 14 percent. Arguments advanced by the carriers supported these or higher increases, for in some cases lower than theoretically justified increases were requested because higher increases might reduce traffic. National did not ask for an increase or submit a brief; it did submit factual information required of carrier parties.

The carriers' positions were taken prior to the two interim increases of 1958 which together resulted in an approximate increase of 10 to 11 percent in passenger fares.

The General Services Administration, appearing under provisions of law[54] as the representative of government purchasers of transportation services, opposed any increase and requested that the Board make such decreases as might be justified by the record. Bureau Counsel were allowed to file their position later. They concluded that a 4-percent increase over levels existing at the beginning of the GPFI was justified, but recommended that the total increase of February, 1958, be allowed to stand until June 30, 1960, to provide a cushion during the period of transition to jet equipment.[55]

To summarize, the airlines asked for about a 15-percent increase; they had received interim increases of 10 to 11 percent; Bureau Counsel, representing the public, wanted only a 4-percent increase to stand; and GSA, on behalf of the government as a consumer of air transportation, pressed for taking away all increases already granted, and more if justified.

It would serve no purpose to analyze the correctness of these particular positions, for conditions have changed since the positions were taken. What follows is a description of the conflicting positions taken on the issue of what standards of rate making should be applied to the airline industry. Congressional committee members and the Comptroller General were concerned over absence of standards

[54] Section 201(a) of Federal Property and Administrative Services Act of 1959, as Amended, 40 USC 481.

[55] Bureau Counsel estimated that this would mean 3.28-percent reduction in fares immediately and 6.39 percent on July 1, 1960. Bureau Counsel's brief, p. 23.

for rate making, and statements of Board members and parties show that all considered that there was a vital need for such standards. Board member Hector, for example, told the New York Society of Security Analysts about the GPFI in a speech in November, 1958:

> Its most important purpose is, or to my mind should be, to establish clear guide-lines and policies—procedures and standards—for the future determination of whether rates are just and reasonable. Its main value is certainly not just a one-shot determination of whether rates are reasonable today.

The basic equation for determining rates is simple. Rates must be such that gross income equals costs plus return for investor. Rate making involves calculations of three elements: income, costs, and fair return. For each element many components must be calculated, and the calculations are never simple. They would not be simple even if parties were agreed on the standards that should govern, because it is difficult to estimate what income and costs will be in a future period—and the objective must be to make the equation work for a future period. But parties in rate-making proceedings rarely agree on standards.

On subsequent pages an attempt will be made to clarify the main issues on standards on which there was contest in this case. Enough detail will be supplied (1) to show the difference in positions of parties, and (2) to throw some light on the problems of feasibility in use of the standards. The material will be presented under the following headings:

1. Basic Views: Liberal Return vs. Strict Costing
2. Determination of a Fair Return
    Basic Approaches
    Profit (Margin-of-Return) Method
    Rate-of-Return Method: (A) The Return Rate
        Cost-of-Capital Approach
            Capital Structure
            Interest Costs
            Cost of Equity Capital
        Alternatives to Cost-of-Capital Approach
        Capital Gains—an Additional Rate-of-Return Issue
    Rate-of-Return Method: (B) The Rate Base
        Prudent Investment vs. Property Used and Useful
        Inflation

BASIC VIEWS: LIBERAL RETURN VS. STRICT COSTING

Although no one used the label "Liberal Return vs. Strict Cost-ing" in the GPFI, the term does describe the basic difference in approach between the airlines and Bureau Counsel.

The general position of the airlines was that they should be al-lowed more liberal returns, that is, higher earnings, than those considered reasonable for traditional utilities, such as railroads or gas and electric companies.

One basis for this argument was the immediate need for fi-nancing a two–and–one-half–billion–dollar expansion program. The transition to jet equipment would require enormous expenditures for planes, ground facilities, and other items. The carriers argued that the required funds could not be obtained from the capital markets unless returns were relatively high.

In addition, many carriers emphasized the promotional objective of the regulatory act under which CAB operated. Thus, Eastern's trial brief stated that provisions of the act "are unique among sta-tutes regulating common carriers of persons and property and other utilities. No other regulatory body entrusted with control of utilities is so specifically charged with duties of promotion and develop-ment."

Primarily, however, the airline case rested on an argument that the industry was different from standard utilities. The argument emphasized the dispensability of airline service, competition within the industry and with other forms of transportation, rapid obso-lescence of equipment, instability of earnings, and the insecurity created by high operating ratios (ratio of expenses to gross in-come).[56] It was asserted that the airlines were more comparable to

---

[56] See, for example, American's trial brief and its brief.

manufacturing industries than to utilities,[57] and hence were entitled to a higher level of earnings.

The legal basis for this argument was the "corresponding risk" doctrine of the Supreme Court. Two cases were repeatedly cited. The first was the Bluefield case, in which the Supreme Court said:

A public utility is entitled to such rates as will permit it to earn a return on the value of the property which it employs for the convenience of the public equal to that generally being made at the same time and in the same general part of the country on investments in other business undertakings which are attended by corresponding risks and uncertainties; . . .[58]

The second was the Hope case, where the same court said:

The return of the equity owner should be commensurate with returns on investments in other enterprises having corresponding risks. That return, moreover, should be sufficient to assure confidence in the financial integrity of the enterprise, so as to maintain its credit and to attract capital.[59]

This emphasis on liberal returns, comparable to those in industries of higher risk than utilities generally, was the point of departure in the airline case. Bureau Counsel started at a different point. Their approach was strict application of the cost principle:

Passenger fares should be based upon the costs of providing passenger service, including the fair and reasonable earnings which are the cost of attracting capital. The costs to which the fares should be related should be the lowest reasonably attainable under honest, economical and efficient management.

These costs should be determined for "a representative period of reasonably extended duration." Costs should also be "predicated upon economical and efficient use of the carrying capacity of the aircraft in terms of the seats installed," or, differently stated, upon realization of optimum load factors. The representative costs were in general determined from historical periods considered by Bureau

[57] See particularly Delta's trial brief.
[58] Bluefield Waterworks and Improvements Co. v. Public Service Commission, 262 U.S. 679, 692 (1923).
[59] FPC v. Hope Natural Gas Co., 320 U.S. 591, 603 (1944).

Counsel to be representative. Since Bureau Counsel assumed that the same level of rates must exist for all carriers, they used weighted averages of the figures for individual lines.

Bureau Counsel argued that if costs, including capital costs, were covered, then financing of the jet program could be completed. They denied the validity of comparisons with manufacturing companies which were presented. As for the regulatory act, Bureau Counsel, too, stressed the promotional purpose, especially in the concluding pages of their 340-page brief. In addition, however, they stressed the Board's duty under Section 1002(e)(1) of considering the effect of rates upon the movement of traffic. To promote air transportation and move more airline traffic "the Board should require that the proper level of earnings be attained through high load factors and low fares."

The airlines did not question the relevance of cost figures. They did maintain that Bureau Counsel's figures were not representative of future conditions or sometimes even of past operations. Bureau Counsel did not deny the need for a return that was relatively high in comparison with the standard utilities. They did deny that returns should be determined by those of manufacturing companies. The differences in attitude were constant and were reflected in positions taken on various issues.

DETERMINATION OF A FAIR RETURN

Basic Approaches. Probably no question of public policy has produced so much controversy as: What return is fair and reasonable for a regulated industry? From the leading case of *Smyth v. Ames* in 1898[60] to the Hope case in 1944[61] the standard set for rate making in decisions of the Supreme Court of the United States was fair return on fair value. In the Hope case the Court announced that this method of rate making was not essential, that the test of rates was not the method employed but the "end result." Rates that were fair both to consumers and to investors would not be held invalid merely because of the failure to follow a particular method, whether fair return on fair value or other method.

---

[60] Smith v. Ames, 169 U.S. 466 (1898).
[61] FPC v. Hope Natural Gas Co., 320 U.S. 591 (1944).

The vague "end result" test may be an appropriate guide for courts in their task of passing upon the reasonableness of what regulatory commissions have done, and it has the merit of allowing commissions to use different methods. But commissions and legislatures seem to feel the need for a more definite guide in setting rates. The search for this something more definite was the objective of the GPFI.

In the GPFI, Bureau Counsel stood on traditional ground: the return for investors to be included in fares should be described in terms of return on a rate base (fair value of properties or investments). This is the fair-return, or rate-of-return, method. It encompasses two elements: (1) return rate; (2) rate base (value).

An entirely different method was proposed by Eastern (one of the Big Four) and a number of the smaller carriers as a group. They favored what is variously called the profit, margin-of-return, or operating-ratio method. In this method the investor's return is described as a percentage of gross income. The profit margin—or differently stated, the margin of return—is the ratio of profit to revenue, figuring profit after payment of all costs, including income taxes, but before payment of debt charges. The complement is the operating ratio, which is the ratio of the total of operating expenses, depreciation, and all taxes to revenue.

Several of the carriers, including American, Braniff, TWA, and United, favored dual or multiple standards. United argued in its brief for use of the profit (margin-of-return) method for "checking results otherwise obtained." American's position was stated as follows: "The traditional rate of return—rate base approach should not be abandoned, but because of the nature of the air transport industry the operating ratio technique should be used in conjunction with it." Expert consultants presented by different airlines argued for high returns, some on the basis of rate of return, some on the basis of margin of return, some on still other bases. The ATA thought all these studies had merit but believed "the soundest approach would seem to be to use these various expert studies as establishing points of reference—minima for the workable level of earnings to attract capital—rather than as absolutes in themselves." The ATA's and American's basic position was that of the Hope case: "The end result, not the mechanics of reaching the result, is all important."[62] The end result in this instance was that same "encouragement and development" of the airline industry stipulated in Section 2(a) of the act under which the CAB operated.

GSA rejected both the profit and the rate-of-return methods. It accepted Bureau Counsel's case as to the inadequacy of the profit-margin method and the carriers' case on the undependability of cost-of-capital estimates—which was the Bureau Counsel's method of figuring rate of return. GSA stood simply for reducing costs and raising revenues through improved load factors (carrying more passengers with the same plane capacity), possibly through extended coach service.

Profit (Margin-of-Return) Method. The profit method is a departure from usual methods of government rate fixing but has been used or recommended for certain industries. The airlines arguing for the profit method found legal and other expert support for their position in three places: (1) the definite trend of ICC decisions toward use of the method in motor carrier cases; (2) the increasing tendency toward local use of the method in setting transit rates; and (3) a report on rate regulation for the bus industry by a special committee of the National Association of Railroad and Utilities Commissioners in 1952.[63]

Advocacy of the profit method by Eastern and the smaller trunk-line companies was grounded on the economic characteristics of the air-transport industry. Compared with railroads and gas, electric, and telephone utilities, it is an industry in which capital investment is low in relation to the amount of sales. Stated differently, capital costs are relatively low and the operating expenses (labor, fuel, and the like) are relatively high as percentages of total sales. In such an industry the profit margin, which is the margin covering capital cost, will tend to be low.

The airlines explained their position for the profit method by making comparisons of industries with respect to expenses and capital turnover. Capital turnover is the number of times capital is used each year. Thus, a corporation that has an investment of $20,-

---

[62] The quotation is from American's brief, p. 2. For similar statements of the end-result standard, see Justice Douglas's opinion in FPC v. Hope Natural Gas Co., 320 U.S. 591, especially 604 (1944).

[63] Printed as Appendix 3 to Delta's brief.

000 and sells $100,000 in a year has a capital turnover of 5, while a corporation with $100,000 investment and sales for a year of $20,000 has a capital turnover of 0.2. Eastern's brief contained a comparison of industries for 1955 (see Table 2).

TABLE 2

Comparison of Industries for 1955

Industry	Rate of Capital Turnover	All-Expense Operating Ratio	Profit Margin*
Water Utilities Class A and B	0.21 times	74.3%	25.7%
Electric Utilities	0.30	79.9	20.1
Class I Railroads	0.38	88.8	11.2
Bell Telephone System	0.41	86.4	13.6
Gas Distribution and Pipe Line Utilities	0.47	85.8	14.2
Domestic Trunk Airlines	1.78	95.0	5.0

* This column has been added by the author. It is obtained by subtracting the figures in column 3 from one hundred.

In addition, Eastern's expert witness, H. B. Dorau, presented an analysis for 195 unregulated industrial companies showing as a weighted average (derived from aggregate dollar amounts for all companies) a capital turnover of 1.76 and a profit margin of 7.4 percent.[64] The capital turnover was practically the same as for airlines, and Eastern argued that it should have substantially the same profit margin as industrial companies. (Eastern asked for 7 percent.)

Eastern's expert witness discussed also the relations between the two factors discussed above and a third—rate of return. The relations can be arithmetically stated. "Thus," stated Dorau, "if the capital turnover is 0.5 and the margin of return is 20%, the rate of return must be 10%, for the investment is twice as large as the revenues, and a return that is 20% of the revenues is, therefore,

[64] Which brought a return on capitalization of 13.1 percent.

10% of the investment." Hence, where R is rate of return, M is margin of return, and C is capital turnover,

$$R = M \times C \text{ or } M = \frac{R}{C}$$

It was argued that the rate of return customary for utilities would in the airline industry bring a low margin of return and a small margin of safety over costs. If rate of return is 6.0 percent and capital turnover is 1.78, then M is 3.36. A margin of return of 3.36 percent, it was claimed, did not provide a substantial safety cushion against an increase in operating costs.

The bigger operating cushion could, of course, be provided by a higher rate of return, which Bureau Counsel recommended for other reasons. For Eastern and the smaller airlines the conclusion was that rate of return was not a satisfactory measure of risks. They were arguing that the rate-of-return approach was inappropriate where the risks of an industry were associated with high operating expenses and with volume of business rather than with capitalized expenditures.

It was further argued in support of the profit method that it was simpler than rate of return to administer because it looked only to the income statement and avoided the necessity of a rate base determined for each enterprise in the industry.[65] Dorau said:

Any notion that a formula such as the "Rate Base—Rate of Return" formula can be applied to a diverse group of enterprises within an industry or area with the same or comparable precision and certainty as to an individual enterprise in control of its market by benefit of an exclusive franchise is economically and administratively naive and assumes a mathematical impossibility.

Obviously there would also be administrative problems in use of the profit method: If the method were used, what should the amount of the margin be? Eastern argued for 7 percent on the basis of Dorau's testimony on the weighted average profit ratio for 195 industrial companies. J. Rhoads Foster, expert witness for the eight intermediate carriers, claimed they should have a margin of not less than 10 percent. Bureau Counsel questioned whether these companies should be compared with airlines, noted that the components

[65] Stressed in Delta's brief.

of the industrial figure were untested, and maintained that the industrial figures were for a relatively good year—1955. Bureau Counsel did not see any satisfactory means of determining return without referring to the amount of money invested and to the return investors would require on that money.

The full substance of Bureau Counsel's reply to arguments for the profit method may be condensed: Volume of expenses or revenue gives no clue as to what investors will require in order to place their money in an industry (supply price of capital); in the capital markets investors are interested in return on capital rather than expense-earnings ratios; regardless of how often capital is turned, the amount of risk is limited by the amount of capital committed; operating ratio is analogous to cost-plus, for as expenses go up so also does the dollar amount of the profit margin; with respect to leased property the operating-ratio method means the public pays twice—as an operating expense and as a return element on this expense;[66] a fair rate of return will provide an adequate margin of return; carriers desire the proposed method to disguise the returns made and thus enhance the possibilities for greater returns; the operating method is not simpler to administer because an operating ratio must be related to a rate of return in order to have meaning and significance. In short, return on capital is what is significant in determining whether rates are too high or too low, and no other method can escape reference to this standard.

Rate-of-Return Method: (A) The Return Rate. The fair rate of return is a percentage ratio applied to a rate base. Under rate-of-return–rate-base theory a utility is entitled to collect revenues sufficient to equal all reasonable expenses, including depreciation and taxes, plus a fair return on the rate base.

1. Cost-of-Capital Approach. In this case Bureau Counsel and the carriers favoring use of the fair-return approach agreed that rate of return was to be determined, exclusively or primarily, by cost of capital.

For determination of cost of capital, decision must be made on

---

[66] Some carriers lease planes, and they would find an advantage in the profit method. Under the rate-of-return method, they would get a return only on what they owned; under the profit method, return would be figured on sales. In the latter event it would be logical to disallow lease cost as an operating expense.

three elements: cost of debt; cost of equity capital (common stock and surplus); and capital structure, that is, the proportions of debt and of equity capital. Decision on each of these three involves many judgments, and the factual information for these judgments is often of questionable reliability.[67]

   a. Capital Structure—In business financing some funds will ordinarily be borrowed, usually in the form of bonds. This is the debt element in capital. Other funds will be obtained from common stock issue and surplus. This is the equity or ownership element in capital. The ratio of debt to total capital (debt plus equity) is called the debt ratio, and the proportions of debt and common equity determine the capital structure.

   Since debt capital can ordinarily be obtained at a lower cost than equity capital, a high debt ratio reduces the cost of capital. But since payment must be made regularly on debt, while dividends on common stock can be passed, a high debt reduces the financial safety of the enterprise. Hence, deciding the amount of money to be raised by debt financing means striking a balance between economy and safety.

   The capital structure may have a large influence on the amount of revenue needed and hence upon the level of rates. The connection between debt structure and rate making was illustrated by an airline witness who showed that if interest rates are 4 percent, and common stock holders require 16 percent, a total rate of return of 13 percent would be required if the debt ratio was 25 percent, while a rate of return of only 10 percent would be sufficient if the debt ratio were 50 percent.

   The BAO, in all its calculations of capital cost, relied heavily upon the report prepared for it by Paul Howell Associates, financial and utility consultants. The most frequently referred to airline exhibits were the studies of David A. Kosh, managing partner of David A. Kosh Associates, and of W. C. Gilman and Co., engineers. As the appropriate debt ratio for airlines, Howell recommended 40 percent, Kosh and Gilman 25 to 30 percent. Bureau Counsel recommended 45 percent for the Big Four and 50 percent for the other eight carriers, while the airlines stood

   [67] In the GSA's brief, the "cost-of-capital" approach was rejected because of "unreliability of basic data."

for the 25 to 30 percent recommended by the industry's expert witnesses.

The BAO case rested substantially on the actual and imminent debt structure of the carriers, on the assumption that fixing rates on a lower debt figure would create a windfall for the carriers. Witness Howell found that projections by the Big Three (American, Eastern, United) showed expectation of a debt ratio of nearly 50 percent by the end of 1958. Bureau Counsel's brief summarized projections as follows: "The Big Four carriers themselves forecast 49.1 percent debt, 1.9 percent preferred stock, and 49.0 percent equity as at December 31, 1958, and the other eight carriers forecast 54.2 percent debt and 45.8 percent equity for 1958."

The carrier position, on the other hand, was that "sound regulation should be based on the 'optimum' capital structure and not on the actual capital structure," so that airlines would be given a chance to improve their capital structures. It was argued that it was the duty of the CAB to encourage the development of sound capital structures with an adequate margin of safety.

What was an adequate margin of safety? One test was coverage, that is, the number of times net income covered debt cost. Witness Kosh sought the answer on the amount of coverage needed by posing this question: "What capital structure must the airlines have so that they may have the same protection against a decline in coverage below minimum levels, as is now available to the electric utilities, and the telephone utilities?"

Since a coverage of two times was a criterion often used by fiduciary institutions in determining whether securities were eligible for legal investments, Kosh compared the increase in expenses which would reduce utility and airline coverage to two times. Obviously, the wider operating ratio of the utilities would provide a greater margin of safety. One comparison showed that, on certain assumptions deemed to be reasonable, an increase in expenses of 16.1 percent for the Bell System, 15.0 percent for electric utilities, and only 9.3 percent for United Airlines would reduce coverage to two times, and that 23.5 percent for the Bell System, 35.0 percent for electric utilities, and only 10.5 percent for United would reduce coverage to one time.

Bureau Counsel set forth, in contrast, that under the assumptions on which they were making recommendations to the CAB (rates of return, debt cost, and the like) the actual coverage rate before federal income tax payments would be 9.22 percent for the Big Four and 7.12 percent for the other carriers. Bureau witness Howell, projecting his recommendations, arrived at 11.07 percent.

The dependability of the estimates on each side was questioned by the other. Howell's total presentation was less dependent upon projections of figures. His chief points were:

1. Under deft ratios that had existed since 1951 (ranging from 32.1 percent to 28.4 percent of total invested capital) fixed debt charges were covered by net income from twenty-one to twelve times, without including capital gains.

2. What is really important is the amount of cash to cover interest charges. Depreciation is a bookkeeping record and leaves the cash represented in the depreciation account in the business. The depreciation set aside by carriers for 1955 exceeded $112,000,000, which provided a substantial margin of safety for interest expenses that totaled only $7,379,000.

3. The reasonableness of his recommendations for debt ratios was substantiated by airline management and borrowers: (a) Management had not been reckless in borrowing up to existing ratios. (b) The president of United Airlines had testified before a Senate committee that a "40% debt ratio was not an unreasonable ratio," and the president of Delta Airlines had testified in the Six Percent case that a 50-percent ratio was appropriate. (c) Most of the airline debt had been obtained from institutional loan officers, who were responsible trustees.

b. Interest Costs—Cost of existing debt is easy to calculate. In estimating this element in the rate of return, the problem is the uncertainty with respect to future interest rates. Bureau witness Howell made an analysis of existing debt cost, that is, interest rate on the outstanding debt of $293,000,000. For the Big Four the average interest rate was 3.68 percent, for the Little Seven 4.14 percent, and for Capital 5.18 percent. He estimated prospective costs as of the end of 1958 at 3.93 percent for the Big Three (excluding TWA) and 4.77 percent for the Little Eight. On the basis of these figures and the cost of American's preferred stock, Bureau Counsel recommended use of 4 percent for the Big Four and 4.8 percent for the other eight carriers in computing the cost of debt capital. It was argued that it was not necessary to speculate on future interest rates because the airlines had "already contracted for a large part of their capital requirements for several years ahead."

American's witness Gilman looked at the future and recommended allowing an interest rate of 5 percent, which he considered "conservative" in view of his estimate of long-range costs of 5.5 percent. American's brief noted the conjectural nature of future interest rates and concluded that 4 percent was "a bare minimum," but that Gilman's figure of 5 percent "likely remains the more realistic figure" for future capital. United accepted the 4-percent figure but noted it was almost certain to be exceeded. Braniff thought the higher costs on Continental's recent financing should be considered, and American thought the 4.25 percent on its latest borrowing showed some discrepancy in BAO calculations. TWA thought exclusion of its interest figures in Bureau Counsel's projections for airlines for the future was not adequately justified and that BAO figures were "plainly inadequate for the period after 1958."[68]

The differences on this item were not differences in principles, but were related, except for TWA's contention, to the issue as to whether adjustment should be made for prospectively higher interest rates.

c. Cost of Equity Capital—American's brief noted that the "really critical difference" between its position and the position of Bureau Counsel was in estimating the cost of equity capital.

The search for a figure on cost of equity was an effort to determine a fair return for existing stock and a return that would allow sale of future stock. One difficulty in the use of historical data was the fact that during the postwar decade 55 percent of equity financing was through the retention of earnings and 27 percent was through the conversion of senior securities (bonds or preferred stock). The complexities of the search for a figure on return on equity are in part revealed by the following:

Bureau Counsel relied exclusively on "the earnings-price ratio approach" which is the relationship between twelve months'

[68] The BAO's reasons for exclusion were that a large part of TWA's business was international and that its capital costs (which were higher than the Big Three's) reflected the special circumstance of a single large stockholder.

earnings and the market price of stock. On its face this may appear simple, but an analysis of the methods used by Bureau Counsel's witness Howell will show many complexities. Howell made his calculations of the ratio as follows:

1. Capital gains were included in earnings. Capital gains on sales of equipment are intermittently and irregularly a significant item in airline earnings; they are included in airline unadjusted reports on earnings and contribute to unevenness in airline profit figures. Howell balanced the arguments on inclusion or exclusion of capital gains, concluding that sophisticated investors would exclude capital gains in their calculations, but that many investors do not read the "fine print." He decided to include capital gains. Moody's reported earnings, which included capital gains, were used.

2. He used "market capitalization of concurrent earnings," rejecting allowance for a "lag" in investor knowledge of earnings, as revealed a few months earlier.

3. He chose as a representative period for calculation of ratios that from 1951 to 1957 (for 1957, twelve months ending June 30). This period, it was asserted, had the advantages of recency, stability, and extended length.

4. He used for each year the simple arithmetic average of twelve monthly closing stock prices.

5. The annual averages were weighted from one to six inversely (the weight of six for 1957, one for 1951).

6. The calculations were made for the Big Three (excluding TWA)[69] and the Little Eight. He reached a time-weighted average earnings-price ratio of 11.0 percent for the former and 12.1 percent for the latter.

7. An adjustment upward of 15 percent was made to reflect factors, such as costs of sales, leading to underpricing of stock at time of subscription. With this adjustment the cost-of-equity-capital figure for the Big Three was 12.9 percent[70] and for the Little Eight 14.1 percent.

8. No adjustments for the future were made because evidence

[69] Excluded because of (1) its substantial operations in international transportation, (2) the close holding of 75 percent of its stocks, (3) an unrepresentative year, and (4) the substantial backing of TWA by Hughes Tool Company.
[70] The equivalent of 17.6-percent increase over 11.0 percent.

showed that none of the Big Three, at least, planned any new issuances of stock.

The BAO accepted these figures.[71] Combining them with its interest rate figures of 4.0 percent for the Big Four and 4.8 percent for the other eight and a debt-equity ratio of 45–55 for the Big Four and 50–50 for the others, it reached its recommended cost-of-capital (rate of return) figure of 8.9 percent for the Big Four and 9.45 percent for the remaining trunks.

United's witness Kosh prepared elaborate estimates of cost of capital on the basis of earnings-price ratios. Kosh's methods were in general similar to Howell's. The more substantial differences, according to United's brief, were two: Kosh used the years 1950 to 1956, or 1950 to June 30, 1957, though he questioned the value of 1957 figures. Kosh justified his choice of years as reflecting a full half-cycle of earnings from the high 1950 to the low 1955 or 1957. Inclusion of 1950 increased the earnings-price ratio. Exclusion of 1957 would also. The other difference was that Kosh took a simple average of the ratios for each year. United's brief stated that if Howell had used 1950 and a simple average of annual figures he would have reached an earnings-price ratio of 13.81 percent and that if he had also eliminated 1957 the figure would have been 14.15 percent. This, said United, gives credence to Kosh's conclusion of 13.53 percent for United, 13.06 percent for the Big Four, and 12.77 percent for the Big Three, which Kosh rounded up to 14.0 percent because of his choice of lower alternative factors in his calculation.[72]

Thus, two experts using the same technique arrived at results not widely divergent but substantially at variance, nevertheless: 12 percent in one case, 14 percent in the other.

American's witness Gilman and American's attorneys regarded the earnings-price ratio as unsatisfactory by itself. American's brief pointed out that (1) though investors are buying futures, there is no way of measuring future market capitalization of earnings; (2) market prices do not always move proportionately with earnings changes; and (3) the ratio may be unreliable because of inclusion of nonrecurring earnings, for example, capital gains. Witness Gil-

[71] The Big Three figures were adopted for the Big Four.

[72] Kosh used a lower figure on acquisition cost of new capital than had Howell, namely, 10 percent instead of 17 percent.

man's analysis of the cost of equity capital included (1) the earnings-price ratio, "(2) relationship of earnings per share and net proceeds per share in recent trunkline sales, (3) rate earned on common equity for the trunklines and for certain other utilities, (4) rate earned on book value of stocks of manufacturing companies, (5) relationship of book value to market price of stocks of the airlines and other companies, and (6) comparative percentages of revenues available for common stock." His judgment, taking into account these factors and the risks of the industry, was that equity holders should have 15 percent.

Other airlines attacked the reliability of earnings-price ratios as a test of cost of capital. TWA noted that these ratios were more erratic for airlines than for utilities. Braniff argued that such ratios had value only under certain conditions, including among others a cluster of earnings-price ratios for the firms in the industry,[73] and stability in earnings-price ratios, stock prices, and dividend rates. None of these were characteristic of the airline industry. Eastern argued, "there is no known technique" for determining cost of airline equity capital, and plumped for the margin-of-return approach. The fullest condemnations of the earnings-price ratios came from witnesses who favored the margin-of-return method, namely Dorau and Foster.

2. Alternatives to Cost-of-Capital Approach. Although American and United presented cost-of-capital testimony through expert witnesses (Gilman and Kosh), both argued for using additional ways of arriving at the rate of return. TWA, in particular among the other carriers, emphasized these other approaches.

American presented its investment plans and then set forth the earnings that would be necessary to support them. It thought this testimony presented the CAB with a unique opportunity to measure against reality the results of the theoreticians' analyses of cost of capital.

The three carriers presented expert testimony from persons familiar with the operation of security markets and the habits of investors. "Expert observation" by such persons constituted, in United's opinion, "an alternative approach" to cost-of-capital inquiry.

---

[73] Howell found a cluster for the Big Three, not for the others.

The most forceful conclusion came from Arthur H. Tully, limited partner in Hayden, Stone and Co., who said, "Much as I love aviation in all its aspects, as an investor I wouldn't touch airline securities with a ten foot pole." Benjamin S. Clark, partner in White, Weld, & Co., listed eight criteria of investments considered by professional investors and found airline securities lacking on all but two. United's witness McClintock testified airline securities were unattractive and that a rate of return of 12 percent would enable the airline industry to be competitive in the money markets.

United's brief most fully summarized the testimony of financial experts. The summary included, in the main, these points:

1. Airline stocks are avoided by professional investors—investment trusts and insurance companies hold little airline stock, and holdings by institutional investors have declined.

2. Airline stocks are given poor market ratings—for example, the best rating by Fitch Publishing Co. for any airline stock is a "B."

3. Airline stocks are poorly regarded by the stock market—as measured by their market performances over past years.

4. Airlines have been unable to raise adequate equity capital on reasonable terms—causing the debt ratio to go "dangerously high."

5. The credit standing of the airlines is marginal—for example, the highest rating by Moody's for any airline debt is "Baa," which is a rating for "lower medium grade" securities.

Bureau Counsel replied to these arguments. It was alleged that the carriers' contention was "basically an appeal to the emotions rather than a matter of substance." If the projections on costs of operation and rate of return in its presentation were sound, then the airlines would have earnings to support the jet program. The BAO made an extensive analysis on two points. First, it found that the carriers had placed firm orders with manufacturers for 256 jet aircraft and 150 turboprop aircraft. Some carriers had substantially met their requirements. It analyzed the equipment program of each carrier to show the substantial completion of financing or the ability to finance the jet program. Second, it analyzed the cash flow estimates of carriers to show that funds would be available for the jet programs.

The facts lay in figures. The basic question remained: How useful a supplement to other evidence was testimony of financial experts on investor preferences? Were the cost figures, with all their imperfections, a more reliable basis for determining rate levels?

3. Capital Gains—An Additional Rate-of-Return Issue. Capital gains result from the sale of equipment (usually planes) at more than depreciated book value. It has been the historical practice of the CAB to consider capital gains as "other revenue" of carriers in determining in open mail rate cases the amount of need for mail subsidy.[74] Capital gains were deducted from the amount of subsidy paid. In 1958, however, Congress provided that this should not be done where the capital gains were spent for flight equipment or deposited in a flight equipment fund.[75] The primary interest of Congress was in assisting local carriers to purchase planes to take the place of DC-3's.

The airlines' position in the GPFI was that capital gains should be excluded from the revenue projections on which passenger fares were fixed. One argument was that these gains fluctuated, being large in years in which old planes were sold and new equipment purchased, and small or nonexistent at other times. Another was the unpredictability of future capital gains. In the end the airline position on capital gains was unopposed by Bureau Counsel, who commented as follows:

Potential future capital gains are not capable of accurate measurement. . . . Accordingly, it is appropriate to view such potential in the nature of a cushion for the transition to the jet age in view of possible temporary earnings-abnormalities associated with the introduction of new aircraft types.[76]

Rate-of-Return: (B) The Rate Base. When the rate-of-return method is employed, a rate base must be calculated. The rate base is

[74] Confirmed by the Supreme Court in Western Air Lines v. CAB, 347 U.S. 67 (1954).

[75] Pub. L. 373, 72 Stat. 84 (1958), amending Section 406(b) of the Civil Aeronautics Act (April 9, 1958).

[76] Two comments: (1) It was feasible to include capital gains in open mail rate cases, for determinations were for past periods; it is, on the other hand, impossible to predict capital gains for a future period. (2) If there are substantial capital gains it is the result of incorrect rates on depreciation. The way to avoid windfalls to carriers through capital gains is accurately to regulate depreciation allowances.

the calculation of value on which a return is to be estimated. The BAO and the carriers differed significantly on matters affecting the dollar total of the rate base.

1. Prudent Investment vs. Property Used and Useful.   The carriers had placed with manufacturers substantial deposits of money for new aircraft. These were called equipment deposits. The carriers contended that these amounts should be included in the rate base. Disallowance of these deposits would reduce the rate base by about 15 percent. Bureau Counsel recommended their exclusion from the rate base until the equipment was placed in service; interest would be allowed on the deposits in the interim and this interest capitalized as part of the rate base when the equipment was delivered. Thus, the issue substantially was over deferral of any equity return above an interest cost figure until the date of delivery of the equipment.

The carriers argued that the rate base should be the amount of money prudently invested in the business, that is, the amount of money invested unless the investment was dishonest or wasteful. Equipment deposits would be included. All three of the cost-of-capital experts—Howell for Bureau Counsel, Kosh for United, and Gilman for American—contemplated this method of determining the rate base. American's brief stated that this was the "prudent investment" theory advanced by Justice Louis O. Brandeis in the Southwestern Bell Telephone case, wherein he said, "The thing devoted by the investor to the public use is not specific property, tangible and intangible, but capital embarked in the enterprise."[77] It also cited other cases from regulatory experience.

Bureau Counsel recommended use of "depreciated original cost of capital used and useful in the business." Equipment deposits would be included with capitalized interest charges when the equipment was "used and useful." This was stated to be in accord with long-standing CAB policy in mail rate cases. A number of state commission decisions in support of the policy were cited.

American's brief argued that the act of Congress in 1958 on capital gains supported the airline position. The act stated that amounts deposited in the re-equipment fund "shall not be included as part of the carrier's used and useful investment for purposes of Section 406

[77] Missouri *ex rel* Southwestern Bell Telephone Co. v. Public Service Commission, 262 U.S. 276, 290 (1923).

[on mail rates] until expended as provided above." The negative implication, said American, was that after amounts are "expended as provided above," they are included in the Section 406 rate base. Also, "expended as provided above" plainly includes "payments on account of the purchase price" referred to earlier in the act. The brief quoted supporting statements from the congressional history, including one from the Senate committee report. The brief admitted that technically the language required only that equipment deposits resulting from capital gains realized by a subsidized carrier should be included in the carrier's rate base, but argued that such a limited interpretation would be an anomaly. It would discriminate against the subsidized carrier who, instead of being fortunate enough to have capital gains for use on new equipment, was forced to use other earnings or to obtain outside financing for the purpose. In the latter event, the carrier would have an even stronger equitable claim for inclusion of invested funds in the rate base.

2. Inflation.   The most controversial issue in utility rate cases has been whether the rate base should be determined on the basis of actual cost of properties, insofar as the expenditures were prudent, or on the basis of reproduction cost (cost of replacing properties). Where inflation has taken place since existing properties were constructed, utilities have usually argued for reproduction cost. In this case there was no extensive treatment of the issue. This may be accounted for in part by the fact that airlines were replacing their old equipment, and perhaps also by the fact that Bureau Counsel's method of calculating the rate of return sought to include in this factor the investors' estimate of the future. Some of the carriers did argue, however, that if the fair-return–rate-base method were used, an inflation increment should be included in the rate base.

Bureau Counsel had sought at the prehearing conference to limit consideration in this case to valuation of assets at original cost, but the Board had left the determination of relevance of evidence to the examiner's discretion.

American, which accepted the rate-base method, based its argument on prudent investment theory. It argued at length for inclusion of equipment deposits but made no argument for adjustments for inflation. Bureau Counsel thought the answer to arguments for such adjustments was simple: "The earnings-price ratio adequately reflects investors' estimate of the economic future. Thus, any further adjustment in the rate of return is unwarranted." Decisions of regulatory bodies and experts were cited in support of this contention.

United denied that adjustments for inflation were reflected in earnings-price ratios and cited the testimony of expert witnesses Kosh and Walter A. Morton in support of its denial. United favored an increment for inflation through adjustment of the rate base. This could be done through periodical re-evaluation of the invested capital or through re-evaluation of physical assets, but in either case the pitfalls of reproduction cost could be avoided by trending the rate-base value by use "of a suitable price index." United stated, however, that its request for a 17-percent increase in passenger fares included no increment for inflation.

COSTS AND REVENUES

Load Factors. If the basic equation—gross income must equal costs plus return—is recalled, it will be seen that revenues and costs, as well as return, must be estimated before rates are fixed. The most significant influence on cost is the load factor. In fact, Bureau Counsel stated that the load-factor determination "is the most important, single rate making element open to the judgment of the Board."

Load factor is the rate of use of capacity. President C. R. Smith of American defined load factor as "the percent of seat-miles produced that are actually sold." A load factor of sixty means, therefore, that 60 percent of the seat capacity was ticketed.

With a high load factor, costs per unit of sale will be low and rates can be low. An error in estimating the load factor when setting rates could mean the difference between high and low earnings. American's brief stated that a difference of one point in the load factor (for example, between 65 and 66 percent) represented for it $5,600,000 at 1957 fare levels.

Bureau Counsel argued that airline passengers should not be burdened with the cost of excess capacity. They took, therefore, this position: "The Board should deliberately incorporate an optimum load factor for each carrier in the fare level." Rates should be set on the assumption that management would achieve the highest attainable load factor. This would force efficiency in schedule planning and equipment purchase, and would be the means of attaining the objectives of Section 1002(e), one of which was adequate service "at the lowest cost consistent with the furnishing of such service." Another standard in the Act was the effect of rates upon the movement of traffic. In conformity with these standards "the Board should require that the proper level of earnings be attained through high load factors and low fares."

Bureau Counsel argued that "airline management is both responsible [for] and capable of exercising control of load factors over reasonably extended periods by tailoring capacity to the requirements of traffic." This control could be affected "within narrow tolerances." In support of this position Bureau Counsel noted, particularly, the stability of load factors achieved from 1953 to 1956; the solutions being developed for the "no-show" problem (that is, failure of passenger to appear); the relatively small investments as compared with utilities—which meant greater flexibility with respect to expansion and contraction of equipment; the substantial and continuous growth of airline traffic; and the removal of nonsked coach competition. At the same time, it was believed that temporary factors, such as (1) the increase of competition since 1955, (2) the availability of new equipment, and (3) the general recession dating from 1957, did not prevent carrier control of load factors over reasonably extended periods.

Bureau Counsel offered the load factors attained in the five-year period from April 1, 1953, to March 31, 1958, as a valid standard of future attainable load factor. This excluded the high load factors of the Korean war period and included the relatively unfavorable period since the middle of 1957. Excluding Continental and Northeast, whose route patterns had been so substantially changed as to vitiate past experience, the weighted average revenue passenger load of 63.1 was obtained from the 1953–1958 period. Load factors varied from 67 percent for American to 58.9 percent for Western. On the basis of figures for these years an average load factor of 63 percent was recommended for the trunks.

The industry attacked these positions. It was argued that load factors were not controllable "within narrow tolerances" and that the figure set for the companies was unattainable in the period for which rates were to be set. In addition to competition, new seat capacity, and recession, many difficulties were stressed. Included among other factors were community pressures for service, seasonality, requirements under certificates for service to low traffic points, and other certificate obligations for service. Stability in load factors in 1955 and 1956, said United's brief, was due to external factors rather than management control. Braniff elaborated on the difficulties of maintaining load factors in the development period following new service authorizations by the CAB. But the heart of the airline case was that the load factors recommended by the BAO exceeded the airlines' projections of future attainable load factors.

Load factors reflect a balance between service and economy. Frequent flights and ample seating capacity result in more adequate service; but if a large percentage of the seats are unfilled, the cost per passenger will be high. Airline briefs recurringly referred to the fact that the CAB had given notice of inadequate service as one reason for making competitive route grants. Airlines, ran the argument, were to be caught between the CAB's standards of service in route cases and its load-factor standards in rate making. The ATA cited three recent cases in which the Board had found that particular operations of certain carriers were conducted with excessive load factors. American said the argument that service in the five-year period 1953–1958 had been adequate in other than a legal sense should be approached with caution in view of shortage of equipment and the Board's route decisions in 1955 and 1956 requiring extensive new competitive services.

Bureau Counsel set forth the legal precedents for its position that the Board could legally incorporate into the rate level load factors which were reasonably attainable and which reflected a quality of service that was adequate and efficient. But the airlines took the position that the Board had no authority to incorporate an optimum load factor into the level of rates. The Eastern brief declared:

Two general principles must be recognized. First, the Board may not use fare changes to encourage or discourage particular practices which it feels help or hurt development of the nation's air-transportation system. Second, like the presumption of innocence in a criminal case, a public ultility's management is presumed to be honest, economical and efficient until the contrary is proved on the record.

Not much attention or citation of authority was given on the first proposition, but airline briefs argued at length, with citation of authorities, that the Board must accept airline judgment on adequacy of scheduling and other matters affecting load factors unless managerial judgment was proven to be inefficient. "The test of proper fare is not the Board's concept of appropriate operations, but whether operations as conducted and proposed by the airlines themselves represent honest, economical and efficient management," argued American.

What load factor will be realized? What load factor is attainable? These are questions of judgment on future fact. The issue of principle remains, however: Should the Board assume a reasonable optimum load factor in determining prospective airline earnings for rate-making purposes? Or should it limit its consideration to the actual load factor that is anticipated by airline management for the future? The former sets a standard for attainment by airline management; it forces management to give careful attention to the earnings factor when making decisions on schedules and purchase of equipment. Is this a proper objective in a rate proceeding? Does the CAB need an instrument to prevent overexpansion in competitive markets? But would this be accomplishing by indirection the control over scheduling which the act denies? And what should be the balance between public and private discretion? How will the best judgment be made as to the proper amount and quality of service?

Of interest is the contrast in positions taken by airlines and by Bureau Counsel on two issues: capital structure and load factor. As to the first, the airlines argued that sound rate regulation would encourage an "optimum" capital structure; Bureau Counsel, that rates should be based on actual and imminent capital structure. As to the second, Bureau Counsel argued for encouragement of an "optimum," and airlines for acceptance of the imminent as projected by them.

Operating Expenses, Depreciation, Taxes, and Passenger Revenues. Full discussion of operating expenses, depreciation, taxes, and revenues would lead deep into labyrinths of figures and away from standards of rate making. Hence only a few highlighting comments will be made.

For operating expenses the BAO sought to set up a standard cost figure stated in terms of cost per available ton mile.[78] Carriers pro-

[78] "Available ton mile" as used here means the lift capacity of the aircraft, modified by uses made of the space—for example, two hundred pounds per passenger, plus baggage, times the number of miles flown.

jected cost estimates in five-year forecasts. Some of the carriers found no objection to Bureau Counsel's operating expense calculations. This was explicitly stated by Eastern and tacitly admitted by American. On the other hand, some carriers (for example, Capital and United) attacked the BAO's figures. Since the bureau computations were based on averages, it was expected that reactions would differ.

There was, on the other hand, general objection to depreciation standards used by Bureau Counsel. As for other items of expense, Bureau Counsel arrived at an estimate of depreciation cost per available ton mile. They rejected carriers' projections for the future as conjectural, believing that experience over a past representative period was more reliable. Using reported depreciation for the twelve years 1946–1957, they found the average ton-mile figure to be 2.45 cents. This they recommended for use in this proceeding.

Bureau Counsel also used another method for fixing depreciation. This followed the conventional practice of basing depreciation on two variables: estimated uniform service life of equipment and estimated residual value at end of the service period of the equipment. They recommended for rate-making purposes the use of a service life of seven years for piston-powered aircraft and ten years for jet-powered, and a residual value of 15 percent plus a built-in overhaul cost of 5 percent. (Seven years had been accepted by the Board in some past cases for piston-powered aircraft; 15 percent residual had been required in reporting rules.)

The airline attack on these proposals included these chief objections: (1) since it was an average, the 2.45 figure was high for some and low for others; (2) the figures were far lower than those projected by the airlines for 1959–1961; (3) the residual-value estimates were too high; and (4) the service-life periods were too long, at least for some types of planes.

United noted the decision in *Alaska Airlines v. Civil Aeronautics Board*, 257 F.2d 229 (1939), that the CAB had no power to regulate depreciation figures in connection with uniform reporting requirements. It denied, therefore, the CAB's right to do so in rate proceedings and argued that it was a proper principle of rate making that management be allowed a range of discretion in connection with depreciation expense. Carrier determinations that were reasonable should be accepted. (It should be recorded, however, that exclusion of capital gains from earnings would remove the automatic corrective for excessive depreciation allowances.)

On taxes the major argument was whether the difference between "normalized" taxes and taxes paid under the accelerated depreciation provisions of Section 167 of the Internal Revenue Code should be counted as earnings. Bureau Counsel's position was that it could be assumed that continued investment in new operating facilities would permanently defer the payment to the government of this difference, and hence that the difference was an actual saving. The industry answer included: (1) this is unsupported conjecture; (2) it assumes Section 167 will remain law forever; and (3) even if these things were true, it was contrary to congressional intent, which was to promote economic expansion by giving industry the benefit of liberalized depreciation.

American set forth as one of its four points of difference with Bureau Counsel the latter's projection of anticipated passenger revenues. American argued that the projection did not take account of the prospective increase of coach service as a proportion of total service, and hence of a decline in revenue per passenger mile.

An Additional Issue: Value of Service

Bureau Counsel took the position that value of service to customers should not be considered in fixing rates, but only costs of service. Some of the carriers argued that value of service should be considered, and Delta's brief summarized the case fully. This brief set forth:

1. That the ICC, and the Post Office Department in mail cases, recognized that value of service was a legitimate consideration;

2. That two guides for rate making in the Civil Aeronautics Act obviously involve value-of-service considerations: (a) effect of "rates upon the movement of traffc" and (b) "the inherent advantages of transportation by aircraft"; and

3. That value-of-service considerations were large—improved service, frequency of scheduling, faster transportation, and the like. Airline transportation offered the public a big "bargain"; airline service had been greatly improved over the past decade, with little

or no cost increase to the passenger; airlines should receive additional returns because of the value of the service rendered.

The Weak-Strong Carrier Problem

The examiner requested that briefs consider "whether a price should be fixed that would result in opportunity for proper profit for the average carrier, for the most poorly situated carrier, or for carriers determined on some other basis."

Bureau Counsel noted that the existence of competition on most routes prevented setting different rates for different carriers. Rates "should meet the costs of the bulk of the industry, both in terms of numbers of carriers and volume of traffic. . . . the weighted industry average costs are of great significance in determining the general fare level." These might require modification if one or more carriers unduly weighted the average, but "the industry averages should be the major determinative when the individual carriers' revenue needs cluster reasonably close to the weighted averages."

Similarly, Delta's position was "that the nature of trunkline transportation is such that the Examiner and the Board cannot avoid fixing the passenger rate level on the basis of averages for the trunkline industry as a whole." This bulk-line method, as it was called, fitted the pattern developed by ICC. Delta's president testified, "The Board must not attempt to solve these problems through theoretical computations based upon peculiar situations of individual carriers." To the extent that the rate level was insufficient to allow each carrier to earn a fair return, the Board, in Delta's opinion, should be prepared to equalize earnings through strengthening route awards or subsidy.

On the other hand, the GSA started with the provision of the Civil Aeronautics Act that the Board in fixing rates "shall take into consideration . . . the need of each air carrier for revenue" and concluded that "an attempt by the Board to regulate the entire industry by an average rate of return for the air carriers as a group, would be inconsistent with that Act."

Several of the airlines took the position that rates should be high enough to allow each carrier to make a fair return. In Northwest's opinion this followed from the promotional responsibility of the CAB and, more important, it would give carriers financial strength

AN ADMINISTRATIVE CENTER AT WORK

to experiment in new low-cost transportation. Capital referred to the "marginal economic position" of the smaller carriers and contended that "the possibility" that some carriers would earn a higher rate of return than others should not "lead the Board to set rates which will effectively eliminate, by forced merger or bankruptcy, that portion of the industry with a lesser earning position." Once again, Capital noted that fare structure needed to be considered if short-haul services were to be adequately compensated. United thought that when the CAB decided a carrier's services were needed and when its management was efficient, the Board was under obligation to allow fares that would produce the service. Eastern argued that the Board should approve the highest fares needed by any carrier, subject only to the limitation that, if no increase in total revenue resulted, fares should not be raised. It thought the CAB "should undertake an examination of how suspension of unprofitable services might aid the weaker carriers" and that the Board might "encourage the absorption of a chronically weak carrier by a larger one which can support it."

American's position was different and was carefully grounded on a legal base: The CAB should not attempt to fix a price at all; rather, it should determine whether the proposals advanced by the carriers were lawful. "The Act contemplates Board prescription of rates only if it is determined that carrier-set rates will be unjust or unreasonable, and even in that event the Board need not set actual rates, but can confine its actions to setting maximums, minimums or both." To attempt in this case to set a price lawful for all carriers would lead into "a hopeless morass." In this case, except for "mavericks" asking 12.5 or 20 percent, the requested increases centered on 15 percent. The Board should grant this and allow carriers to determine, "as a matter of business judgment," how far to apply the allowed increases.

Hence, the examiner had several answers to his query:

1. Set rates on the basis of averages.

2. Set rates high enough to yield a return for each carrier (subject perhaps to Eastern's proposed limitation).

3. Approve all proposals for "lawful" rates and leave to carrier judgment determination of whether to charge the maximum allowed. The difference between this alternative and alternative (2) is not

entirely clear because of the uncertainty as to what would constitute a "lawful" rate.

ADJUSTMENT OF RATES

It will be recalled that the examiner requested the parties to submit opinions on the "legal and economic feasibility" of automatic adjustments of passenger rates. All parties agreed on the nonfeasibility of regulatory adjustment of rates according to formula.[79]

The "fuel" escalator clauses, which appear with frequency in rate schedules of electric, as well as manufactured and natural gas, utilities, are the commonest form of adjustment provision. It was generally agreed that adjustment clauses based upon cost factors were inappropriate for the air transport industry. Braniff's brief referred to the fact that 50 percent of a gas utility's costs are for purchased gas, but that there was no comparable single item of cost in air transport except wages, which comprise about 45 percent of airline costs. But questions were raised by the companies about automatic escalation for wage changes. For example, would an airline be justified in covering a $75,000 wage for pilots in rate increases? Or assuming wage cost reductions through purchase of electronic equipment, how would automatic adjustment be calculated? Bureau Counsel noted that costs might not all move in the same direction.

Bureau Counsel's chief objection to escalator clauses was that they removed or reduced incentives to lower cost through improved efficiency. Escalator clauses embodied the cost-plus principle. Particularly objectionable would be clauses based on total costs. Added to the cost-plus objection was the fact that such increases might have an adverse effect upon the amount of traffic, which would be contrary to the promotional objective of the statute.

Use of the sliding-scale method of adjusting fares and earnings was also rejected. Braniff's brief reviewed experience with the technique in utility regulation, concluding that it had broken down where there were major changes in conditions, that it became com-

[79] The longest discussions of the problem were in Bureau Counsel's brief (pp. 31, 318–339), and Braniff's brief (pp. 56–66). Some carriers left treatment of the matter to others, but it was considered in briefs of American (pp. 114–116); Delta (pp. 93–96); Northwest (p. 66); TWA (p. 65); United (pp. 107–110); ATA (pp. 89–90); and GSA (pp. 73–75).

plicated even in the simple situation of single-firm supply of utility service, and that it had no value in such a volatile and complex industry as air transport.

Bureau Counsel said, "The sound development of the dynamic industry will follow a pattern of peaks and valleys. To attempt to level the curve may well interfere with the desired development." As in other parts of their presentation, Bureau Counsel emphasized the CAB's policy of viewing rates over "long run representative periods."

United's attorney viewed the main difficulty in automatic adjustment as inability to foretell the future to which rates were to apply. TWA feared it would lead to too frequent reopening of rate proceedings.

American argued that automatic adjustment by regulatory decision was illegal. Rates could not be changed without carrier petition except after notice and hearing. Escalator clauses were part of fixed schedules and were included there by carrier initiative. Bureau Counsel noted that escalator clauses meant a delegation to the industry of regulatory responsibilities and that the Federal Power Commission had "held that escalated increases must conform to the usual rate-making procedures."

The ATA's brief argued that airline managements should not be tied to a formula but should be allowed "a substantial measure of discretion in pricing their services." Delta argued that automatic adjustment would be contrary to the purpose of the act. It "anticipates that competitive forces, reasonably controlled by the Board, will exert a downward pressure on fare levels, while at the same time the Board is enjoined to hold a floor under fare levels so as to avoid cutthroat competition." If floor and ceiling were both sharply restricted through an automatic formula, "the normal drives to reduce costs and increase revenues are removed, and the shift is toward a 'cost-plus' theory of rate regulation."

Bureau Counsel thought "attention should be directed to the relative speed" of the CAB in the interim changes during the GPFI proceeding. They hoped, along with some of the carriers, that, as United's brief put it, "the development of sound rate making principles will clear away much of the debris with which the instant proceeding has been cluttered and will permit the expeditious handling and determination of requests for either upward or downward adjustments in passenger fares." Northwest's brief even suggested that "once the basic issues are decided it would be logical and desirable to explore methods by which the necessary fare changes could be accomplished expeditiously and without the necessity of extensive formal proceedings."

THE EXTENT OF PUBLIC RESPONSIBILITY

Involved in many of the issues discussed above is the broader question of managerial discretion versus commission judgment. Carriers, particularly American, have claimed that the Board could not legally substitute its judgment on several of the issues for that of the carriers.

The challenge by American was presented, as has been described above, on load factors, depreciation, uniform rates, and adjustment of rates. The effect of this challenge was to present the basic question of loose versus tight public control. The argument of the carriers for an optimum debt ratio had the same effect.

American's argument rested heavily on interpretation of CAB powers under the Act in two 1958 decisions in the District of Columbia Court of Appeals, neither of which related directly to rate making. In *American Overseas Airlines v. CAB*, 254 F.2d 744 (1958), it was held that strike losses, not proved to be the responsibility of management, had to be considered in fixing mail rates for a past period, and that the CAB should not go outside standards prescribed in the act. One test was "honest, economical and efficient management." "The statute contemplated, we think, that the figures, past or prospective, of the operation of the carrier in question be used unless some item or items are due to dishonest, inefficient, or uneconomical management. In such event, the Board must make a finding as to the effect" (p. 749). In *Alaska Airlines v. CAB*, 257 F.2d 229 (1958) (certiorari denied) it was held that the CAB had no authority, under reporting provisions of the Act, to regulate depreciation—an authority vested in certain other regulatory commissions.

American recognized that the rate-making standards of the Act were different from standards considered by the courts in the cases mentioned above, but it argued that the legislative history showed

Congress rejected wording that would have subjected airline service to discretionary CAB regulation.

The arguments on this question of loose versus tight regulation were not entirely legally based. The ATA, for example, contended that reliance upon carrier judgment was a practical necessity.

What protection would the public have if the Act were interpreted to limit rate-making jurisdiction to the extent American proposed? Eastern's witness Dorau and Eastern's brief thought competition offered the public the needed protection. Bureau Counsel, in contrast, thought that regulation was created to provide the public with benefits like those competition would provide in an industry not subject to exclusion of entry.

SUMMARY OF ISSUES RELATING TO STANDARDS FOR RATE MAKING

After years of argument and procedural complexities, the GPFI went to the CAB examiner for decision. All parties—airlines, investors, the government, and other consumers—looked forward to the decision about whether fares would be increased, and if so, by how much. But before deciding on increases, the examiner would have to consider many issues concerning standards for rate making:

1. Should rate of return or profit margin be used as the basic standard? Or should these be used as dual standards? Or one as complement to or corrective for the other? Or the two used only as points of reference?

2. If profit margin is used, how shall the appropriate margin be determined? Is comparison with industrial companies a satisfactory approach?

3. If rate of return is used, then there are issues with respect both to rate of return and rate base:

a. As to rate of return: Should actual and imminent capital structure or desirable capital structure be used? Is the earnings-price ratio a sufficient measure of cost of equity capital? Are there any satisfactory alternatives or complementary methods?

b. As to rate base: Should prudent investment or property used and useful be the standard? Should the rate base be adjusted with changes in the price level? Should an attrition factor be included?

4. As to costs and income: Should an optimum load factor be assumed? Should company standards of depreciation be accepted or

should a uniform and reasonable standard be incorporated into the cost figures used in rate making? Should income taxes to be deducted in rate-making calculations be calculated on normal depreciation or on accelerated depreciation?

5. Should value of service be considered in determining rates?

6. What should be the answer to the examiner's question as to whether rates should provide "opportunity for proper profit for the average carrier, for the most poorly situated carrier, or for carriers determined on some other basis"?

7. Is it feasible to adjust rates according to formula? Is it desirable to attempt to make short-range adjustments?

8. Should the regulatory ceiling on rates float loosely over the regulated industry, generously allowing flexibility, or should it press tightly on the industry, allowing only carefully determined costs—including, of course, cost of capital?

The Board's Interim Decisions

Beginning with the order instituting the GPFI on May 10, 1956, and down to the submission of briefs (October 29, 1958) the Board issued ten orders in the proceeding, granted extensions of time by instruction to the examiner on two occasions, repudiated one staff press release, and denied or granted several requests for rate increases. In addition, it took other actions on rates, such as initiating an investigation of family fares and deciding on a Continental Airlines proposal for rate changes.

1. 5/10/56[80]—Instituting the investigation and defining its scope.
2. 7/27/56—Refusing to enlarge the scope of investigation. Granting local service carriers and GSA status of interveners.
3. 8/22/56—Granting leave to intervene to ATA.
4. 10/31/56—Granting leave to intervene to Department of Air Force on behalf of Department of Defense and to Conference of Local Airlines.
5. 2/6/57—Denying BAO's request for restriction of rate-base evidence to original cost less depreciation.
6. 2/7/57—Denying Western Air Lines' objection to BAO's request for information.
7. 3/29/57—Instructing examiner to grant extension of time.
8. 7/11/57—Instructing examiner to grant extension of time.

[80] Date of decision; order issued May 19, 1956.

9. 8/8/57—Consolidating Suspended Passenger Fare Increase case with GPFI. Setting forth additional evidence required.
10. 9/25/57—Denying increase in Suspended Passenger Fare Increase case.[81]
11. 9/27/57—Denying Eastern's request for information.
12. 1/24/58—Suspending proposed tariff of Continental Airlines and TWA.
13. 2/25/58—Granting increase of 4 percent plus one dollar per ticket.[82]
14. 3/13/58—Denying request of American Airlines for elimination of initial decision of examiner or tentative Board decision.
15. 4/30/58—Granting request of Bureau Counsel for four weeks' recess of hearings.
16. 9/30/58—Granting petition relating to applications of Continental Airlines.
17. 10/14/58—Approving elimination of round-trip discounts and reduction of family fare discount.[83]

Most of the Board's decisions related to procedural issues discussed in the preceding section. Some, however, involved substantive issues similar to those presented in the GPFI and were in essence interim decisions on the general rate level and on the principles of rate making.

SUSPENDED PASSENGER FARE INCREASE CASE

In the Suspended Passenger Fare Increase case, decided on August 6, 1957, the Board had denied a requested increase. In an opinion September 25 the Board said:

1. "The issue of possible decreases in existing passenger fares has been deferred until further order of the Board."

2. "In addition . . . the Board [by earlier order in the proceeding] limited consideration of the earnings element to the rate of return to be allowed upon a rate base equal to the original cost less book depreciation of the used and useful assets, and excluded from the proceeding all issues concerning fare structure."

3. Fare levels were to be determined "on the basis of earnings necessary to provide a fair return over a reasonably extended period

[81] Decision announced in press release of August 8, 1957.
[82] Decision announced in press release of January 24, 1958.
[83] Decision announced in press release of October 14, 1958.

which includes both good and bad years." (No party, said the opinion, had taken issue with this approach.)

4. "For the purpose of determining the reasonableness of earnings, we shall use eight percent." (This was the accepted standard in mail rate cases.)

5. Capital gains were to be taken into account in determining earnings. The Board left open the merit of carriers' contentions on this point in the GPFI case, noting only that the contention had no merit in this petition for an emergency increase.

6. "We believe that the heart of this case lies in whether the present [September, 1957] depressed earnings are due to short-term factors or not." The Board's conclusions were that the recent drop in earnings was "due in large measure to the impact of new aircraft and new routes and the integration and developmental costs which ensue," and that carriers who received major route awards could be expected to show higher earnings.

7. ". . . management has the obligation to tailor schedules to the need of the market once sufficient experience has been gained to determine the need." Overscheduling was blamed, in part, by the Board for the decrease in the load factor. To the contention of the carriers that the Board must accept management decisions that all schedules are necessary unless inefficiency is proved, the Board answered that this would frustrate rate regulation, for thousands of schedules would need to be checked and proof developed to show inefficiency on any of these.

The statements of Board position on investment base, rate of return, and capital gains were made pending argument and decision on them in the GPFI. The Board's position was clear that the issues on standards remained open for decisions in the GPFI. Moreover, the examiner had taken no position on the issues in the Six Percent case, having certified the record to the Board without an initial or recommended decision. Finally, positions taken might be affected by new evidence now called for to substantiate the carriers' claim that financing difficulties faced the industry.

THE ONE-DOLLAR–4-PERCENT CASE

The reader will recall that the decision in August, 1957, denying an increase was followed by one on January 24, 1958, granting an increase of 4 percent plus one dollar per ticket. The opinion in the one-dollar–4-percent case (issued February 25, 1958) is interesting on four counts:

1. The Board's decision was made, without hearing, on the basis of "detailed staff analyses" beginning in December, on the earnings position of the carriers. This was government on "an expedited basis" and possible, of course, only because the decision was accepted by the carriers.

2. In spite of statements in its opinions and before a congressional committee that it would look at earnings over an extended period, the Board accepted the downward trend in business conditions over three months as evidence of inability of airlines to continue their normal growth:

The deceleration in market growth reported for September, October and November, 1957, assumes greater significance than might otherwise be the case, because of the concurrent downturn in general business conditions. Manifestly, we cannot, on the basis of a three months' development alone, predict with certainty that the rate of traffic growth will continue to be substantially below prior years. However, where, as here, it occurs as a concomitant of a general business downturn, and where the immediate business outlook remains as uncertain as it is, the probabilities are in favor of a below normal rate of traffic growth. This being the case, and the carriers having already experienced depressed earnings, we can no longer safely assume that the depression in earnings is only transitory. The simple fact is, that at least for the near future, it is unlikely that the carriers can reverse the downward trend in earnings without an adjustment in fares. This means that, under current fare levels, the depressed earnings experienced in 1956 and 1957 for a sizable number of trunkline carriers will probably continue into 1958 until decision is reached in the General Passenger Fare Investigation.

3. The Board took note of the fact that its own expert staff—Bureau Counsel—had in the GPFI endorsed returns of 8.9 percent for the Big Four and 9.45 percent for the remaining trunklines and that this was the lowest rate of return recommended in the GPFI.

4. The Board noted that the form of increase—a one-dollar flat increase—would be helpful to the smaller, short-haul carriers. Thus, the Board recognized that structure as well as level was significantly involved in current rate issues.

POSITIONS OF BOARD MEMBERS

Board orders and opinions were issued without designation of authors and were prepared in the Opinion Writing Division of the Office of General Counsel. Nevertheless, there were some signed concurring and dissenting opinions in several of the rate decisions. Analysis of the backgrounds of 1958–1959 Board members and of their positions as revealed in nonunanimous Board opinions is illuminating both about the rate issues in the GPFI and about the possible effects of diverse opinions of Board members in a complex case.

Chan Gurney was the member with longest service. Gurney was born in Yankton, South Dakota, in 1896 and was educated in the Yankton public schools, after which he went into business with his father in the Gurney Seed and Nursery Company. He built and operated a radio station and was president in 1932–1936 of the Chan Gurney Oil Company. A Republican member of the United States Senate from 1939 to 1951, he was appointed by President Truman on March 12, 1951, to a vacancy on the Board and was reappointed by President Eisenhower.

Gurney had consistently voted for fare increases in this series of proceedings. In 1952, when the Board granted a one-dollar-per-ticket increase, suspended the proposal for elimination of round-trip discounts, and first ordered the GPFI, Gurney dissented on the suspension portion of the order. In 1953, he voted to dismiss the GPFI and was with the Board in its statement of the cyclical theory of rate making, which at the time was given as justification for the current high earnings rates. He dissented from the Board's denial of an increase in the Suspended Passenger Fare Increase case. On the one-dollar–4-percent increase he dissented and favored a one-dollar–10-percent increase. On a Continental Airlines' "package" proposal, with some increases and some decreases, he voted on September 30, 1958, for suspension, on the ground that it would not produce any material increase in total revenue. He concurred in the vote for the October, 1958, increase. He wrote very brief opinions but emphasized the need for a "financially strong industry" and his belief that the need of the carriers was critical.

At the opposite pole was G. Joseph Minetti, appointed to the Board in 1956. Minetti was born in Brooklyn in 1907, received a B.S. degree from Fordham University and the LL.B. and J.S.D. degrees from St. John's University, taught in St. John's Pre-Law Division for two years, and then engaged in private practice of law. Except for military service during World War II and brief periods of law practice, Minetti had been in government service since 1937. He was special assistant district attorney, Kings County; attorney in the Antitrust Division of the Department of Justice; first deputy commissioner, Department of Investigation, New York City; commissioner of the Department of Marine and Aviation, New York City; executive assistant to the deputy mayor of New York; commissioner of New York City's Board of Transportation; and, finally, for about two years prior to his appointment to the CAB, a member of the Federal Maritime Board. He belonged to a number of fraternal, veterans, professional, and political (Democrat) organizations.

Minetti was with the majority in the denial of an increase in the Six Percent case. He dissented from the Board's decisions to grant the one-dollar–four-percent increase in February, 1958, and the increase in October, 1958. In a concurring opinion on American Airlines' petition for skipping the examiner's decision (March, 1958) he stated that "any future interim fare increase, prior to the final resolution of the issues in this Docket, will, like the last one, prejudge many of the issues." He had taken the position that the need was for promotional fares to attract new customers. In his dissent in the one-dollar–four-percent case he thought that extending the increase to coach fares was "especially regrettable," and that this was "a shortsighted way of promoting aviation." As for Continental's package proposal, he concurred in the suspension but indicated approval of the economy proposals for coach service and regretted these could not be separated from the rest of the package.

Harmar D. Denny was appointed to the Board in 1953. He was born in Allegheny, Pennsylvania, in 1886, obtained B.A. and LL.B. degrees from Yale and the University of Pittsburgh, and from 1938 to 1950 was investment counsel for a Pittsburgh firm. He was director of public safety in Pittsburgh in 1933–1934, Republican candidate for mayor of Pittsburgh in 1941, and a Republican member of Congress, 1951–1952. He served in both world wars—as a bombing pilot in the first and an air force officer in the second.

Denny was one of the three who, in dismissing the GPFI in 1953, subscribed to the idea of a staff investigation and to the cyclical rate-making theory. In the Six Percent case, he concurred with the majority in denying an increase but stated that he did not agree with some of the reasons and conclusions. He was passing upon whether the carriers needed interim relief, but wanted to retain an open mind on the issues in the GPFI. He was one of the majority of three in the one-dollar–4-percent increase and with the four-man majority that granted the October, 1958, increase. In the Continental Airlines fare request he was, judging from Commissioner Hector's remarks, against across-the-board increases. He had, therefore, occupied a middle position on the issues presented since the date of his appointment and had voted with the majority on every occasion.

The chairman of the Board was James Randall Durfee. Born in Oshkosh, Wisconsin, in 1897, he was a student at Huron (South Dakota) College, and was a law graduate of Marquette University. He practiced law in Antigo, Wisconsin, after 1927, and was district attorney, then court commissioner, then from 1951 to 1956 a member, and for three years chairman, of the Public Service Commission of Wisconsin. He was appointed member and chairman of the CAB in 1956. He was a Republican.

In the rate cases Durfee usually voted with the majority and without separate opinion. He concurred in the denial of a rate increase in 1957 and in the grant of the two increases in 1958, but he was one of two dissenters from the Board vote to disapprove the Continental package. He had expressed the opinion that airlines must tap new markets by offering lower-priced services.

The youngest and newest member of the CAB was Louis J. Hector, appointed in 1957. He was born in Fort Lauderdale, Florida, in 1915, graduated from Phillips Andover Academy, Williams College, and Yale Law School, and studied at Oxford. He had been attorney in the Department of Justice, assistant to the Under Secretary of State, on the staff of the Office of Strategic Services in China, a private practitioner of law in Miami, Florida, and president of the Hector Supply Co. in Miami. He was appointed by President Eisenhower to fill one of the Democratic places on the Board.[84]

---

[84] The Civil Aeronautics Act of 1938 and the Federal Aviation Act of 1958 both provide that no more than three members of the Board be appointed from the same political party.

Hector, too, had generally been with the majority. But like Minetti he had put his individual opinion on record more frequently than the other three. Concurring in denial of American's petition for skipping the examiner's decision, he thought the denial ought to be more forceful, for the petition would hamper the BAO, which represents "the general public welfare rather than any individual interest." He stated, "We would all be much better off if general passenger fare level standards had been developed some time ago." In the Six Percent case his concurring opinion stated that he thought the airlines had given "little real evidence" to support the claim that a fare increase was necessary for jet-purchase financing, and he gave an outline of information needed similar to that in the Board's five-year forecast request. He concurred in the two increase decisions in 1958, and dissented with Durfee against denial of Continental's package. At this latter point Hector summarized his views fully.[85] The financial problem of the airlines was real but the answer difficult:

They need greater profits. So far as fares are concerned, this problem is being attacked in two directions. First, the carriers wish to obtain greater revenue from the passengers they are already carrying. Second, they wish to accomplish a substantial increase in the overall number of passengers. Since an increase in fares in a soft market would normally discourage traffic rather than encourage it, it is clear that there is no simple, easy formula for attaining both of these goals.

To Hector it was "clear that stimulation of new traffic is the most important job of the airlines today." Continental was attempting to increase its family tourist traffic. "What Continental was trying to do is standard American business practice in the face of declining business profits and static volume."

All of this sounded like Minetti's position. But Minetti, and apparently Denny, would not approve of a fare increase, including one on regular coach service, to balance the promotional (family) fares. Hector would approve because of his "healthy respect for the system of management discretion" and desire to avoid a "series of board investigations and decisions." He pointed up what he called the "temporary paralysis" of the Board:

[85] In the Matter of Applications of Continental Air Lines, Inc., Order E-13037 (September 30, 1958).

The Board has reached its result in this case by a curious set of circumstances. One Member [Gurney] has refused to vote for any part of a package tariff which involves substantial discounts or lower fares. Two Members [Denny, Minetti] have refused to vote for that part of a tariff which involves across-the-board increases. Thus the Board would seem to be on dead center, unable to approve any tariff which combines fare increases and promotional discounts.

Curiously, it may be added, the Board would not be in an improved position to consider "fare increases and promotional discounts" after the GPFI. That investigation had been restricted by design for the purpose of limiting a judicial type of inquiry to manageable dimensions. And perhaps, due to the passage of time, it had been restricted to the wrong issues. It dealt with the level, not the structure, of rates—with how much carriers ought to make, not how they could or should make it.

SIGNIFICANCE OF BOARD OPINIONS

The opinions in the interim decisions revealed the quandary of Board members on the rate problem. They offered little guidance to the CAB staff in preparing a case for presentation to the examiner. They indicated that the complexities of the rate problem extended not only to level but also to structure of rates. Finally, they showed the importance of appraisals of the rate problem by individual members of the Board. If the composition of the Board remained unchanged, the inevitable appeals from the examiner's decision would be considered by a divided Board and on a record that did not include evidence on the issues of rate structure that some members considered to be vital to resolution of the rate problem.

The Examiner's Decision

Examiner Wiser's opinion was released on May 27, 1959, to become final after ten days if exceptions were not filed within that period. The opinion was 189 pages in length and was supplemented by 114 pages of tables and charts. The main points in the opinion are here summarized, following substantially their order in the examiner's discussion:

1. A section on "Legal Principles" quoted from three cases—

Bluefield case, Hope case, and *FPC v. Natural Gas Pipeline Co.*[86]—
listed the five standards in Section 1002(e) of the Civil Aeronautics Act, quoted the part of Section 102 of the Act which gave the Board a mandate for "encouragement and development of an air-transportation system," added that it "appears obvious . . . that the public would be best served by an industry" characterized by sound economic conditions, and concluded: "All findings and conclusions herein have been made on the basis that the encouragement and development of such an air-transportation system is a paramount consideration" (p. 10).

2. On the jet-aircraft acquisition program, it was concluded that although there were errors and shortcomings in Bureau Counsel's presentation, the fact was established that sufficient contractual arrangements had been made for the completion of the program "if opportunity for a reasonable earnings rate is afforded" (pp. 13–14).

3. The discussion of "Rate of Return" (pp. 15–86) was introduced by "General Considerations": "The criteria available for determining reasonableness of profits of utilities is provided by the fact that the utilities do obtain their capital from the competitive markets" (p. 17). The trunkline industry is in a risk position far above that of utilities generally, and capital cost increases with risk. Witnesses from the banking and investment world "painted gloomy pictures" of the airlines' ability to attract capital. The contracts for jet equipment generally are conditioned by tests on financial condition. "The profit element (including interest on borrowed funds) is a relatively small item in the total cost to the public. . . . to have doubled the profit element [from January 1, 1947, to December 31, 1956] would have required only a nine percent increase in fares . . ." (p. 27). Income taxes should be considered as business expense and the "analyses in this proceeding . . . look to return on investment or return margin after taxes unless otherwise indicated" (p. 28). The issues on return are " (1) whether the return should be based on a percentage of capital invested or on a percentage of revenues, and (2) the proper percentage to be permitted" (p. 28).

4. It was concluded that "fair return on investment is the proper

[86] Bluefield Waterworks and Improvement Co. v. Public Service Commission, 262 U.S. 679 (1923); FPC v. Hope Natural Gas Co., 320 U.S. 591 (1944); FPC v. Natural Gas Pipeline Co., 315 U.S. 575 (1942).

measure of the profit of the trunkline carriers for rate-level regulation" (p. 74). It was "a more direct, certain, and reliable manner than an allowance of operating ratio" (p. 74). The main argument was stated as follows: "The investors furnish capital—nothing else"; "The subject of the risk is the money invested"; ". . . the extent of profits in relation to investment is the inevitable ultimate test of an investor"; and "It is an obvious anomaly to speak of determining the charge for capital in terms of a percentage of something other than capital" (pp. 75, 76, 80). As to simplicity of administration, the record did not show any "simple method of determining the proper operation ratio"; determining this ratio "is fraught with far greater uncertainty and vagueness" than rate of return on investment (p. 82). Also, operating ratio is a cost-plus arrangement; it is relatively untested in courts, only one federal court decision having been cited. Though operating ratio was a "valuable tool" for certain checking purposes, even here it was subject to "serious weakness" (p. 86).

5. After summarizing at length the testimony of the separate rate experts on such matters as cost of debt, cost of equity, and debt-equity ratio these conclusions were reached on the percentage of return:

a. On cost of debt: 4.5 percent is the reasonable estimate for the Big Four and 5.5 percent for the other eight.

b. On cost of equity: 15 percent is the reasonable cost for the Big Four and 17 percent for the other eight. The earnings-price ratio was declared to be "the most significant indicator of capital cost" but it had "many deficiencies." It was said that "the air carriers are relatively comparable in risk to the manufacturing companies . . ."

c. On capital structure: Bureau Counsel's argument for use of "actual capital structure" was accepted, for "use of the hypothetical structure and an optimum debt ratio gives a windfall to the equity holders" (p. 50). Bureau Counsel's figures of a debt ratio of 45–55 for the Big Four and 50–50 for the other carriers was accepted as the actual structure which would obtain in the next few years.

d. On overall return: application of the above figures on debt cost, equity cost, and debt-equity ratio results in overall returns of 10.25 percent for the Big Four and 11.25 percent for the other eight.

6. On rate-base issues it was concluded:

a. That prudent investment rather than the assets used and useful was the appropriate standard, and hence that equipment deposits on purchases should be included in the rate base. It was said that the effect of the argument of Bureau Counsel was to consider the deposits "as all debt-capital" (p. 60).

b. That the argument for adjustment of the rate base to recognize the effects of inflation was "without merit" since it was "the preponderant view of economic opinion that the cost of capital based in large measure on earnings price ratios includes an allowance for the risk of inflation" (pp. 55–56).

7. On "Future Operations, Revenues, and Expenses" (pp. 87–166), the following determinations, in addition to those on capital costs, were made:

a. Bureau Counsel's proposal for incorporation of an optimum load factor into the fare level was rejected. As to level of service required by considerations of national policy: "It is beyond argument that the Board not only certificated additional competition in part because the carriers had in many instances failed to provide a satisfactory volume of service, but that the Board expected and anticipated an increased volume of service and decreased load factors to result and thought that end desirable" (p. 107). Hence, the load factors of the past five years could not be used as a test of adequacy of future service, as proposed by Bureau Counsel. Moreover, the carriers' forecasts did not show possibility of realizing the optimum load factor in any year (p. 119).

"The most important problem is whether an attempt by the Board to establish standard load factors in regulating the general level of fares is consistent with the economics of the air-transportation industry and with the functions of the Board assigned by the Federal Aviation Act" (p. 107). As to economics, factors limiting managerial capacity to achieve an optimum load factor were noted, and the carriers' assertion that incentive to make a profit would control decisions on schedules was accepted. As to legality, guidance was provided in several cases but primarily in *American Overseas Airlines v. CAB,* in which the Board was denied the power to infuse general policy considerations on labor disputes into the determination of mail pay.[87]

The matter of fixing an optimum load factor involved "a determination of policy as to the extent to which the Board as a governmental agency should determine by regulation of rates the type of product produced by the airlines and to what extent this type of determination should be left to the interplay of economic competitive forces . . ." (p. 113). Guidance for the Board lay in the American Overseas case; moreover, the Board had in many decisions indicated its "reliance upon competition to bring efficiency and high quality of service" (pp. 119–120). It had refrained "from attempting to exercise precise control of levels or adequacy of service in its regulation of the general fare level. Such controls are better exercised by continued monitoring in licensing proceedings . . ." (p. 120).

b. On traffic estimates: the reasonableness of carriers' traffic estimates for the five-year period as a whole was accepted. As to the effect on traffic of "a relatively limited change of about 15 percent at this time" in rates, the business judgment of carrier managements "should be allowed to prevail unless clearly shown wrong" (pp. 94–95). The judgment of the carriers had not been shown to be in error.

c. On cost expense estimates: it was noted that Bureau Counsel had set up standard unit costs and had contended that these could be met. It was "found that the bureau has failed to support its proposed unit costs as standards for the future" (p. 136). However, Bureau Counsel's argument that labor productivity increases would balance other increased costs was found to be supported by carriers' estimates that operating expenses would start downward in 1959.

d. On depreciation: Bureau Counsel's proposal of a representative depreciation figure of 2.45 cents per available ton mile, based on a twelve-year average, was rejected. Likewise, carriers' argument that the American Overseas case precluded anything but accepting the carriers' depreciation figures was said to go "too far." "The determination of depreciation charges is a part of ascertaining

[87] American Overseas Airlines v. CAB, 254 2nd 744 (1958).

costs" (p. 146). The historical method of estimating depreciation on the basis of a seven-year serviceability of larger post-World War II aircraft types and ten-year serviceability of turboprop-jet aircraft was accepted. This had been proposed by most parties, including Bureau Counsel, in an alternative to its representative ton-mile figure. Bureau Counsel's proposal for estimating residual values at 15 percent was accepted but without any addition, as proposed by Bureau Counsel, for overhaul expenses. No residual value was placed on engines.

e. On taxes: it was concluded that federal income tax expense should be based on normal taxes that would be paid under straight-line depreciation, and that accumulated reserves for deferred taxes should be excluded from the rate base.

8. It was concluded "that establishment of a system of automatic adjustment of fare levels for air transportation is not practicable at this time" (p. 163).

9. After noting that costs per mile increase with decreases in trip length, that evidence in the Large Irregular case, Docket No. 5132 et al., showed that the two one-dollar surcharges added to each ticket ($1.00 in 1953 and $1.00 in 1958) "still leave a substantial lack of matching between price and cost at certain mileage levels" (p. 165), and that "the addition of $1 more surcharge would bring price and cost into relatively substantial agreement" (p. 165), it was said:

Fare-structure issues were excluded from the general-level phase of the proceeding and an order covering them cannot issue at this time. However, it is recommended that the Board give consideration to, and receive the views of the parties on brief and oral argument with respect to, temporary authorization of a structure change along the lines above indicated to remain in effect from the effective date of the general-level order in this proceeding to a date when any evidence necessary to decision may be heard and acted upon. (p. 166)

10. The "General Conclusions" at the end of the opinion included these: [88]

a. The domestic trunkline industry failed to earn a fair return in

[88] The examiner did not consider or even refer to value of service or capital gains.

1957 and 1958, and the forecasts placed in evidence show that fare levels in effect prior to 1958 will not produce a fair return in the years covered by the forecasts.

b. Bureau Counsel's proposals for standard load factors and representative costs are "inconsistent with law" and "impracticable" (pp. 167–171). "The carriers' forecasts, except as shown not to represent reasonable estimates, will therefore be used to judge the reasonableness of the fare level . . ."

c. "The only proposed earnings standard justified by the record . . . is the rate of return on investment. . . . Operating ratio can be useful as a check" (pp. 171–172).

d. Since it is impracticable for one carrier to charge different fares than another over the same route segment, "the problem becomes one of industry regulation" (p. 172). The position of American and certain other parties that setting rates on averages would be unlawful would have the effect of taking away the Board's power to regulate rates. Carriers whose needs are not met by rates fixed on averages could petition for higher rates, but competition "would preclude them from charging such rates except on some few noncompetitive segments" (p. 175).

e. Since the reasonable rate of return has been found to be 10.25 percent for the Big Four and 11.25 percent for the other eight carriers, and the Big Four account for two-thirds of the industry's investment, the weighted average return needed by the industry is 10.6 percent.[89]

f. There should be a reasonable middle ground between "the keyhole-view and a long-run-view approach"; rates, therefore, should be "designed to place 1959, 1960, 1961, and 1962 into a reasonable level" (pp. 176–177). When earnings fall below 10 percent in a particular year, a financial danger point is at hand and consideration should be given to raising the fare level; when the five-year earnings' figure is above 10 to 12 percent, consideration should be given to lowering the rates unless yearly figures show a declining trend.

g. In the light of the forecasts of the carriers, the elements of error

[89] The Board's final opinion in the GPFI (at p. 25) showed that an industry weighted average return of 10.6 percent in 1958 would have yielded individual carriers from 6.09 to 13.95 percent, except for Northeast, which would have incurred a deficit of 3.30 percent.

in the forecasts, the poor results of the past three years, the tendencies of revenues, expenses, and profits, the need for reasonably stable fares, and "all other facts, circumstances, and considerations shown in the record," it was concluded that the passenger fare level should be fixed 12 percent above that in effect prior to February, 1958. "This can be effected with little change in the present temporary rate pattern if an additional surcharge of $1 is added" (pp. 188–189).

Board Consideration and Decision

Exceptions to Examiner Wiser's decision of May 27, 1959, were filed by Bureau Counsel, GSA, and ten airlines within the ten days allowed by CAB regulations. This brought the case to the Board for its deliberation and decision.

When a case is appealed to the Board, the record of the case before the examiner moves to the Board, and attorneys are provided an opportunity to present briefs and oral arguments on the issues on appeal. The ensuing process of decision contrasts sharply with that at the examiner stage. The examiner's decision is that of a single person who has a limited assignment of cases and who lives with each case through its development. The Board's decision is that of a group of men with many responsibilities and limited time for each case presented for decision.

Each Board member has a legal assistant, but the aid given by him is spread over many matters. The chief assistance to the Board on a large case comes from the Opinion Writing Division of the Office of the General Counsel. It is staffed by attorneys from Grades 11 to 15 and is supervised by an associate general counsel at Grade 16. The primary responsibility of the Opinion Writing Division on a case is to prepare an opinion that reflects the Board's reasons for its decision. The persons responsible for preparing an opinion sit in on deliberations of the Board, except those in executive session, to discern as fully as possible the thinking of the Board. They share the interest of the Board members in sharpening the issues for deliberation. To meet this need, it is the practice of the division, after briefs are presented and before oral arguments are given, to prepare a statement of issues that sums up the issues and the arguments thereon without any evaluation of the merits. It is general practice, also, to present at a later stage a list of questions for instruction. This may in effect create an agenda for the Board's deliberations.

A member of the Opinion Writing Division is assigned to a case when it is appealed to the Board. Working under the supervision of the associate general counsel and aided perhaps by other attorneys, he will prepare an opinion after the Board reaches a decision. The opinion will be reviewed by or for the associate general counsel in charge of the Opinion Writing Division, and, technically at least, will be cleared in the general counsel's office for consistency with precedent, clarity, accuracy, adequacy of findings, and legal errors. It will then go to the Board, after which revisions may be made on suggestion of Board members.

Since the provisions of Section 5 of the Administrative Procedure Act providing for separation of functions are not applicable to rate proceedings, the Board is free to consult with members of the staff in rate cases. Nevertheless, in a case where, as in the GPFI, the BAO has taken a position in the proceedings, the Board avoids consultation with its personnel. The Board may seek advice on legal issues and information on past policy from the general counsel. It avails itself also of the services of the Office of Carrier Accounts and Statistics, which maintains data on airline operations. The Opinion Writing Division is responsible for procedural assistance, but the chief examiner will take care of such details as setting dates for filing briefs and allotting time for oral arguments.

In the GPFI the Board's deliberations covered one full day, two half days, and a portion of another day. Part of the deliberations were conducted in executive session, but present during most of the deliberations were the legal assistants of Board members, the associate general counsel in charge of the Opinion Writing Division, the opinion writer in the case, and two other attorneys—one from the Opinion Writing Division, the other from another part of the Office of the General Counsel—who had had experience in rate cases. The importance and complexity of the case led to the participation of these several specialists in the Office of the General Counsel in the preparation of the opinion.

On June 10, 1959, acting promptly on the appeals, the Board directed the Opinion Writing Division and the chief examiner to coordinate the mapping of the issues to be argued, the approximate time allotments, and other details for hearing the case. One week later the Board set July 15 as the date for filing briefs and July 28–29 for oral arguments. Briefs were filed and hearings held as scheduled. The issues were divided in three parts for oral argument, and a small group of attorneys selected by the airlines, and others representing the BAO, GSA, and ATA, presented arguments.

On August 11 the Board considered a date for the beginning of its deliberations, the month of August having been set aside for review of the voluminous record. The Board voted to commence its deliberations on September 1, but with recognition that extension of this date might be necessary because of the possible inability of one Board member to participate before September 15. However, several months' delay followed due to changes in Board membership.

Between the oral argument in the GPFI and the Board's final order in the case, three of the five Board members were changed. Remaining were Gurney, who had been most favorable to rate increases, and Minetti, who had been least favorable. The first change occurred when Hector resigned in September, 1959. He was succeeded on November 16 by Alan S. Boyd, like Hector a Florida lawyer. Boyd, who was thirty-seven years old, had attended the University of Florida, had received the LL.B. degree from the University of Virginia, had served in the armed forces during World War II and the Korean action, had practiced law in Florida, and had served as general counsel of the Florida Turnpike Authority and as a member of the Florida Railroad and Public Utilities Commission (1955–1959; chairman, 1957–1959). He had been named the outstanding young man of the Florida Junior Chamber of Commerce in 1956.

On November 16, 1959, Whitney Gilliland replaced Denny, who had resigned. Gilliland served approximately one month remaining in Denny's term and was reappointed for a six-year term to expire December 31, 1965. He became chairman of the CAB in May, 1960. Gilliland, who was fifty-five, had attended Iowa State College and the University of Nebraska. He was admitted to the bar and practiced law in his home state of Iowa. From 1938 to 1941 he was a state district judge. He served as assistant to the Secretary of Agriculture in 1953, as chairman of the War Claims Commission from 1953 to 1954, and as chairman of the Foreign Claims Settlement Commission from 1954 to 1955. He was Republican state chairman in Iowa from 1947 to 1950 and chairman of the Executive Committee of the National Republican Strategy Committee in 1949. In 1959–1960 he served as president of the Federal Bar Association. Like Boyd, he had had no experience in aviation.

Chairman Durfee resigned in May, 1960, to become a federal judge. He announced to the Board on September 22, 1959, that he would not participate in the decision in the GPFI, but he did participate in certain interim decisions; in fact, his vote was necessary to break a tie on several occasions. He was still on the Board when it made its tentative decision in April, 1960. His successor, John S. Bragdon, did not take part in the decision or sign the final order.

Thus, in the fall of 1959 two Board members resigned and a third announced that he would not participate in the decision in the GPFI. The decision in the case was made by a majority composed of two new members (Boyd and Gilliland) and Gurney, who had served since 1951. Minetti concurred only in part.

Prior to the final decision in November, 1960, the Board had announced interim decisions. On three occasions it announced, without Minetti's concurrence, that it would extend existing rates, reflecting the intermediate increases given February and October, 1958, "pending final decision in its General Fare Investigation."[90]

On March 15, 1960, Boyd and Gilliland announced that they had become familiar with the record and were qualified to participate in the decision. A tentative vote on issues relating to standards in the GPFI was announced in a press release on April 29, and on June 17 further announcement was made that domestic trunkline carriers would be permitted on July 1 to raise passenger rates by 2.5 percent plus one dollar per one-way ticket—the latter increase and the existing jet surcharges to expire June 30, 1961.

Though the Board had announced its vote on most of the issues in April, full explanation came in the opinion of November 25. The opinion of the Board was given in seventy-seven typed pages. It went directly to the points at issue without preliminary statement of statutory standards, legal principles, or economic objectives.

The Board stated that much had been gained from the proceeding in the definition of standards with relation to the "profit element,

[90] Announcement on June 18, 1959, extending tariffs through December 31, 1959; on November 23, 1959, extending tariffs through March 31, 1960; and on February 25, 1960, extending tariffs through June 30, 1960.

rate base, depreciation, and taxes" (p. 4). What conclusions did it reach on standards for rate making?

1. As in the examiner's decision (Item 4, examiner's opinion), the operating ratio method was rejected, it being stated that "only the rate of return on investment indicates the appropriate end result" (p. 10).

2. The rate of return (Item 5, examiner's opinion) was determined as follows: Cost of capital was declared to be "a paramount consideration," but the techniques of constructing it "are complex and necessarily involve large areas of judgment." The Board judged that an overall return of 10.5 percent was required, which was close to the examiner's judgment of 10.6 percent. But the Board did not agree with all of the examiner's constituent conclusions on rate of return.

a. On cost of debt: the examiner's conclusion of 4.5 percent for the Big Four and 5.5 percent for the other carriers was accepted, Bureau Counsel's argument for lower figures being rejected.

b. On cost of equity: for the Big Four, 16 percent, and for the other eight, 18 percent, were substituted for the examiner's figures of 15 and 17, respectively. The Board found generally that earnings-price ratios were not precise indicators of capital cost in an industry with earnings instability. Specifically, they did not reflect fully the risks in the airline industry, particularly "the unique risks stemming from re-equipment" for the jet age. In addition, regulation of fares on a bulk-line basis, rather than in accord with the needs of each individual carrier, added other risks for the carriers and justified "a rate at the upper limits of reasonableness."

c. On capital structure: the Board concluded that the examiner had correctly based the rate of return on actual capital structure, but he had underestimated the percentage of debt. It substituted 50 percent debt for the Big Four and 55 percent for the other eight for the examiner's figures of 45 and 50, respectively.

d. Summary: Table 3 (p. 32) summarized the results (see p. 240).

3. On rate-base issues (Item 6, examiner's opinion), the Board accepted the examiner's conclusion that equipment purchase deposits should be included in the base. On the other hand, it rejected the examiner's conclusion that exclusions from the "prudent-investment rate base should be limited to dishonest, wasteful, or im-

TABLE 3

Overall Rates of Return

Industry Unit	Security	Capitalization %	Security Cost %	Weighted Cost [of Capital] %
Twelve Trunks				10.500
Big Four				10.250
	Debt	50	4.5	2.250
	Equity	50	16.0	8.000
Other Eight				11.125
	Debt	55	5.5	3.025
	Equity	45	18.0	8.100

prudent expenditures (pp. 33ff)." It excluded investments and special funds not used and useful in the airline business, such as National's investment in a Miami television station. To prevent double charging, it excluded charges that had been made to operating expenses but that appeared on the books as surplus, and certain other items already included in cost of debt. These exclusions were made in line with Bureau Counsel's exceptions to the examiner's decision.

4. On "Future Operations, Revenues, and Expenses" (Item 7, examiner's opinion), the following conclusions were reached:

a. On load factors and standard costs: on these items the Board thought that Bureau Counsel had "undertaken to achieve a worthwhile objective." It rejected carriers' argument that the American Overseas Airlines case precluded the use of standard load factors and standard costs, though it added that it was "clearly not the function of the Board to assume the role of management." At the same time, the Board stated that the unreliability of past forecasts of results and the magnitude of the changes in the transition to jet equipment made it necessary to await a more stable period before standards could be set (pp. 42–56).

b. On depreciation: the Board accepted the conventional straight-line depreciation method with appropriate residual values on which the examiner had based his decision. It also accepted his decision on the service life of different kinds of equipment. On the other hand, it corrected his decision to place a 15-percent residual value on engines, as on other equipment, and to allow 5 percent of the airframe cost to be included in the residual value. It made one other adjustment that would allow, in some instances, a somewhat higher depreciation allowance.

c. On taxes: the Board upheld the examiner's determination that the income tax allowance should be normalized and that tax reserves should not be included in the rate base.

5. As to the rate level, the Board considered two problems, which it referred to as problems of "Application" of standards (p. 70):

a. On period to be considered (Item 10f, examiner's opinion): the Board concluded that rates should be regulated to produce a reasonable return over an extended period of time, although it said short-term considerations should not be ignored, and it refused to accept "any mechanical device" such as the examiner's proposed "5-year moving average formula" (p. 71).

b. On the unit of rate making (Item 10d, examiner's opinion): the Board agreed with the examiner's conclusion that the "bulk-line" or industry approach should be used. Under this approach rates would "be set at levels that would meet the average of the costs, including return, of the bulk of the industry." It said, however, that it did not follow the reasoning of the examiner. He had argued that rates should be set to achieve "the same kind of result that would obtain in the open market-place" (p. 73). The Board said this was not one of the statutory rate-making standards. One of these was to "consider" the need of each carrier, but this was only one of five factors set forth in the statute. The statutory standards, particularly the effect of rates on the movement of traffic and the need in the public interest for transportation at the lowest rate, militate against setting rates in terms of the need of the least profitable carrier. On the other hand, to set rates on the basis of the needs of only the most favorably situated carrier would "have a disastrous impact" upon many carriers and the development of transportation generally.

At the end of its opinion (pp. 76–77) the Board declared that "general fare increases cannot be regarded as the panacea" for the weak-strong carrier problem. It named four other tools that could be used to seek a solution of this problem: (1) revisions in fare structure that "might well result in bringing costs and revenues of the individual carriers into closer alignment"; (2) permission to weaker carriers to charge higher rates, though competition would prevent their using these "except on some noncompetitive segments"; (3) route realignments; and (4) subsidy payments.

Minetti dissented on three of the determinations made by the Board. He thought that "in recognizing equipment purchase funds and deposits which are related to airplanes not delivered, the Board is charging today's airline passengers with part of the costs of operating tomorrow's airplanes . . ." He objected to granting carriers permission to charge as expense "normalized" taxes, rather than actual taxes paid. But his most significant dissent was on the rate of return. The rate was "higher than . . . allowed by any other government agency in history." It resulted from an excessive allowance for equity capital. He thought the earnings-price ratios overstated investment requirements. He was led to this conclusion by the fact that the period from which the ratios were drawn was that of the highest sustained earnings level in the industry's history. Instead of correcting upward by 3 points, from 13 to 16 for the Big Four, he would stay with the 13 percent revealed by the figures. This would reduce the overall return for the Big Four to 8.75 percent instead of the 10.25 percent allowed by the Board. For the other eight he would allow 14.5 percent on equity capital, making an overall return of 9.6 percent. For the industry as a whole the resulting overall return would be 9 percent instead of 10.5 percent. In all, Minetti concluded that the Board's decision would cost users of airline transportation eighty million dollars annually in excess of reasonable rates.

What did the Board conclude as to the dollars-and-cents level of rates that should be allowed? The majority and Minetti concurred in the decision on this point. As stated in the majority opinion, the carriers' experience for 1958 and 1959 differed "markedly from their own projections" (p. 48). They had not obtained the revenue anticipated, and there were disparities between estimated and actual costs. It was concluded:

In view of the unreliability of the forecasts and the lack of data in the record reflecting jet operations, we are without a trustworthy basis for projecting future results. Under these circumstances, it is clear that we cannot determine the appropriate level in this proceeding. (p. 52)

The decision—four years, six months, and fifteen days after the initiation of the GPFI—was that "meaningful data useful for determination of appropriate fare levels for representative, relatively extended periods" were not available in the "transitory, unsettled stage" of the industry, and "We shall, therefore, terminate this investigation" (p. 52).

Concluding Comments

The CAB has authority to use two regulators: route awards and rate controls. Through its control over routes it can provide for competition between the largest traffic centers, and in the past it has done so. It has not succeeded in equalizing the strength of competitors. Competition among equals might offer more protection for the public than rate regulation over unequals. The effect, however, of a conflict among competitors of equal strength could probably not be anticipated. It could lead to overscheduling, excess capacity, expensive luxury additions to service, destructive rate competition, and possibly to insolvency or return to subsidy. Competition among unequals might lead to elimination of some carriers and an ultimate concentration of control which would destroy the effectiveness of competition as a regulator. Such tendencies may be checked by the supplementary power of setting minimum rates. On the other hand, as experience with duopoly and triopoly has shown, a struggle for a market between two or three competitors serving it does not always lead to price competition. It may lead to promotional advertising and service additions rather than to promotional pricing. The setting of maximum rates may, therefore, be regarded by many as a useful supplementary instrument to ensure the development of a mass airline service.

The tightness and the accuracy of rate regulation for the airline industry will be affected by many factors. Since the strength of competitors will never be completely equated, rate regulation for the industry will probably be less precise than that for monopolistic utilities. Also, the volatility of the industry may prevent accurate prediction, even for short periods, and restrict ability to provide for evenness in returns over successive years. Moreover, the impact of rate making may be affected by the degree of control allowed under the regulatory act.

If the courts were to accept the arguments of the airlines that their estimates of depreciation cost must be accepted as conclusive in rate proceedings, the gap in the CAB's cost control would create looseness in rate regulation. Strict control over the price of airline service could be achieved only by control over factors affecting use of seat capacity, including scheduling.

The effectiveness of rate regulation for any industry may be affected by the degree of success in establishing standards to guide future administrative decisions. Standards should simplify the task of regulation and aid in more expeditious handling of rate decisions. Also, establishment of standards provides the regulator with a comforting sense of fairness and the regulated firms with standards to guide their future actions.

Establishment of standards for setting rate levels does not, however, solve all problems. First, standards may not be durable or precise. Certain standards may have durability: rate of return rather than profit margin, normalized taxes, bulk-line estimates of cost of capital, and inclusion of equipment deposits in the rate base. But 10.5 percent as a rate of return is a figure derived from market conditions and, hence, subject to change. An "extended period of time" is an imprecise standard. Second, issues concerning structure of rates and effect of rates upon the movement of traffic remain open for the judgment of men in particular circumstances. Third, agreement on standards affecting rate levels does not lead to agreement on figures. Cost of capital must be refigured. Expenses and earnings for the future must be estimated. Innumerable issues of fact on cost and income calculation for future periods can be litigated repeatedly.

The difficulty of rate regulation is increased by the procedural requirements. During the lengthy judicialized process, needed adjustments may be delayed. By the time the process is completed, new issues may be more important than those that have been litigated, or the facts in the record may be outmoded by new developments. If rate regulation is to be carried on with a reasonable measure of effectiveness, revisions in procedural methods may be required. A crucial item is the extent and kind of hearing for rate making that will contribute both to fairness to parties and to effective government. What degree of accuracy in decision should be sought? Is it possible to consume many months with cross-examination and other elements of the testimonial process and yet produce unusable figures? Whether 142 days of hearings and whether the kind of hearings held in the GPFI were necessary for fairness and effectiveness are matters for careful thought.

A further problem is the need for definition of roles and relationships in government rate making. To what extent and on what matters should Board members be treated as judges by parties at interest, by congressmen, and by the President and chief officials in the executive branch? The issues of ex parte conversations between Board members and private parties and between Board members and members of the executive and legislative branches are difficult to resolve. So is the question of what supervision and direction Congress should legitimately exercise. One of the most difficult problems is definition of the types of decisions to which protections like those for judges should be extended. There is also the question of whether Board members, as agency heads, should remain judicially aloof in proceedings such as the GPFI, even though this means giving little guidance and direction to their subordinates who carry the agency's responsibility to represent the interest of the general public.

CHAPTER **6**

The Air Transport Association

The basic characteristic of a system of regulated private supply of a service is coparticipation by persons and institutions in private and public sectors. In contrast to public ownership and management, functions are allocated both to governmental and private agents. Basically, this is achieved through statutes which define areas of activity for public administrative authorities and leave the remainder to private agents.

The participation of the private parties is not limited, however, to functions reserved to them as private functions. Necessarily, they are brought into the public arena through their own petitions to government agencies and through actions initiated by these. They will seek to obtain favorable, or to avoid unfavorable, decisions respecting their interests. This may be done through formal channels of access, such as administrative proceedings or congressional hearings, or through informal processes, such as personal contacts or appeal to public opinion. Through a variety of means the private agents will get inside the governmental process itself, and what on its face appears to be public action is a resultant of forces mounted in part, perhaps almost exclusively, from the private sector.

In addition to these influences exerted on government from private positions, private parties are sometimes incorporated into the regulatory process by requirements for their consent and collaboration in the making and administration of policy. A system of public-private collaboration is institutionalized to the extent that neither the public nor the private agents can move without the cooperation of the other. Illustrative are the arrangements for regulation of agricultural production and prices—referendums through which farmers approve or disapprove of production limitations and farmer committees to administer regulations. However, specific provision for this coparticipation of private with public authorities is exceptional and is regarded with suspicion by those who fear impairment of public purpose or unequal representation of private interests.

In commercial aviation, as in other industries, private interests are aggregated in large measure through associations. The most significant of these is the Air Transport Association (ATA). It assists companies on a wide range of technical matters that are of interest to them in their private capacities. It represents them in forums of public policy decision. In addition, it serves as an instrument for industry coordination in an unusual system of public-private collaboration that has the effect of incorporating the private structure into the public regulatory pattern.

Some of the activities of ATA have been displayed in earlier chapters. A more extended discussion of its operations is merited, both because of its importance in the universe of activity being described and because of the general neglect of associational activity in descriptions of the regulatory process. The study that follows gives first a general description of ATA's functions and its organization and methods of operation. This is followed by a case study to illustrate the system of public-private collaboration and by comments on what is revealed with respect to such collaboration.

ATA's General Position

The ATA represents part of the commercial segment of the consumer-service organization of air transport. That is to say, in the first place, that it does not represent manufacturers of aeronautics equipment, nor air pilots, nor the military, nor communities receiving air service, but it does represent air transport companies; and second, that it represents only those companies which are engaged in certificated service over regular routes. Its membership, defined in its Articles of Association, includes operator members and associate members. Operator membership is available to carriers that have legal authorization to conduct scheduled air transport service under a certificate of public convenience and necessity, and associate membership is obtainable by foreign air carriers having permits for scheduled air transport service. Only operator members have voting rights in the Association.

The Association's general position in the universe of commercial aviation is affected by a number of factors. First, it is internally a federation and subject to the limitations which characterize such structures. Although the commercial interest in regular aviation service provides much cohesion within the structure, there are elements of pluralism in the interests represented. International and domestic, trunkline and local service, passenger and cargo, and helicopter certifications create different, often conflicting, as well as shared interests. Also, companies strive separately for income potential from favorable route grants and for income realization from sales; and this striving, sometimes competitive, creates separate interests, and judgments thereon, that lead to conflicting positions on many policies. In addition, the ATA is, like most federations, composed of members of unequal strength, which leads to additional complications in developing programs of action.

The diverse and competitive interests of the companies circumscribe the area of Association activity. Thus, ATA must stand aloof from the contests among its members for routes. Thus, also, the differences in interests, and in judgments on ways of meeting these, support the inhibitions of the antitrust laws against coordinated activity with respect to rate structures and levels. Although all carriers are interested in high returns, they each pursue independent rate policies judged to be income producing for their respective companies. The Association has, therefore, stayed out of rate cases, a notable exception being the General Passenger Fare Investigation, as discussed in Chapter 5. Because of carrier differences, even this intervention was for limited purposes. Policy judgments of carriers may cause deep divisions, the classic instance being the three-to-two split among the five big carriers over whether the desirable public policy was "Once off subsidy, always off."

Associational activity is dependent, therefore, upon discernment of common interest and upon much mutual adjustment of different interests and views. Achievement of these results places strains on leadership different from those existing in organizations where power is allocated from the top downward.

Second, the Association is a point of convergence in a communications net between its internal components and its external environment. The environment is complex, and although the regulatory segments of that environment are rather stable the technological influences are unusually volatile. The activities of the Association are responses to signals from the environment and from its members. Yet with respect to the environment, as well as to its members, it has no power allocation commensurate with the demands the signals place upon it. In contrast to government agencies, it has no command authority over any portion of its environment. The only coin its officers can use in communications with the external environment is influence. This influence accrues only from aggregation of unity among its members and from resiliency and susceptibility of the environment.

A third factor is the extraordinary diversity of the Association's activities and the resulting complexity of the organization through which it operates. Its activities are much more diverse than those of either of the major regulatory agencies with which it is in constant contact. It is, in fact, the one structure which most nearly encompasses in its activities all the matters which comprise the universe of commercial aviation supply. This enlarges its potential for a comprehensive view and for coordinative activity, but it also has contributed to complexity in the structure and operations of the Association and to considerable deconcentration and dispersion of responsibility within it.

Finally, in contrast to the aforementioned factors, there is a feature of the regulatory pattern which strengthens the Association and allocates to it a kind of regulatory-coordinative function. Section 412 of the regulatory acts of 1938 and 1958 provides that carriers may file agreements with the Civil Aeronautics Board with respect to pooling of earnings, rates or classifications, improving safety, eliminating destructive competition, or other cooperative working arrangements, which the Board may disapprove if "adverse to the public interest, or in violation of this Act"; relief from the antitrust laws is granted for actions taken in pursuance of such agreements. The significance of this with respect to the Association is that it may serve as an instrument to coordinate the views of the airlines in the formation of agreements and to implement the agreements. The Articles of Association of ATA are themselves an agreement approved by CAB, and the Association is continuously assisting in making or amending agreements and in their implementation through enforcement procedures or otherwise.

The role of the Association and the limitations on it in industry agreements will be developed in later portions of this chapter. It is sufficient to conclude here that industry agreements approved by a regulatory agency are an exceptional feature in American regulatory patterns, and that the provision for these enlarges the role and strengthens the position of the trade association.

The functions of ATA were classified for the author by one of its officials. The first function is to serve as a focus for the airlines' communications with the regulatory agencies and other parts of the government on all matters of industry-wide interest. There are matters which the carriers cannot appropriately or easily handle individually. For example, the fight for a more adequate organization for safety than that administered by the Civil Aeronautics Authority (see Chapter 4) was led by ATA. The carriers did not want to say individually, "We have had a lot of near misses lately; we need to replace CAA." Although ATA itself found it hard to take this position publicly, it was nevertheless, in the words of one of its officials, "the blade on the bulldozer." It bore the brunt of the interaction between the existing agencies and the industry.

The second major function is the reverse communication function of informing the industry of actions taken or contemplated by the regulatory agencies and Congress, and, more important, formulating judgment factors for its members for assessing the effects and values of such actions. ATA conducts analyses and planning with respect to government actions which no company is equipped to do as fully.

The third function is coordination of industry views. This is regarded as essential because of the vulnerability of every group that competes for favorable public policy. In aviation, the military has a tight organization and strong political influence. "General aviation" users and miscellaneous consumers of airline service are numerous and widely dispersed at the grassroots level, and thus potentially are able to exert influence through many channels. The commercial airline industry, not tightly integrated and having a relatively small number of members, believes that it needs a compensating arrangement for agreement upon, and for protection and promotion of, its vital interests.

The fourth function was stated to be enabling the small airlines to share the high-priced expertise of both the larger airlines and the ATA itself. Through ATA's Operations Department technical knowledge can be made available to all companies.

This summary of functions and the preceding comments together supply clues for classification of ATA's functions into two categories. One is the representative function—that of representing the industry-wide interests before government and in the wider forum of public opinion. This is a function which is common to trade associations generally. The other is the internal coordinative-regulatory function, which has two parts: the coordination of industry views toward common policy positions, which is essential for the performance of the representative function and hence characteristic of all trade associations; and coordinative activities on a technical level. The two are often blended in a highly developed, quasi-regulatory role which sets ATA somewhat apart from other trade associations. A closer look at ATA's organization, functions, and operations, and then a case study, will provide deeper insight into the two categories and the significance of a private multi-functional, coordinative instrument in the mixed private-public system of supply of aviation service.

ATA's Structure and Performance

ATA's organizational pattern is designed to facilitate industry coordination on all those matters on which there is an industry-wide interest. This is accomplished to some extent for virtually every phase of commercial air transportation except rate decisions. The resulting structure is unbelievably diverse and complex.

There is, on the one hand, an integrative structure which is conventional in type, relatively simple, and also relatively small in size. At the top of this structure is a board of directors, a president of ATA selected by it, and several vice presidents or assistants to the president. There are the usual types of specialized staff services, including those of the treasurer's office, the office services section, the library, the research and economics staff, and the Legal Department. Besides the Legal Department there are departments for each major substantive activity: Public Relations, Federal Affairs (national agency contacts), Public Affairs (state and local representation), International Services, Finance and Accounting, Traffic,

Operations, and Personnel Relations. The total number of officers and employees below the board of directors on December 31, 1966, was 177.

Service in this, the bureaucratic structure of ATA, places unusual demands on persons. They must have technical competence in their respective functions comparable to that in the industry and in the government. They must, in addition, be able to bear extraordinary tensions inevitably created in operating between a volatile and sometimes hostile external environment and a semipluralistic industry.

There is, at the same time, for industry coordination, a lightly integrated structure that is complex, that is uniform in general features but variable in details, and that engages the participation of numerous industry officials. In almost every kind of activity engaged in by the Association there is a conference or committee structure that brings together the top-level airline men knowledgeable on that activity. In its most developed form the top level of organization is a "conference." The conference is formally organized through bylaws and an agreement approved by the CAB. Under the conference there is usually a group of committees and subcommittees appointed to fulfill special roles of problem solving or procedural policy formation. These committees are staffed by the subordinates of the top-level men who make up the conference. The committee members are not members of the conference; they only report to the conference.

ATA's own bureaucratic structure is related to this industry coordinative structure by having members of its staff serve as secretary to each of the conferences and committees. The corresponding ATA department head usually serves as executive secretary of the conference and its most important committees. Typically, one or more assistants then handle the lesser committees and subcommittees. Thus, the general pattern is industry group relating to corresponding ATA unit.

The structure is most elaborate for those groups of activities which relate to the operational side of airline service. The committees and subcommittees served by the Operations (primarily engineering operations related to safety) and Traffic (interline ticketing, baggage transfer, and other functions) departments of ATA number in the dozens. They sometimes have functions which are administrative and quasi-regulatory with respect to operations. They serve also as representational units to communicate with the vast and differentiated array of private and governmental organizations in the external environment. However, since so much of the work is operational or procedural, and technically specialized, and frequently also inwardly coordinative instead of externally representative, it can be conducted without the necessity of attention and vigorous leadership from topside officials of ATA. Policy making and operational coordination is extremely decentralized to diverse types of specialists.

The pattern is different in significant respects for the functions which are more highly representative. The Federal Affairs, Public Affairs, Public Relations, International Services, and Legal departments of ATA have responsibilities which are more diverse and which cut across the functional divisions for specialized activities. Their work regularly also touches sensitive relationships with the external environment. This brings them into close relationship with each other and with the president of ATA. In sensitive areas, policy making, although coordinative of industry interests and views, is necessarily centralized within ATA. It will be seen, also, that the same thing has been true of the Personnel Relations department.

These two aspects of ATA's own structure and operations should be distinguished from housekeeping and service functions performed by it for independent organizations. For the Airlines Clearing House the administrative work is done by the Chase Manhattan Bank, but ATA supplies legal service without charge. Similarly, the Universal Air Travel Plan Committee, a joint International Air Traffic Association-Air Traffic Conference committee, is supplied legal services by ATA for a charge.

EXAMINATIONS OF ATA STRUCTURE

It should not be surprising that a complex structure, comprising both representational functions similar to other associations and coordinative and quasi-regulatory functions peculiar to ATA has been the subject of inquiry. ATA itself employed a management consultant firm which reported in March, 1962. The thrust of the report was that the diffuseness and technical nature of ATA's operations impaired its ability for anticipation of policy problems and coordination of industry positions on these. It found that "Industry members had operated in a highly individualistic fashion." It said that the conferences and committees of ATA were concerned primarily with technical and procedural matters and attracted a disproportionate amount of time and effort from the Association's executives. It recommended a reconstructuring of ATA with abolition of all conferences except the Air Traffic Conference, reduction of the number of committees, and greater integration of activities under the Board of Directors.

More significant was an external inquiry, reflective of a hostile environment, into ATA's organization and operations. The Antitrust Subcommittee of the House Committee on the Judiciary (Celler Committee) issued on April 5, 1957, a comprehensive report on "Airlines" which was in essence a report on ATA.[1] The report was critical in tone and conclusion. It sought to show that ATA was unrepresentative of its membership, being dominated by the large carriers. As to the general impact of the Association, it stated, "It is apparent that officers of the certificated carriers and officers of the Air Transport Association have entered into many agreements and have undertaken various activities pursuant to these agreements in order to prevent growing outside competition and to assure continued control over air transportation by the members of the 'established industry'."[2] Among the activities noted were attempts of carriers through ATA to persuade the CAB to deny operating authority to new applicants for all-cargo service, a public relations campaign conducted by ATA against new entries to air transport service, and joint opposition to nonsked participation in the Joint Airline Ticket Offices plan (JAMTO). It concluded: ". . . the committee is of the view that a substantial number of ATA's activities for its member carriers involve serious antitrust problems."[3] It recommended action by CAB, including a restriction of Section 412 approvals and an investigation of ATA.

The Celler Committee's investigations, of which the report on "Airlines" was one result, gave rise ultimately to tensions among the components in the public-private structure affecting the airline industry. The tension between the committee and the CAB was reflected in the inquiry of the former with respect to a passenger

[1] *Report of the Antitrust Subcommittee of the House Committee on the Judiciary*, 85th Cong., 1st Sess., Airlines (April 5, 1957).

[2] *Ibid.*, 183–184.

[3] *Ibid.*, 187.

fare investigation in 1956. In turn, the initiation of the investigation by CAB upset the friendly spirit between that agency and ATA. Within ATA there was a feeling that the passenger fare case was ill-timed and the result of congressional pressure on the Board. On the CAB's side there was resentment in 1958 over ATA's campaign, largely through the press, to gain a favorable regulatory attitude.

As a consequence of these developments, CAB, taking formal notice of the Celler Committee's recommendation that it investigate ATA, instituted on March 10, 1959, "a general inspection and review of the activities and practices of ATA . . . to determine whether the Board should continue its approval of the organization of ATA, and if so, whether the Board should impose further conditions to such approval."[4] ATA denied its subjection to inspection by the Board, but ultimately accepted inspection of an estimated 1,600,000 pages of files, records, and documents. It persisted in its denial with respect to all documents on which it claimed attorney-client privileges, and was upheld in District Court.

In the inspection-and-review proceeding the Board insisted on changes with respect to ATA's and its associated organizations' structure and operations in line with limitations implicitly suggested by the content and tone of the Celler Committee report. The contest over access to documents led the Board also to insist, as a condition of continued approval of ATA's organization and operations, on guarantees of its right to access, which it considered essential for the kind of supervision the Celler Committee had thought it ought to exercise.

Most of the Board's objectives were accepted in an offer of settlement by ATA on July 16, 1962, but on two matters, subsequently to be noted, the Board's final order terminating the investigation on April 2, 1964, went beyond the terms of the proffered settlement. The significance of the order is that ATA is subjected to regulations affecting both its private representational function and its coordinative and subregulatory function as the price for its approval under Section 412. The result is to formalize a set of balances between a private association and a supervisory public agency.

The Board's order[5] clarified the requirements with respect to

4 Order E-13597 (March 10, 1959).
5 Order No. E-19260 (January 31, 1963). See also Order No. E-20409 (January 29, 1964) and Order No. 20641 (April 2, 1964).

filing of bylaws of ATA's associated organizations. The Board had held in 1939 that the Air Traffic Conference's bylaws were not an agreement requiring filing, but ATA's Articles of Association were approved in 1940 and bylaws of additional conferences were approved in later years. The Board now took note of the expansion of conference activities over the years. Although it concluded that "The spectrum of activity of the conferences is so broad that it is apparent that efficient operation of a scheduled carrier requires the facilities provided by these conferences," it declared its obligation to supervise the conferences. It found that bylaws were agreements, and required, as a condition of continued approval of ATA's Articles, that the bylaws of its conferences or divisions be filed for approval. A second requirement was that ATA's Articles of Association be amended to provide for equal voting, on an unweighted basis, for each regular member. This requirement reflected the opinion of the Celler Committee that weighted voting allowed a small number of large carriers to dominate ATA's proceedings and resulted in an integration of control dangerous to the public interest. CAB imposed still an additional requirement in its 1964 order: each of five classes of carriers (domestic trunklines, international trunklines, local service, helicopter, and all-cargo) was, unless all members of a class elected otherwise, to have representation on ATA's board of directors each year. This requirement, designed to ensure fair representation, had the incidental effect of giving one carrier, the only certificated all-cargo carrier, continuous representation. The requirements will not, it should be noted, ensure equality of representation in ATA's affairs. Service on ATA's numerous committees is expensive to airlines; also, there is more talent and more urge for leadership in the large airlines.

To enable the Board to discharge its "responsibility for keeping surveillance over trade association activities," requirements for reporting to CAB were imposed. ATA and its conferences were instructed to report all resolutions, contracts, and agreements required to be filed under Section 412 as determined by the Board. Minutes of membership meetings of ATA and its conferences were also to be submitted to the Board. In addition, "a full statement of any public relations campaign or program" was required to be submitted to the Board within thirty days after its authorization. This requirement, which thrusts at the heart of private associational activity, was supplemented by others. Reacting to public appeal through information media by ATA on docketed cases, the Board in effect made applicable to ATA, its conferences, and their officers the "Principles of Practice," which inhibit interested parties from giving statements to communication media designed to influence the Board's decision in a hearing case. Also, reflecting the Celler Committee's concern over unrepresentative decisions or courses of action, it required appropriate opportunity for all affected or concerned members of ATA to participate in consideration of publicity programs; it also required affirmative disclosure by ATA of the extent of its representation of members in any instance in which it had reason to believe that any members disagreed with the publicity statement.

The Board was particularly concerned with disassociation of the function of publishing consolidated tariffs from the policy-making structure of ATA. It saw a valuable service both to the public and the industry in such publication, but it was sensitive also to anti-trust implications. It thought that this was a technical activity different from usual trade association functions and rejected a proposal of ATA's for continued supervision by an ATA official. It accepted housekeeping connection with ATA but required that the substantive functions not be under the control of any officer of ATA. The function has now been organized under a Tariff Corporation.

The most difficult problem in arriving at a conclusion of the inspection-and-review proceeding was the framing of rules concerning access by the Board to documents. The Board believed that none of the reforms through which it sought to make its surveillance of ATA more adequate would be effective if it were to be confronted in the future with claims such as had been made in the past of attorney-client privilege. It was concerned with "the potentially coercive effect on smaller carriers of over-centralized legal representation," with "potential interference with the Board's access to differing points of view," and with the danger of "collusive activities." On the other hand, ATA felt strongly that it was necessary to protect its interest in confidential discussions with the carriers it represented. The solution embodied in the order is multifaceted. The Board's right to access to all nonprivileged records is restated. Confidentiality of legal advice and of communications is accepted for the broad range of purely internal relations within the ATA structure: ". . . among officers or employees of ATA or its instrumentalities, or individual members of its committees, etc., with respect to the activities of ATA or its instrumentalities, or of such committees, etc. . . ." This allowance is conditional upon ATA's keeping all such documents segregated, reporting to the Board quarterly their number, and upon request furnishing the Board with a list of such documents with date, author, and addressee of each. A different rule is prescribed for the relations between ATA and its members:

ATA shall so conduct its affairs as to preclude it, its officers or employees from engaging in the practice of law in such a manner as to create a claim of privilege against disclosure to the Board of information or documents based upon an alleged attorney-client relationship between it, its officers or employees on the one hand and its members on the other.

The restrictions imposed on ATA in the final order in the inspection-and-review proceeding are accompanied by another imposed in 1959 that ATA finds particularly obnoxious. CAB Rule 263[6] provides that an air carrier association, its officers, or its employees may participate in Board proceedings only if the articles of the association provide for it and if the Board grants leave therefor. Leave is ordinarily to be granted only where the association (1) represents its own financial or property interests as distinct from those of its members, or (2) acts as a conduit of factual information, or (3) represents named members at their request, subject to the condition that an interested member or the Board may ask withdrawal of the association on the ground of diversity of interest within the association. The routines imposed by this rule are, of course, very restrictive. The scope of the prohibition can be determined when experience shows whether the Board will construe it as a limitation only on formal participation in formal proceedings or whether it will be used to inhibit informal contracts with the Board and its staff members.

MAJOR REPRESENTATIONAL DEPARTMENTS

To present an adequate picture of ATA's operations it is necessary to describe in some detail the functions and operations of its separate departments.

[6] Issued June 16, 1959, 24 F.R. 4882.

Before the Government and the Public. Certain of ATA's departments are engaged almost exclusively in representing the airline industry before the government and the public and in the coordination of industry views for that purpose. The Public Affairs Department, which deals with state and local governments, has an elaborate organization for carrying on activities which are customary for a trade association. There is a public affairs committee composed of a representative and an alternate from each airline, and a smaller executive committee. For each state one or more airlines are designed as coordinators of legislative activity. There is also a group of field coordinators supplied by the airlines. The air transport industry is vulnerable to state taxes—particularly fuel taxes—and to state legislation affecting insurance, licensing, and many other regulatory matters; it also has interests in promotion of airport services through state and local action. The Public Affairs Department maintains sources of information through which it can learn about measures proposed, or measures to be proposed—pressure to avoid introduction of a bill is regarded as a more desirable technique than pressure to kill a bill. The department analyzes about two thousand bills per year and conducts the kinds of research required for effective representation of airline interests. The head of the Public Affairs Department is the focal point in information gathering and the action program which follows. Sometimes he testifies before legislative committees himself, but the bulk of the work in the separate states and cities is done through the collaborative industry structure.

For representation of interests before Congress, ATA has a Federal Affairs Department. Functions stipulated for it include supply of factual information to congressional committees and individual congressmen, presentation of views of the airline industry to Congress, and coordination of airline activities on congressional matters. The last function is not always successfully accomplished. There have been instances of breakdown of normal liaisons within ATA itself, the Federal Affairs Department not having received notice of courses of action pursued by other departments. But the usual limitation upon the department is the lack of consensus among the airlines. Moreover, the department sometimes finds it difficult to enlist the cooperation of airlines in presentation of the industry's case. The airlines have their own well-developed contacts with

Congressmen—giving them some ability to exert influence, but they wish to conserve this influence for their particular ends.

The methods used to influence Congress are affected by the special position of the airlines and ATA. A listing is maintained of airlines serving and points served in each congressman's constituency. Information is known on attitudes of key members and on channels of influence to them. The potential for affecting votes within a congressman's constituency may be made the basis for an attempt to influence his action. This bargaining aspect of influence is, however, less utilized than by many associations. The personal influence of Stuart G. Tipton, ATA president, and Leo Seybold, head of the Federal Affairs Department, accrues largely from confidence in them established over the years. Significant, moreover, is the possibility for winning by sheer weight of the case, presented in public interest terms. The public service aspects of airline service are emphasized. It is known that key figures like Senator Monroney have strong convictions on the public service of airlines (may even, it has been said, feel "a mission"), may have no political reasons for taking a particular position, or may (as one ATA official said of members of the Ways and Means Committee) have so many pressures on so many issues that another one is absorbed "in the mass." The identification of airline service with the public interest is facilitated in the case of airlines by congressmen's intimate knowledge of a service they frequently use.

The volume of work for the Federal Affairs Department is reflected in the Annual Legislative Summary of the Air Transport Association for the 1961 session of Congress. Bills of interest to the industry numbered, in the House alone, fifty-six in the Commerce Committee, forty-two in the Ways and Means Committee, twenty-eight in the Judiciary Committee, ten in the Post Office and Civil Service Committee, ten in the Rules Committee, forty-eight in eleven other committees. Also significant is the record of frequency of testimony and formal submittals by ATA: of the former, seven in the Senate and ten in the House, and of the latter, three in the Senate and five in the House.

A third major representational department is the Public Relations Service. Until 1955 this service was primarily a so-called staff service, its main function being to supply information to the airlines (including that for the airlines' publications for employees), and only irregularly and without overall planning supplying information to the public press. In 1955 ATA's Board of Directors authorized an active and positive public relations program, now referred to as a line activity of the Association. The Association's staff is supported by a committee organization, composed of a central committee of public relations directors of airlines and regional committees representative of airlines in the regions.

While the objectives and methods of the service are similar to those of other industry public relations services, specific attention has been directed toward three purposes. One is to create public understanding of the essential function of profits in the airline industry. Another is to develop belief that the airlines are efficiently, honestly, and responsibly managed, and that this is a positive good and creates a consequent need for limitations on government regulation. The desire is to preserve understanding of management prerogatives and the dangers of extending regulation into managerial details—into "everything in sight without regard to the amount of public interest involved," says one ATA official. The third purpose is to increase public appreciation of the FAA and CAB and of the need for these agencies to function without susceptibility to public pressures.

An illustration of the focusing of these objectives in an action program is found in the activities of the ATA during the period of the General Passenger Fare Investigation, as revealed in CAB's records of the inspection-and-review proceeding. A general public relations program was conducted with the specific, practical, and related aims of softening the New York money market and obtaining a favorable decision from CAB on legitimate earnings levels. ATA records were quoted on the objectives of the Public Relations Service: "Gaining support of the financial community both for satisfying future capital requirements and for helping to ensure an equitable regulatory climate." The Finance Committee of ATA's Board of Directors reported this objective as having "the highest priority." A letter from Willis Player, ATA vice-president for public relations, stated: ". . . a basic point is that, apart from the merits of the issue, the climate of public opinion will have a great deal to do with the mood of our regulatory agency, when it begins to examine the level of our earnings." The ATA campaign included press releases and suggested editorials, for example, "The state of

Wyoming, as well as the nation as a whole, has reason to be . . ."
As for the GPFI, Mr. Tipton stated at a Public Affairs Committee
meeting that he hoped the members would continue to pursue the
subject and wield any influence they could with Chambers of Commerce, Rotary Clubs, and other groups to bring to their attention
the need for a fare increase.

It will be recalled that CAB reacted vigorously to the active public
relations of ATA. Sensing a need for defense, it both inhibited statements to the press by interested parties to influence Board decisions
and encumbered ATA's planning of public relations programs.

A further set of activities is conducted through the International
Services Department. As explained by the ATA vice-president of
this department and his assistants, the activity falls into four parts.
One is to consolidate and report the position of the United States
flag international carriers to the Department of State and the CAB
with respect to bilateral negotiations with other countries. The
department may be able to exercise little leadership where the
economic interests of competing lines differ. On the other hand, it is
engaged sometimes in reconciling the carriers' positions and also in
explicating or drawing together the positions of the government
agencies. Second, the department tries to influence the development
of the substance of government policy on international aviation.
Thus, in the event of a White House study it may submit data and
views to the study commission. It is concerned always that economic considerations of the airlines not be overlooked under pressures to consider foreign policy objectives. This is a danger particularly felt when policy making is raised to the presidential level.
It is a danger of which ATA is especially conscious because foreign
airlines are usually wholly or partly government operated and it is
felt that national prestige and honor, or other national policy objectives, may prevail easily in their positions over strictly business
considerations. This situation makes it imperative, from the airlines' viewpoint, that strong emphasis be placed on the economic
needs of airlines in the American position. Also, one problem in
international aviation policy where Association activity may be
helpful, it is felt, is overcoming the lethargy within a government
which must be active in so many matters that its attention to any
one kind of problem is less than those concerned with it may wish.

The third kind of activity is facilitation of foreign transport, that is, cutting down on the red tape involved in getting passengers and cargo in and out of the United States. The department works before the State Department and Congress to reduce or eliminate visa requirements; with the Bureau of Customs, Immigration Service, Public Health Service, and the Department of Agriculture to cut down on the time and difficulties in their inspections; and with the Department of Commerce to simplify export controls. Finally, the department supports in whatever ways it can the promotion of international travel and trade. It worked, for example, for the establishment of the United States Travel Service.

On Personnel and Industrial Relations. There is a Personnel Relations Conference and a department on personnel relations in ATA. The conference functions through an executive committee, under the chairmanship of an airlines representative, and with an executive secretary, who is ATA's vice-president for personnel relations. Actually, however, the nature of the work requires more concentration of responsibility and more informality in relationships than in many ATA activities, and hence the vice-president carries the main burden of the responsibility. His department supplies true staff services to the airlines on such matters as selection and training of personnel, executive development programs, and relations with government departments on personnel matters. Increasingly, however, the main purpose is "balancing the airlines position at the bargaining table." This calls for accumulation of data prior to bargaining, and for consultations with carriers which move cautiously at the border between legality and illegality. Since carrier differences on industrial relations policies may lead to whipsaw action by unions, and since such differences do exist, there is advantage to the carriers in Association activity which produces unity of position. The desirability of unity is enhanced by the existence of the Mutual Aid Pact, under which a trunkline on strike is given assistance from a carrier fund to which each of the signatories to the pact contributes.[7] It is evident that millions of dollars in airline revenues can be involved in negotiations, and hence that the services of ATA in coordinating carrier positions on matters at issue can be among the most valuable of the services of the organi-

---

[7] The Mutual Aid Pact first became effective for six participating airlines on October 20, 1958, and was approved by CAB in Order No. E-13899 (May 20, 1959).

zation. On the other hand, consultations either must not be open or must not produce a collective solidification of position which will substantiate a union charge that the requirements of the Railway Labor Act for collective bargaining are being violated. It is noteworthy that a substantial portion of the documents which ATA claimed were privileged in the inspection-and-review proceeding related to industrial relations, and that CAB felt impelled to initiate an investigation of such matters in 1960.[8]

Technical Coordinative and Regulatory Functions. The features of the technical coordinative, and—largely incidental—regulatory, activities are common to the several technical functions and are readily obvious to the observer. They have been described generally already, and hence the specifics can be summarized briefly. First, the central conception is the conference, which is the name given to the sum-total of the activities of each of the several fields of activity. There are three major conferences—Airlines Operations, Finance and Accounting, and Air Traffic—each with its own bylaws defining organization and purpose. Second, the basic organizational conception of the conference is that it is representative. Each conference represents all the membership in the conference as a whole, which has an elected president and vice-president, and functions through committees on which a convenient number of the airlines are represented. The committees usually represent the specialized bureaucracies of the airlines, bringing together persons with technical competence in particular aspects of airline operations. Third, service and coordinative roles are performed for the conferences and the committees by the bureaucracy of ATA. Each conference has an executive secretary who is head of a department of ATA, and who in the case of the Operations Conference also serves as chairman of the conference, and each committee is served by a secretary from the ATA department. The primary function of the technical departments of ATA is to service the conferences and their committees. Fourth, the conferences themselves and many of their particular functions are given legal standing and public legitimacy by an agreement approved by CAB. The agreement is a flexible instrument of public supervision. In the year 1961, for example, the Air Traffic Conference filed with CAB six new agreements and seventy amendments

[8] Order No. E-15413 (June 20, 1960).

to existing agreements. Fifth, the role of ATA, formally defined as a service role, is in practice defined by two circumstances: The day-to-day operations are technical in nature and hence are conducted, until major policy questions arise, without the active participation of the top leadership in ATA; the conferences and the committees operate by unanimous consent, and hence any leadership of the ATA bureaucracy must be through brokerage of company positions —in essence a political function of consensus building. The statement of one department head that ATA cannot lead in anything perhaps only obscures the nature of the coordinative function. Finally, public supervision over the conference activities is formalized in the terms of the agreements and amendments thereto, and in whatever provisions are included for reporting to CAB.

The range of activities of the conferences is so extensive that illustration by reference to some of the major activities is all that is possible. The Airlines Operations Conference was created to deal with the airlines' "mutual operations problems." Virtually all phases of engineering problems are included in the work of committees. One emphasis is on safety problems, with consideration of these running the gamut from aircraft fires to development of safety regulations pertaining to new aircraft. Committees are concerned with such things as the Air Traffic Control System, all-weather operations programs, and training curricula for flight crews. For example, much attention is given to adequacy of weather maps and to distribution of aeronautical charts and maps. Another activity is the coordination and preparation of operating specifications for the airlines' intercommunications system, for example, with respect to passenger reservations that require interline service. One of the oldest functions is coordination of airline needs with respect to supply, attention being given to such things as standardization of manufacturers' parts catalogues, packaging of repair parts, and pooling of commonly needed parts.

The Finance and Accounting Conference's officials proudly assert their historical function, dating from 1940, in aiding CAB and the airlines in the development of the uniform accounting system. The conference's committees plan also for uniform ticketing, interline ticketing settlements (operating through a clearing house), uniform handling of air-cargo claims, and more favorable insurance policies for airlines and airline travelers. In recent years the conference has been particularly interested in the use of electronic data processing in airline accounting, statistics, and reporting. Basically, the purpose of the conference in its various activities is standardization and simplification of airline procedures .

The Air Traffic Conference deals through its numerous committees with a great variety of technical functions, but to a greater degree than for the other conferences these functions may have more than a technical significance. On the technical side, for example, are all the arrangements for interline ticketing and interline baggage transfers. Formerly included also was the development of the consolidated tariff schedules. The removal of this function under constraint from the CAB to an independent corporation emphasizes the fears of the CAB and the Celler Committee that traffic committees could be instruments of agreement or understanding going beyond technical matters. The Air Traffic Conference is concerned with many matters which have a direct interest to the public, such as excess baggage charges, interline connection schedules, passenger and air freight service improvements, and market development. It also operates, under the Air Traffic Conference Sales Agency Agreement, a regulatory function over travel agencies, which are listed for service by the conference and operate under standards prescribed by it.

The Celler Committee report attacked the validity of carrier control of entry into the business of selling airline tickets. It noted: "The overall effect of the Board's course of conduct with respect to travel agents has been to confer on the certificated carriers farreaching regulatory powers over the travel agency industry which the Board itself does not have statutory authority to regulate in the first instance."[9] Because of evidence shown during the Celler Committee's hearings of its concern over regulation of travel agents, the CAB investigated the matter and ATA revised its procedures to meet objections which were prevalent among travel agents. Sponsorship of a carrier for a travel agent was dropped as a requirement for listing for service, and procedures for appeal were established, with final opportunity for arbitration, in case of denial of an application for service or of actions objected to by certified agents.

The regulatory functions of the Air Traffic Conference with re-

[9] *Report of the Antitrust Subcommittee*, 85th Cong., 1st Sess., Airlines, 215.

spect to the airlines themselves are best illustrated in the work of the Office of Enforcement. The resolutions of the conference cover every conceivable aspect of interline passenger travel or air freight shipment—from the size of the passenger ticket to the proper procedures for the prompt handling of misdirected baggage. Strict conformity with the resolutions avoids conflicts within the industry and serves a public function in providing the public with the convenience and efficiency of an integrated public transportation system. The airlines voluntarily set up an Office of Enforcement in 1956. It seeks to prevent breaches of resolutions before these occur, by conducting a continual system of spot checks, by visits to airline offices to observe procedures, and by guidance to airline personnel in interpreting resolutions. When, however, breaches are alleged, the office conducts an investigation to determine the facts, with the airline being provided an opportunity to present its defense. The office may, if it decides there has been a violation, levy a fine. The airline may appeal by asking for arbitration proceedings before an impartial panel selected from the American Arbitration Association.

Turning from specific activities to a more general observation, it is noteworthy that the conference activity provides a continuing grid over which airlines may maintain communications with each other on their common operating problems and with the service, coordinative, and leadership structure of ATA. Its benefits to the airlines must be judged to be substantial because of the large amount of time they contribute to it and because of the extent to which they have subjected themselves to it. It may also, if confined largely to technical coordination and regulation, contribute to efficient, economical, and convenient public service, and thus have a significant role in commercial aviation service. It should be added that, in addition to this internal communication grid, the conference structure sets up additional representative positions through which the airlines can be jointly represented on the larger communication grid which encompasses the entire interacting structure of commercial civil aviation supply. Through conference officials the airlines are represented before manufacturers, insurance companies, travel agencies, and other private organizations. They are represented in innumerable lines of communication and association with government agencies. The lines reach to the FAA, CAB, Weather Bureau, Post Office Department, and many other government agencies. The Airlines Operations Conference has, to illustrate, cooperated in many ways with FAA—making suggestions to it, developing cooperative programs in advance of FAA determination, and participating jointly with it in committees, task forces, or teams.

Many years ago Pendleton Herring concluded that on the technical plane the purposes of government could not be served without industry cooperation.[10] The conference structure of ATA has provided on the industry side an instrument for this cooperation. It has been publicly legitimatized by exercises of the authority of CAB to approve agreements.

The No-Show–Oversale Proceedings

The internal coordinative and regulatory function of ATA through the conference machinery can be illustrated by a case study. For this purpose the no-show–oversale agreement of 1961 is selected. By "no-show" is meant the failure of a passenger to appear for transportation after he has purchased a ticket or made a reservation and not asked for cancellation. By "oversale" is meant an overbooking by an airline which results in inability to provide a passenger with transportation which has been committed to him.

Attention is focused on procedural aspects, with inclusion of only enough attention to substantive problems to illuminate the difficulties in achieving collaboration. The temporarily connected in-flight services discussions are given brief attention. The discussion here follows the pattern of the development of the case, and hence centers initially on the no-show deliberations.

Certain general aspects of the no-show–oversale proceedings are noteworthy. The proceedings have been described by participants as typical of the way ATA's coordinative procedures operate in numerous undertakings. There was a sufficient parallelism between public policy objectives, reflected through the CAB, and private industry aims, reflected in ATA committee action, to provide a setting for ATA coordination. Public-private cooperation was apparently necessary if the results desired were to be achieved: the Board probably lacked legal authority to impose by its order alone a no-show–oversale plan, and certainly would not by its own action have intruded

---

[10] E. Pendleton Herring, *Public Administration and the Public Interest*, p. 192.

as deeply into problems of managerial detail as a no-show–oversale order would have entailed; industry action without Board approval might well have been illegal. The case shows the fragile and elusive nature of industry consensus on policy matters, and the difficulties in converting policy aims into workable operating procedures. It highlights the vital role of ATA mechanisms in integrating the carriers' views into a policy and operational agreement. The mechanisms included, of course, both the industry representation and the participation of ATA's officials. The role of the latter illustrated in this case is followership more than leadership and is essentially mildly aggressive mediatory.

There were two atypical aspects of the case. One was that it originated in a conference called by the CAB. The other, more significant, was that CAB's consent was obtained for the consultations leading to an agreement. The general rule governing "prior approval" of carriers' meetings and consultations is that any matter that does not directly concern rates may be discussed and agreed upon by the carriers, who then must submit the agreement to CAB for its approval. Because the no-show plan called for a penalty on the passenger (at one time called a "reservations service charge"), it was generally agreed that prior approval for discussions was needed. On a further element in the early discussions—in-flight fringe services to passengers—ATA attorneys felt that prior approval was not required. When this too was included in CAB's formal authorization for discussions, ATA's assistant general counsel informally contacted CAB officials to express the hope that a precedent for prior approval for "services" talks was not being established.

The initiating CAB conference was held on September 28, 1961. The eleven domestic trunks existing at this time had been invited to a conference to discuss the general financial condition of the trunklines. The year 1961 had been disastrous for the trunks—their net loss being $34,568,000—and the Board was concerned. The carriers suggested that they would be aided financially if they could cut out frill services on coach flights and penalize "no-shows." The Board's response was, in effect, "Well, go ahead with the discussions and we'll authorize these by order." The order, subsequently prepared, allowed discussion through October 31 of in-flight services and of "ways and means of curtailing 'no shows,' including the imposition of penalties." It provided for notice of meetings so that a CAB representative could attend, for keeping of minutes and filing of these with the Board, and that any agreements should be filed with the Board for its approval in accordance with Section 412.[11]

Following CAB's authorization, the structure for discussions was quickly established. Since it was a traffic matter, Jack M. Slichter, vice-president for traffic and head of the Traffic Department of ATA, was automatically responsible for service and coordination in the discussions. He would be assisted by John A. Lundmark, assistant vice-president for traffic and executive secretary of the Air Traffic Conference of ATA. Immediately upon discovery of the words of the authorizing order, a correction was requested to allow ATA participation. Lundmark, in a letter to Chairman Alan S. Boyd of CAB, pointed out that "past experience with industry-wide meetings" had shown the value of ATA's secretariat functions, of occasional service of a member of its staff as moderator of discussions, and of staff supply of "specialized knowledge and experience on an industry-wide basis, in particular technical fields which may be involved as the discussions progress." On the following day CAB authorized attendance of ATA employees "to perform secretariat or other informational functions"—a guarded and limited authorization which could not possibly be a realistic description of Slichter's role in the discussions.

To represent the CAB, either Irving Roth, chief of the Bureau of Economic Regulation, or Bruce Miller, head of the Trunklines Section, Routes and Agreements Division, Bureau of Economic Regulation, attended meetings of the committees which were constituted for the discussions. The first of such committees, which will be referred to as the parent committee, came into existence on October 5. A meeting on that date brought together twenty-two representatives of ten of the eleven trunklines, and Slichter and Roth. Later meetings were usually attended by a fluctuating number of persons from the trunklines, sometimes by representatives of local-service airlines, and by Slichter and Miller. The bulk of the committee was formed by the vice-presidents, directors, or managers of traffic, or some division thereof, in the respective trunk-

[11] Order No. E-17515 (September 28, 1961).

lines. They frequently came with the understanding that they would have the authority to commit their airlines, even by signing formal agreements. The first action of the committee was to elect Rex Brack, senior vice-president of Braniff, as chairman. At the end of two days of discussion there was agreement to form a working committee on the no-show problem, referred to thereafter as the *ad hoc* committee. "Terms of reference" were outlined for this committee, and the chairman instructed the representatives of American, Eastern, United, Lake Central, Mohawk, and Piedmont airlines to designate appropriate representatives to serve on the committee. For this committee E. K. Rhatigan, director, Ground Passenger Services of American Airlines, became chairman. The trio of Slichter, Brack, and Rhatigan would be responsible for calling meetings, maintaining communications, achieving consensus, and reporting to CAB. Consensus would be recorded in agreements approved by CAB. These could, under amendments of the Board's authorizing order on October 5, be adopted as Air Traffic Conference resolutions, thereby making them enforceable by the conference's Office of Enforcement.

In-flight services attracted the first attention of the parent committee—probably because the financial savings could be more substantial and the solutions appeared to be easier than in the case of no-shows. There was also opinion that CAB strongly desired the reduction of frill services. At the first meeting on October 5 nearly unanimous agreement was achieved on elimination of food and drink and seat reservations for coach passengers, and handouts to first-class passengers. The chairman directed that a document be prepared, and all trunks except Continental signed it. A few days later Slichter sought by telephone call to obtain Continental's reconsideration, and thereafter his assistant hopefully requested that the agreement go on the agenda of the forthcoming Air Traffic Conference. At a second meeting of the parent committee on October 30 United presented a revised plan, calling for reductions of food service to coach passengers, but the discussion terminated with the revelation that Continental contemplated a tariff filing for an additional "no-frill" coach service, and in view of this would not accept reduction in services on existing flights. Eastern, however, brought forth a new proposal. Brack was unable to get a meeting on it, but Eastern persisted and Slichter expressed hope in a report to Tipton that an agreement would be reached within ten days. A special meeting on in-flight services was finally held by the parent committee on December 12. A list of frill eliminations was discussed, and disagreement was narrowed to two of these. On one of them only Continental and National held out; on the other—reduction of cost of coach food service—all ultimately agreed to sign. United, however, was not present; and in spite of a direct appeal by Brack, United held out and the agreement was dead. In the end a "bombshell" filing by Continental of its tariff for increased coach services registered the complete collapse of the effort to reduce services.

The in-flight services negotiations reveal the central roles of industry chairman and ATA representative in the search for consensus. They also show the great difficulty of coordination of industry positions, even among members of as small an oligopolistic club as the trunklines and on a matter on which great savings for all are possible.

No-Show Negotiations

From the start the no-show negotiations were more complicated than the in-flight services discussions. For this, there were several reasons. One was the lack of agreement among the trunklines about the seriousness of the problem. The statistical data, of which there were a great deal, did not provide a firm answer on the question of number of seats actually not filled because of no-shows. Often load factors are less than 100 percent, and no passengers are turned away because of prior reservations of no-shows. If turned away, they may be booked on another flight of the same or another airline. Moreover, stand-by or no-record passengers may take over the no-show seats at the last minute. Also, the no-show passenger may be a stand-by on an earlier flight and may board it, thus causing no revenue loss to the airline industry and perhaps not to the airline concerned. There is difference of opinion in the industry on whether the operating losses in making reservations for no-shows are significant, for the same amount of personnel might be required at the reservation stations nevertheless. In addition to these factors, there is uncertainty as to what portion of the statistical percentage on no-shows is due to errors in record keeping by the carriers. United and TWA took the position from the beginning of the no-show discussions of 1961–1962 that the number of passenger-caused no-shows was not substantial enough to be worth the expense and trouble of formulating and administering a plan to penalize them, and Delta expressed doubts about this through the course of the proceedings.

The industry had tried no-show penalty plans on previous occasions—in 1946, in 1954 for coach service, and in 1957. A "Draft Report" of the Bureau of Economic Regulation of the CAB of July 20, 1961, reviewed the no-show problem, and drew carefully balanced conclusions. On the one hand, it said:

> We are, however, reluctant to propose or initiate any No Show penalty plan. The industry's previous history with the No Show Penalty Plan suggests that administrative costs exceeded the benefits of the plan, and from a competitive and passenger service viewpoint the disadvantages of the plan outweighed the No Show problem itself. In the absence of any precise evaluation as to the volume of the true passenger-created No Show any such plan would be difficult to justify.

On the other hand, the "Draft Report" noted the currently inadequate earnings of the airlines and said that "the luxury of empty seats can no longer be afforded." It concluded, "Should the carriers determine that a No Show penalty plan is necessary and come forward with such a plan, the Bureau would be inclined to give it favorable consideration."

A factor which further complicated the discussions was the apparent necessity of obtaining the assent of the local-service airlines: to ensure their cooperation in the administration of a penalty plan, and to allow adoption of an Air Traffic Conference resolution which could be enforced by the Office of Enforcement of ATA. Such adoption could be blocked by a single negative vote. The local-service lines had not been invited by the CAB to the September 28 conference because the trunks were in more serious financial distress and because the problems confronting the trunks appeared to be distinctive. The Board's order of that date did authorize local-service airline participation in discussions. When the initial industry conference of October 5–6 turned on the second day to the no-show problem, six local-service carriers were present. These carriers were opposed in principle to a no-show penalty, and they were concerned because they had not been invited to the CAB meeting. Their position was recognized by Brack in the constitution

that day of the *ad hoc* committee, three of the six places being given
to local-service carriers, namely, Mohawk, Piedmont, and Lake
Central.

Still another factor was the difficulty of devising a workable and
acceptable penalty plan. The technical nature of this problem was
the reason for the establishment of the *ad hoc* committee. The
committee's "terms of reference" were quite general and called for:

   (A) Fixing responsibility with the passenger who "no-shows."
   (B) Fixing responsibility with the airline, and other selling agents,
        for "oversales."
   (C) Fixing responsibility among airlines, and other selling agents,
        for interline "no-shows" and "oversales."

Slichter promptly, in collaboration with Rhatigan, made arrangements for an initial meeting, and informed Brack of these arrangements. The committee met on October 11 with all members present,
but with local-service representatives noncooperative on the no-
show program. Five approaches or plans on no-shows were brought
forward and discussed, and some discussion of oversales followed.
Already, the feasibility of fixing responsibility on a specific airline,
both on no-show and oversale penalties, was prominent in the discussions. It was agreed that the five approaches on no-shows should
be studied by the individual company staffs of the *ad hoc* committee
members, so that coverage, costs, and benefits could be estimated.

Rhatigan's posture was the double one of urging movement and
of waiting for further instructions from the parent committee on
the plans under consideration. He was apparently of the opinion
from previous discussions that the parent committee desired to
submit an agreement to the forthcoming meeting of the Air Traffic
Conference. When he informed Slichter that he planned to speed up
the work of the *ad hoc* committee to make possible a meeting of the
parent committee in the week of October 16, Slichter replied in
effect, "Not too fast; let's work out the best possible solution; it
can be handled at a special session of the ATC." Rhatigan then
suggested to Brack that the matter be put on the agenda of the regular ATC for discussion only. Also, on October 16, Rhatigan sent
Brack two additional plans. The last, Number 7, was Rhatigan's
elaboration of discussions on the day of the first meeting of the
ad hoc committee.

Despite the importance of study of technical feasibilities, the primary center of collaboration was the chairmanship of the parent committee. Brack was at the center of the system of communications. He had the responsibility of reporting each step in the proceedings to the principals, including Chairman Boyd of the CAB and the major trunklines. Copies went also to the already informed secretariat, that is, to Slichter in ATA, and through him, when appropriate, to the local-service, or local-service and helicopter, companies. Since consensus was lacking among the companies on the desirability of penalties for no-shows, the requirements for leadership, if agreement were to be obtained, were unusually demanding. Brack was persistent, confident in the face of obstacles, and patient and diplomatic.

Slichter was backup man to Brack but also much more than that. His position has been described as that of staff aide who normally began operating when Brack would say, "Well, can we do that?" or "What do we do next?" One who attended all the meetings said that Slichter did much to "maintain a good spirit at the meetings" and "a lot of fence mending" between the meetings. It was said that he became most active when disintegration was threatened. His strengths were that he had had long experience in what in the airline industry is termed "passenger services" and that he could maintain an industry-wide viewpoint. In sum, the ATA committee system combines the strength of an industry chairman who is first among equals with a staff aide who is technically competent, has responsibility for continuity of proceedings, and thinks exclusively in industry-wide terms.

Sensing the need for exploratory discussions, Brack took advantage of the universal representation of the airlines at the regular Air Traffic Conference. At an informal meeting on October 25 the several approaches to solution of the no-show problem were discussed and the carriers were asked to communicate their objections to any of them to the *ad hoc* committee. At the meeting the basic differences between the trunks and the local-service carriers came into prominence. The latter were opposed in principle to any penalty plan. They noted that the administrative costs would prevent any participation at all by them in the plan and, in addition, they would suffer a public relations blow by participating in the plan even to the extent of collecting the penalty for the trunk carriers. The local-service lines are concerned with encouraging passengers to travel and are not much worried about no-shows. Pique over their slight by CAB in the issuance of invitations to the September 28 meeting and the real self-interests of the local-service carriers produced a sharp cleavage between them and the trunks.

The second formal meeting of the parent committee was held on October 30, at which time instructions were given to the *ad hoc* committee to pursue plan Number 7. Brack had already asked CAB to extend the authorization for discussions, and an additional month was granted on October 31. The *ad hoc* committee met on November 7 to develop details of the plan, and a third meeting of the parent committee followed on November 11. In the meantime Piedmont had withdrawn from its place on the *ad hoc* committee and Braniff was asked to name a replacement. At the November 11 meeting the remaining local-service carriers withdrew, and from then on were not participants either in the parent or *ad hoc* committee.

The divisions among the trunks had now come to the surface. Delta, prior to the *ad hoc* committee meeting of October 7, expressed doubt about the whole venture, noting that it had one of the lowest no-show factors in the industry. Two survey periods had shown that its ratio of no-shows to passengers boarded was less than 6 percent. It attributed this to "good housekeeping." It did not believe that passengers caused more than 25 percent of the no-shows and thought that if this conclusion were correct, then the potential benefits of a penalty plan would not justify the administrative costs. In addition, it repeated doubts expressed by it in the parent committee that a plan could be successful that excluded the local-service carriers. Other differences among the trunks were recorded by Irving Roth in an information memorandum to CAB members on November 22. United was the only airline that refused to agree to the plan at the most recent meeting, taking the position that the major cause of no-shows in the statistics was poor record keeping, and that this was the problem which should be handled first. But TWA doubted that a passenger-caused problem existed, Eastern wanted more than the other lines—an "air bus" plan with a 100-percent retention of payment if the passenger did not show—and Delta would not sign if local-service carriers in its area were not included. Roth said the meeting had been "adjourned," not "recessed," and that no further meetings would be forthcoming.

Brack had, however, reached a different conclusion. On November 24, after the meeting from which the local-service carriers had withdrawn and which Roth had said had "adjourned" the proceedings, he wired the trunk carriers that "In view of recent developments which indicate firm agreement can now be reached on an industry plan a meeting of the trunk carriers on no shows is hereby called" for November 27. Apparently, United had withdrawn its refusal to sign. No minutes were kept of this meeting and the CAB observer was not present, although Brack had informed Chairman Boyd that the meeting was called. The major development at the meeting was a refusal by National to sign. While it had been assumed that the agreement would be for a 20-percent, five-dollar minimum penalty, National's representative stated that he had flat orders not to accept anything less than a 50-percent, five-dollar minimum, and a fifty-dollar maximum. The meeting quickly adjourned, but Brack negotiated with the trunks by telephone and obtained their agreement to the National proposal. United completed acceptance on November 29, agreeing to the latest proposal only, as it said, to achieve unanimity, and upon condition that its position be stated to the CAB at the time the amended agreement was filed.

The agreement sought solution to the no-show problem, first by setting ticket purchase and pick-up time limits, and second by a reservation service charge rule. This rule provided that any ticketed passenger who asked for refund or for use of a ticket after the scheduled flight departure for which the first remaining flight coupon was validated, would be assessed a service charge of 50 percent (with a minimum of $5.00 and a maximum of $50.00) of the applicable one-way local fare of the first remaining flight coupon, unless the customer simultaneously presented written evidence, provided to the carrier, that he had cancelled his reservation prior to scheduled flight departure for which the first remaining flight coupon was validated. Passengers who travelled on credit plans would be billed for the no-show charge. Travel agents would be responsible for advising passengers of the reservations service charge and for the collection of such charges, with commission of 5 percent.

Brack transmitted the agreement to CAB on November 30. In the meantime Miller had asked and CAB had granted another extension of discussion time to December 15. The *ad hoc* committee met jointly with carrier accounting representatives to work out detailed procedures on December 14. Thus ended the first phase of the no-show–oversale discussions. The approved plan was signed only by the trunks. It provided for no-show penalties on customers, but included no provision for oversale penalties on carriers.

ADDITION OF THE OVERSALES ISSUE

CAB, on January 4, 1962, under a form of proceedings called "ratification of actions taken by notation," directed the staff of its Bureau of Economic Regulation to draft and submit for action by notation an order indicating tentative approval of the no-show agreement, subject to the adoption by the carriers of penalties on oversales. The order would provide, also, for a twenty-day period for comment by interested persons before the Board took final action on the agreement.[12]

A press release had been issued by ATA, on behalf of the carriers, on the date (November 30) when the agreement was signed. The effect was an immediate flush of letters to the CAB. The theme of the letters—so stated in some—was "equal protection for passengers." The letters complained of delays in flight departure, cancellations of flights, the "drastic" nature of the penalties for no-shows, the poor record keeping of the airlines on reservations, and the difficulty of getting telephone calls through to airlines to cancel reservations. But the most frequent complaint was on overbooking and the suggestion was made by a number of complainants that there should be a penalty—a few named the figure of fifty dollars—for sale beyond load capacity; some thought, also, that customers should be given a hearing before CAB approved an agreement. The volume of these letters increased after CAB's announcement of a "twenty-day period for comment by interested persons." The bulk of the letters approved an oversales penalty and some said that it should be larger than that for no-shows because of greater injury caused by oversales. Several suggested penalties for delayed or cancelled

---

[12] Order No. E-17914 (January 8, 1962), tentatively approving Agreement No. 16012.

flights, and one even proposed penalties for "airline-caused missed connections, missed baggage loading, and missed business appointments because of airline delays." The requirement for written evidence of cancellation in the airlines' agreement was the subject of question by travel organizations and companies that knew the difficulties of obtaining written evidence. The General Services Administration objected on February 14 to several aspects of the no-show agreement. The Commonwealth of Puerto Rico requested that the Board bring service to Puerto Rico under the new plan and thus withdraw the existing 100-percent penalty for failure to use or cancel (24 hours prior to departure) "air bus" or "thrift" tickets to and from Puerto Rico, and Congressman William F. Ryan of New York introduced a concurrent resolution in Congress (H. Con. Res. 458) calling upon CAB to terminate discrimination against travelers to and from Puerto Rico. The CAB's files, however, show relatively little attention by members of Congress to the no-show–oversale deliberations.

Oversales, the primary subject of the customer complaints, had had the attention of the CAB immediately prior to its approval for discussions of no-shows in September. In 1960 it had instituted enforcement proceedings against Eastern and National on charges of overbooking. In the Eastern case the Board found that the record failed to establish a practice of overbooking and that unintentional overbookings could not be considered an unfair or deceptive practice or unfair method of competition. In the National case the examiner found the respondent guilty of unfair and deceptive practice in intentionally overbooking flights. National did not deny the charge of intentional overbooking but argued that, on account of cancellations and no-shows, stopping the acceptance of reservations when capacity point was reached would result in empty seats. Its overbooking was characterized as "space management" and is also referred to as "controlled overbooking." The Board was sufficiently impressed with National's arguments that it decided to dismiss the proceeding and institute an industry-wide investigation to "provide the Board with a sound factual basis for the development of Board policy with respect to overbooking." This investigation ended with the "Draft Report" of the Bureau of Economic Regulation on July 20, 1961, from which quotations of conclusions on no-shows have already been given. The "Draft Report" concluded that the turnover in reservations, due to cancellations and changes, was substantial, and that "human error, record discrepancy and time lag" are major factors in creating reservations problems. It noted that the carriers were trying to reduce time lags and record-keeping errors through installation of a multimillion dollar equipment program. It said that seven of twelve reporting carriers indicated that they utilized controlled booking to some extent. As in the case of no-shows, the "Draft Report" took a middle, somewhat equivocal, position on oversales. It said, "There is no conclusive evidence that known overbooking does in fact lead to and create oversales." It was "not recommended that the carrier be required to provide immediate notice of an overbooked status to any passenger overbooked." Yet the "Draft Report" made positive recommendations for passenger protection as follows:

> Notice of a known overbooked condition or status be given to such overbooked passenger as soon as possible but in no event less than twenty-four hours prior to scheduled departure. Any known overbooked condition which arises less than twenty-four hours before scheduled departure would require immediate notice.

Conjecture cannot be avoided on why oversales, connected with no-shows in the discussion of the whole reservations problem in July, got separated from the no-shows discussion between September and January, and then was joined to it again in the Board's decision of January 4. The Board's order authorizing discussions on September 28 made no mention of oversales. The Board was interested in improvement of the carriers' earnings position, and it was a time when the Board was interested also in avoiding any appearance of intrusion by it into management problems of carriers. The carriers, on their part, included oversales in the "Terms of Reference" to the *ad hoc* committee, but the subject faded from the discussions. For this, there were apparently two reasons. First, there was a strong feeling among the carriers that no matter how an oversale compensation agreement was worded, it would not remove the liability of the carrier to a suit for higher damages. They were alarmed by a recent court decision awarding an attorney who had been cancelled out on a flight on which he had a confirmed and reconfirmed reservation both compensatory damages and exemplary damages, the latter in the amount of five thousand dollars; but they did not see how an oversale penalty could be a substitute for their common law liability. Second, therefore, they naturally wanted to avoid the additional costs on them in oversales penalties. The Board had been represented in the meetings of the carriers and knew that no oversales penalty was to be included in the agreement; it must have known also that some of the persons involved in the discussions believed that the Board desired that an agreement be signed. The reasonable conclusion, therefore, is that the Board was sensitive to the complaints from customers following the announcement by ATA on November 30 of the filing of the no-show agreement, and that continuance of this sensitivity after its own request for comments accounted for its refusal to recede from the position taken in the January order.

This refusal came in a direct confrontation with the trunks two weeks after the Board's decision of January 4 and following a rapid series of events. It will be recalled that on January 4 the Board instructed its staff to prepare an order tentatively approving the no-show agreement but conditional upon addition of an oversales penalty. The order was issued on January 8. It approved the no-show plan generally, suggested some clarifications, expressed concern that the penalties might be too drastic, but stated that this could be tested in an experimental run, and hence provided for a test period of six months following March 1. It invited other (local-service) carriers to join the agreement by filing with the Board a notice of intent. On oversales it suggested a higher penalty than for no-shows, specifically "$25.00 or 50 percent, whichever is greater, of the applicable one-way local fare of the first remaining validated flight coupon of the ticket." This was followed by Footnote 10: "Where such minimum payment would not fully compensate the passenger for damages sustained as a result of the oversale, he would be free to claim and the carrier would be free to pay, such additional amount as the circumstances would warrant." The order authorized carrier discussions of these matters during the twenty days allowed for filing of comments by interested persons.

Promptly after issuance of this order Brack called a meeting of the parent committee, and, in view of the invitation of the Board to other carriers to join, Slichter invited the local-service carriers to attend. A few of these were present on January 17 for a lively discussion on oversales penalties, called "Compensation for Denial of Confirmed Passage." The *ad hoc* committee had in the meantime struggled with the wording of an oversales agreement which would conform with the Board's order. But the carriers felt that the language did not solve the legal and practical difficulties created by the Board's Note 10. They felt, moreover, that these difficulties were too great for correction in subsequent tariff filings of the carriers, and that in any event the difficulties could not be corrected before the March 1 effective date. Other concerns expressed were that the twenty-five–dollar penalty was above the price of some tickets, that many oversales were caused by a variety of factors over which the carrier had no control, and that frequently a passenger who was the victim of an oversale was accommodated satisfactorily on an alternative flight. It was decided that a committee should be appointed to confer with CAB. Brack appointed a committee composed of himself, three other airline representatives, and Slichter; and Slichter made arrangements for a conference the next day with the Board.

The committee prepared a report to the Board in which it recalled that the joint objective of the Board and the industry was "to reduce carrier cost and increase revenue without undue burden on the traveling public," and reported that the carriers were divided over whether a combination of a no-show agreement with an oversale penalty would attain this objective. It was stated that the public was in a different position from the carriers in that the former had remedies through "damages, adjustments or reimbursement of expense attributable to oversales, whereas the carriers have no remedy against the no show passenger." It was suggested that discussions of oversales penalties could not be productive until there had been a trial of the no-show agreement. In the discussions which followed the submission of this report, Board members asked many questions and the airline representatives felt that the Board obtained a better understanding of their problems. They found, however, that the Board was determined that it was in the best interest of the public to implement the no-show and oversales penalties at the same time. It granted an extension to February 15 of the time for consultations.

At this stage the effort to achieve concurrence between the airlines and the Board was kept alive by a number of factors: the joint desire of the Board and the airlines to get the no-show agreement in effect; the belief of the airlines that the Board's understanding of their problems would allow appropriate exceptions from oversales penalties for factors outside the carriers' control; and perhaps also the hope of the airlines that an oversales penalty could be framed in such a way as to reduce the likelihood of court suits, or, in event of these, of lower court verdicts. Brack promptly transmitted to the trunks a report on the meeting with CAB and asked that the *ad hoc* committee—as soon as the CAB extension order was issued—finalize the conditions for an agreement so that the parent committee could meet. The *ad hoc* committee did not meet until January 30, allowing time for ATA's legal staff to prepare a proposed tariff rule to encompass both the "reservation service charge" and the "compensation for denial of confirmed passage." When the *ad hoc* committee met for consideration of the tariff rule and other matters, it noted the need of a sixty-day period between completion and implementation of a plan, and Miller suggested that the parent committee could ask CAB to take action by a selected date in order to provide the interim time. The committee agreed to meet again on the night of February 12 to finalize details, and to invite the trunks not represented on the four-man *ad hoc* body to meet with it, so that all airlines could be equally familiar with the details of implementation. Even one member of the *ad hoc* group had been unable to attend all meetings; and when he and a representative of another airline began drafting a separate plan, Slichter explained to them that their plan was similar to that on which the discussions had been based.

Brack transmitted the *ad hoc* committee's drafts and minutes to the trunks and called for a meeting on February 12. At that meeting the differences of opinion among the trunks again threatened the success of the consultations. Delta and Northeast felt strongly that the amount of the no-show penalty should be reduced, but National stated that it was not authorized to go lower, and the matter was passed over. Later, in the oversales discussion there was sentiment for reducing the oversales penalty below the amount suggested by CAB, and it was argued that local-service lines' participation might be more easily obtained if all penalties were lower. American then proposed a package of identical penalties on no-show and oversales—50 percent, with a five-dollar minimum and a twenty-five–dollar maximum. National finally agreed to accept this, with a change to a forty-dollar maximum, and there the decision stood. A second matter that caused division was Delta's statement that it would file a tariff accepting liability for oversales payments only when the ticket was issued on its own stock, that is, by Delta. After a long discussion of the fixing of responsibility, consensus, except for Delta, was finally achieved on these features:

1. Penalties at 50 percent, five-dollar minimum, forty-dollar maximum;
2. Carrier suffering oversale paying the penalty;
3. Plan effective sixty days after CAB approval; and
4. Six-month expiration date.

Delta's representative said he would seek authority to approve. The *ad hoc* committee worked on details that evening, and the parent committee met again the next morning, after which the eleven trunks signed the package agreement. Miller and a carrier representative proposed an effective date of May 1 with CAB approval by March 1. It was agreed that the local-service carriers should be informed and invited to further meetings of the *ad hoc* committee, and ATA was instructed to issue a press release. The terms of the agreement were submitted to the CAB on February 15, accompanied by a letter from Brack arguing for acceptance of the changes in oversales penalties from those suggested in the Board's order of January 8.

It was now time for the Board to act again, and it issued its order on March 1, as Miller had in effect committed it to do.[13] The Board's order was in the form of a response both to the carrier's proposals and to the chief comments received from customers as a result of its invitation for such. This was a rule-making proceeding, and in such a proceeding the Administrative Procedure Act requires that the agency consider "all relevant matter presented." The Board took note of questions which had been raised about the administrative feasibility of the proposals. It declared that it could not make an affirmative finding that the proposals were administratively feasible, but that there was need for a test over an experimental period. It noted the complaints about inability to put through telephone calls for cancellation of reservations and admonished the airlines to correct this. It noted the Department of Defense's request for exemption from the no-show penalty of persons traveling on

---

[13] Order No. E-18064 (March 1, 1964), approving Agreement 16012-A1.

government transportation requests, on certification that it was due to the exigencies of the service and not the fault of the traveler. It ruled that the situation of such travelers was not different from that of many others. But the main attention was to the level and conditions of payment, on which there were public complaints as well as airline proposals. Note was taken of the many exceptions incorporated into the agreement to invalidate claims for oversales payments where carriers could not be deemed to be at fault, and of the reduction of the oversales penalties below those suggested by the Board. At the same time the Board took note of the carriers' plan to continue paying for out-of-pocket expenses for hotels, meals, and similar needs of "unable passengers." It imposed only two conditions on its approval of the proposals. One was for monthly reports on a prescribed form. This form appeared onerous to the carriers in one particular, and on their petition it was modified to their satisfaction. The other condition was one that the carriers were able to accept. The tariffs included a provision which would have precluded the oversold passenger from seeking further redress through the courts. The Board conditioned its approval by a paragraph designed "to make clear that the prescribed penalty is a minimum guarantee of the carrier which, only if accepted by the passenger, would terminate the carrier's obligation."

With two principals—the Board and the trunks now in formal agreement—it was necessary to mediate the breach between the trunks and the local-service carriers. It had been assumed by the trunks all along that cooperation of the local-service carriers would be necessary for effectiveness of a trunk no-show plan, and the trunks had so informed the Board on more than one occasion. Since tickets, interline or otherwise, for transportation on the trunks were often issued on local-service carrier stock and since customers would present themselves to local-service stations for refund, a failure of local-service carriers to "honor" the tariff requirement of the trunk for a penalty would destroy the plan. The trunks could see, moreover, that if it were known by the customers that evasion of the possibility of a penalty could be accomplished by purchase of tickets at local-service stations, they would tend to do so, and that this preference for local-service accommodation could work to the competitive advantage of locals in areas where they and trunks were in competition for traffic. In addition, there was need for the local-service carriers to abstain from voting on an Air Traffic Conference resolution so that it could be passed unanimously by vote of the trunks. The trunks realized that they themselves could be led into competitive exemptions from the no-show penalties, thus destroying the plan, unless it were embodied in a conference resolution enforceable by the Office of Enforcement.

Meditation was a task for Slichter. This was an industry-wide responsibility that under the circumstances could not be fulfilled through a chairman who had actively promoted the trunks' purposes. Also, Slichter was concerned that the local-service carriers not get the idea that ATA was unconcerned with their interests. Slichter's task was not a pleasant one, for he knew that the local carriers' attitude was one of hostility on the no-show issue. He called a meeting, nevertheless, for March 15, at which he reviewed the background carefully and explained the alternatives which were before the local carriers: They could join the plan, they could honor it, or they could do neither. Honoring the plan, Slichter said, would mean that when a no-show passenger on a participant's (trunk carrier's) line presented himself at a local-service station for a refund, the no-show penalty would be assessed.

The local-service carriers had come to the meeting with the idea that they would take no part in the plan. But in the closely knit airline industry this was a very difficult position to take, and the trunks had therefore continued to hope for essential cooperation from the other wing of the industry. However, in spite of Slichter's appeal, the local-service carriers remained adamant. When on March 23 the trunks filed the tariff rule on the no-show–oversale agreement, ten local-service carriers simultaneously filed an exception to the filing. Brack appealed to Boyd for rejection of the exception, and ATA sent a copy of his letter to the local-service group. Obviously surprised by the request for exception, Roth wired the group, stating the usual rule of acceptance of the tariff rules of the carrier supplying the transportation and asking for their reasons. Mohawk replied fully, emphasizing the costs of the plan and the lack of hearing afforded the local-service group by the Board throughout the proceedings. The Board now assumed a mediatory position, Boyd suggesting by letter to Brack the day after receipt of Mohawk's letter that it appeared arrangements could be worked out. A few days later (March 17) the ATC met, and approved, with no negative votes, the no-show–oversale plan. But when Brack reported this to Boyd and suggested that it should lead to the rejection of the local carriers' exception, Lake Central wired Boyd that Brack had misunderstood the vote result. The local carriers, Lake Central said, had abstained from the vote because they thought their position would be taken care of by the exception they had filed.

Mediatory efforts ultimately resolved the conflict. The plan went into effect for the trunks on May 1, and when a prehearing conference on the local-service carriers' objection was held on June 14 before a CAB examiner their resistance evaporated. They had now been assured that all they had to do was assess the penalty on the trunk carriers' charges when a ticket on their own stock was presented for refund, referring other tickets to the participating trunk carrier.

With the agreement filed and approved, tariffs filed and not disapproved, the remaining procedural step for the no-show–oversale plan was adoption of a conference resolution. It has been noted that a resolution was unanimously approved, only trunks choosing to vote, in the Air Traffic Conference semi-annual meeting on March 17. It was then submitted for mail vote, but was rejected—five negative, eight affirmative, twenty-four abstaining. The split in the trunks' voting was due to technical details, which were clarified at a meeting of the trunks on April 27, and a second mail ballot was submitted on April 30. The resolution was approved—eleven affirmative (the trunks), no negative, twenty-seven abstentions. The plan had already gone into effect, but could now be enforced by the Office of Enforcement.[14]

Nevertheless, the fragile nature of the agreement which had been reached—demonstrated already by divisions among the trunks, doubts of administrative feasibility expressed by the CAB, and opposition of the local-service carriers—was exemplified once again when Northwest (a trunk) broke out of the ring of trunks and wrote directly to Boyd on April 4. Northwest said the plan would result in competitive advantage to local-service carriers competing with trunks, would be costly and in many cases ineffective, and would

---

[14] Resolutions of Air Traffic Conference dated May 3, 1962, with later amendments, approved in Order No. E-18399 (June 4, 1962). Subsequent amendments approved in Order No. E-18776 (September 7, 1962).

create ill-will; the real answer to the no-show problem would be a reapplication of a reconfirmation rule.

The divisions within the industry were inauspicious for the permanence of the no-show–oversale plan, which was the subject of a lengthy discussion at a meeting of the ATC in October. An attempt was again made to get the local-service carriers to join the plan as full participants. However, a number of the trunks were not enthusiastic about the plan. They were concerned over the administrative difficulties in implementing the plan and believed that the benefit-cost ratio was not favorable enough to justify it. They were concerned also over disservice to customers, produced often by errors in record keeping. The plan was extended to January 30, 1963, with some minor changes. At that time the Air Traffic Conference resolution was allowed to expire and the trunks continued their tariff rules for oversales penalties but dropped the no-show portion of the tariffs.

COMMENTS

Unity and independence—the rival pulls of the desire for accord on matters of common interest and of the will to protect autonomous judgment on matters of company interest—are shown in the behavior of the airlines in this case. Unity is fostered by the practice and habit of cooperation under ATA mechanisms—which consist of a stand-by pattern of behavior that can be called into operation as needed. The existence of the pattern facilitates unity, even when differences of interest and judgment thereon are highly divisive, as between trunklines, or in this instance between trunklines and local-service carriers. Yet mechanisms cannot maintain accord when differences in interests, or in judgments thereon, persist. Where consensus is lacking, and consent is forced by a desire to agree, then agreement is fragile. In loose associations—that is, those formed by parties retaining separate identities and capabilities for autonomous decision—there are inherent limitations upon concerted action.

Second, the posture of the official regulatory agency is seen here as cooperation with the industry in the attainment of its interests when these can be viewed as concordant with the public interest. Yet there is also responsiveness to consumer interests. There is, thus, sensitivity of the regulatory agency in two directions. Moreover, consciousness of its responsibility is strong and induces a jealous protection of Board prerogatives through short-term authorization and close surveillance of cooperative industry activity. At the same time, the Board is self-conscious about avoidance of the appearance of intrusion into managerial prerogatives. The struggle for balance between jurisdictional assertion and jurisdictional restraint is ever present, and caution on the latter is especially prominent.

Third, there exist possibilities for effective public-private collaboration in regulatory activities. Industry regulatory mechanisms combined with public authorization and oversight can be operational. This is evidenced by the substantial amount of industry coordination on operating matters, achieved through industry mechanisms concentrated in the ATA and carried out with the approval of the CAB. There are tensions between the industry and the CAB, and jockeying for self-protective jurisdictions—revealed in the investigation-and-review proceeding especially. Yet the no-show–oversale deliberations show that the tensions between the public and private structures may be no greater, or even less, than those within the industry structure itself, and that unity in the latter may sometimes be achieved only by influence from the public side.

Thus, this account can be concluded with some suggestions on the public role with respect to private industries. The protection of the public against collusive action injurious to its interests may exist both in the roles of public agencies and in the pluralism of interests and wills in the industry structure itself. Industry pluralism and public regulation have complementary functions where the public policy is prevention of injurious action. On the other hand, where uniformity is an objective, this will ordinarily be achievable in an oligopolistic industry, at least above the purely technical plane, only by public order and sanction. Cohesion in the industry is a fragile reed if unsupported by enforcement of a public rule. Yet public action itself is limited where it is dependent upon private collaboration. Viable public-private collaboration is limited to those areas of policy where continuous consensus within the industry and between the industry and the regulatory authorities can be maintained.

PART III

Evaluation

CHAPTER 7

An Essay in Evaluation

One who chooses the method of intensive penetration into limited areas, as those who choose the broader and perhaps less rewarding search for comprehensiveness, faces the challenge to estimate carefully the significance of what is revealed. The response to the challenge in this instance may be more significant if the stance of the author is clarified in advance.

The approach in this chapter is that of the policy scientist. Harold Lasswell, in his seminal discussion of policy science, said that the policy scientist is concerned "with locating data and providing interpretations which are relevant to the policy problems of a given period." He said, also, the policy scientist is "interested in evaluating and reconstructing the practices of society . . ."[1] Concern for the relevance of his work for policy formation and for the reconstruction of practices is what distinguishes the policy scientist from the neutral scientist.

The posture of a neutral scientist, of course, is difficult to assume, because from the beginning he is likely to be influenced by some standard of utilitarian or ethical relevance. More pertinent here, however, is the fact that much of what either sort of scientist does is the same. The policy scientist, like the neutral scientist, must be interested in discovering regularities of behavior or, differently stated, what are under given circumstances the determined directions or tendencies in what he analyzes. Reconstruction of practices is possible only within some area of practical maneuverability, that

[1] Daniel Lerner and Harold D. Lasswell, *The Policy Sciences: Recent Developments in Scope and Method*, pp. 14, 12.

is, in the area where regularities of behavior are not so fixed that human ingenuity can have no influence on the future shape of things. Expressed another way, both the policy scientist and the neutral scientist, if such there be in social research, share in the quest for understanding what is and what may be—for propositions about, or awareness of, what is so fixed that it cannot be altered or altered only in unusual manner or circumstances, and for knowledge of what is in the normal course of events left open to human manipulation.

In this chapter I try to stick rather closely to this area of interest to all social scientists. In major portions of the chapter the technique is to state propositions and their corollaries, and some of their consequences. Nevertheless, potentials for reconstruction of practices are constantly in mind, and some observations on these are included.

I shall try to state what is illustrated by the studies in this volume with respect, first to social systems, and then specifically to the system of government regulation and promotion. Occasionally I draw on knowledge gained elsewhere (this being my third book on regulation)[2] and venture some conjectures; but the presentation will allow the reader to differentiate these extensions.

Causative Factors in Social Systems

Many authors have emphasized a single type of causative factor in human events—frontiers, technology, the system of production, ideas, great men, or some other. Many search constantly for the single clue upon which to arch a theory or a program of reform. For illustration, from Bodin's concept of "sovereignty" (now renamed "authoritative allocation of values") to the revival of Bentley's "interest group," and the elaboration of the "elitist" theory, thoughtful writers on the polity have harbored hope for a central concept. Searches for an organizing clue have added much to our knowledge, and have also left something to be corrected. I have used the concept of "a universe of social action" (in effect, a social system or subsystem) as an organizing tool; it has the advantages of recognizing multiplicity and complexity in causative factors, and of allowing attention to the policy outcomes of human behavior.

---

[2] Emmette S. Redford, *Administration of National Economic Control* and *American Government and the Economy*.

AN ESSAY IN EVALUATION

Stephen K. Bailey, with perception of the complexities, inventively categorized the influences in the making of social policy as four *I*s: ideas, individuals, institutions, interests.[3] The effects of all these have been illustrated in my studies, and, in addition, a fifth category not listed by Bailey.

My first proposition is that belief patterns (ideas) shape boundaries within which policy decisions are reached (Chapter 2). The obvious corollary is that one who seeks to reconstruct the practices of society must find support in accepted belief patterns, or must modify or transcend them if they are hostile. This is the first requirement for political feasibility. It explains, for example, why expansive political leadership is built upon concepts, such as the New Deal, the Fair Deal, and the Great Society. In spite of discussions under such labels as "symbols" and "consensus," and in political science of the strong emphasis by David B. Truman on "rules of the game,"[4] I have found no case illustrations in the literature on the regulatory process showing the importance of belief patterns prior to the study presented here as Chapter 2.

My second proposition is that individuals do influence the trends in policies and, hence, that no strict view of social determinism can be accepted. Commissioner Eastman was important in the passage of the Civil Aeronautics Act (Chapter 2), Senator Monroney in the enactment of the Federal Aviation Act (Chapter 4) and in other decisions (Chapter 3), Board Member Boyd and industry representative Brack in the development of the no–show–oversale agreement (Chapter 6), and Congressman Celler in impulses to new activity in the Civil Aeronautics Board (Chapters 5 and 6). In none of these cases is it possible to say that the roles assigned to the men, or the socialization process affecting those roles, determined completely the actions taken by them. In each of the cases the results could have been different if other men had filled the strategic posts from which influence was exerted. The proposition stated above is not in conflict with the illustrations of social determinism that support the proposition that sometimes individual action is fully determined by external influences.

[3] Stephen K. Bailey, *Congress Makes a Law: The Story behind the Employment Act of 1946*, p. 240.

[4] David B. Truman, *The Governmental Process: Political Interests and Public Opinion*, particularly pp. 159, 348–349, 448, 511–516.

The corollary follows that there is nearly always an element of chance in decisions. Just as the placement of Chief Justice Marshall, or more lately of Justice Black or Justice Frankfurter, made a difference in constitutional law, so the imagination, vigor, and judgment of strategically located congressmen, consultants, or other individuals can affect economic policy.

An additional corollary is that there will always be some inadequacy in theories that postulate social causes for decisions or courses of action. The various social theories—interest group, Marxist, Weberian—are based on the assumption that the roles of actors are determined. They do not allow for the facts that looseness in the social system and a lack of rigidity in the flow of events give opportunities for the imagination, aggressiveness, or even aberrant behavior of men. We are reminded that the leadership of Lenin allowed the Marxists to skip a stage of history postulated in their own deterministic theory, and that the informal activities of actors in administrative organizations often conflict with the defined roles assumed in Weberian theory. This means partial defeat both for the neutral scientist, seeking causative explanations, and the policy scientist, seeking a more certain route to human advance than the uncertainties of individual behavior. We need, however, more research on the extent to which the actions of so-called leaders are determined by assignment of functions and socialization within groups or structures.[5]

The studies in this volume support another proposition: Institutions (as used here, meaning merely organizational or structural arrangements) have a significant impact on policy development because they provide channels for the aggregation and assertion of influences, and for accommodation and choice among values (preferred ends). Merle Fainsod has argued that institutions can "tilt the scale" in the contest of interests.[6] This volume substantiates his thesis, because it shows how a strategic position in an organization is a factor that creates opportunity for influence on the course of

[5] For an example of such research see Richard F. Fenno, Jr., "The House Appropriations Committee as a Political System: The Problem of Integration," *American Political Science Association*, LVI (June, 1962), 310–324.

[6] Merle Fainsod, "Some Reflections on the Nature of the Regulatory Process" in Carl Joachim Friedrich and Edward S. Mason (eds.), *Public Policy, 1940*, p. 320.

events. Organizations are centers for representation of particular interests or values: the Federal Aviation Agency for safety, the CAB for "public" purposes in economic regulation, the Air Transport Association for airline companies' interests. Organizations are positions through which interests can be adjusted: congressional committees (Chapter 3, particularly), the CAB, even the ATA (Chapter 6). It is organizational position—creating the opportunity for playing a role—which provides individuals with ability to exert influence. Monroney (Chapters 3 and 4), Stuart Tipton (Chapters 3, 4, and 6), and members of the CAB (Chapter 6) have had opportunities to tilt the scales because potentials for influence were concentrated in the structures that gave them their positions.

The studies indicate further that the creation of new organizational positions, or the strengthening or weakening of old ones, can be an effective means of restructuring the practices of society. Perhaps the outstanding example in this volume is the strengthening of a particular value—namely, safety—through the establishment of a stronger organization devoted to that goal. One must hasten to add that institutions, like all other factors, have their limits. The limits, as will be shown in the next section, may narrow substantially the potentials for reform. The organizational positions will have no effect if they have no consonance with the setting of forces; they are themselves influenced, as well as being influencers; and their influence is further dependent upon the grasping of opportunities by individuals.

With respect to interests, it is difficult—perhaps impossible in view of the fruitful contributions of so many scholars—to say anything today that is not repetitive. Certainly, the propositions that all government action, if rational at all, is a response to men's interests, and that the response is made under influence from asserted interests, are central in modern political science. Some subpropositions which are illustrated in studies in this volume are:

1. Regular and continuing interest representation centers in functional subsystems, such as that created for air transport by the interactions of administrative agencies, committees and subcommittees in Congress that are primary working centers on commercial aviation, and the interested private associations. Normally, the reconciliation of interests and the choices among values are made within the system (see Chapter 3, especially). The studies

here (particularly Chapter 3) support the conclusions of Arthur Maass, in his study of the Army Engineers, and J. Lieper Freeman, in his analysis of services to Indians, that the establishment of national agencies to administer programs results in a system or subsystem that is triangular in structure and operates with interlacing of influences from the three corners.[7]

2. The diversification of interests in a modern subsystem like regulated air transport will be very complex, showing representation in multiple centers of many values (see especially Chapter 3 on diversification in general, and Chapter 6 on intra-industry diversification).

3. Interests gain strength through aggregation in institutional positions. This is particularly illustrated in the story of the passage of the Federal Aviation Act (Chapter 4). On the other hand, the coordination necessary for aggregation may be more difficult in private associations than many have believed it is (see Chapter 6 on the Air Transport Association).

4. Interests variously described as latent, unorganized, or potential do get some representation. This is illustrated most clearly in the response of the CAB to consumer complaints in the no-show–oversale case (Chapter 6). It can be seen also in the enactment of new legislation for protection of the safety of passengers (Chapter 6), and is reflected in the initiation of the General Passenger Fare Investigation but not to any substantial extent in the results (Chapter 5).

5. Interests seek, in addition to immediately favorable policy outcomes, protection of established representational positions (see next section).

More generally, we may say that the impact of interest influences cannot be placed in proper perspective except through an understanding of the total complex of interrelated influences. Interests are themselves created out of conditions and modified in their content and directions as these change.

In addition to the foregoing statements affirming the four *I*'s, another proposition is illustrated: technology, and resources for its

---

[7] Arthur Maass, *Muddy Waters*; J. Leiper Freeman, *The Political Process: Executive Bureau-Legislative Committee Relations.*

use, are basic in the development of social systems and social policy. Unfortunately there is no *I* for this factor; we can, however, call it the *TR* factor. We saw in Chapter 1 that for air commerce "technological developments in a setting of adequate resources generated many new interests which in turn pushed out a multitude of organizational centers." Technology gave rise to an industry, to new social relations, and to the demand for a pattern of social control (resulting in the Civil Aeronautics Act). Resources made possible subsidies to support the expansion of the industry, and also research and development to improve the facilities for service. The studies in this volume provide many specific illustrations of the influence of technology on policy. The introduction of the jet produced a temporary but severe drop in airline earnings that made the General Passenger Fare Investigation fizzle out in indeterminacy of factual data. Technological changes have produced the volatility in the industry which led the CAB to establish an earnings standard that is high in comparison with that for other regulated industries. The low earnings in the transition period while jet technology was being adopted also created the setting for the no-show–oversale agreement. Technology produced the hazards, and also the opportunities, for a system of safety control, which accounted for the Federal Aviation Act.

In Chapter 1, I defined ecology to include these factors of technology and resources, as well as society's general institutions and belief patterns. There has been so much study of the intimacies of behavior within organizations, and of interest and power group influences, that it may be useful to reassert the need for constant attention to the base factors of technology and resources in system and policy development. John Gaus urged, almost alone, this emphasis in public administration,[8] and more recently Fred Riggs has shown the fertility of study of this type.[9] The present study, like most others, assumed these two factors. Its attention to ecology was accordingly limited to belief patterns and to institutional systems. The special interest was in the latter, even to a particular type of system. I turn now to a summary of the features of that system which are illustrated by the study.

[8] John M. Gaus, *Reflections on Public Administration.*
[9] F. W. Riggs, *The Ecology of Public Administration.*

Institutional Attributes of Regulatory Systems

Civilian transport in the United States is a system of service through regulated private enterprise. In the light of the studies collected here, it has the following pertinent characteristics, not all of which are unique to regulated enterprise, though all are important for an understanding of it, and all have policy consequences.

1. The core of the system consists of structural centers (companies and associations) energized by a dominant value that can be called, alternatively, the profit motive or the business motivation.

Company executives may have other motivations, to be sure, and these are especially present in the airline industry: adventure, in creating organization and service and in using new techniques; prestige, in controlling the line serving a network of interconnected cities; expansion—apparently a drive characteristic of successful Americans; and pride, in safety and service records. There are also the personal motivations of the rank and file, which include good workmanship, advancement in rank and pay, sociability with fellow workers, and others—common to workers in all organizations, whether business, public, or quasi-public. But money in the till sufficient to show profits on the ledger must be the overriding objective in a private enterprise, and this quality does not change with public assertion of other objectives. It must, moreover, remain a test of the health of regulated private enterprise. Without profits (whether or not with public subvention), it must deteriorate, or be supplanted by direct public management.

The dominance of this motivation on the actions and attitude of the industry is illustrated at numerous points in the studies in this volume. The industry sought public establishment of regulated competition, based on limitation of entry, to end insolvencies and to ensure future profitability; the Civil Aeronautics Act of 1938 was the result (Chapter 2). The industry fought for military business and against the nonskeds (Chapter 3). It wanted safety protection but was concerned also that the costs to the industry would not be excessively high (Chapter 4). It tried to prevent a passenger fare investigation; and when that came, it sought through both legal and public-opinion forums to gain an earnings standard and cost allowances to produce a high level of return (Chapter 5). The industry has tried through its organization to promote attitudes favorable to high returns and to influence directly those who can make decisions affecting profitability (Chapter 6). Its attitude toward the regulatory agency changed when that agency seemed to threaten profit potentials (Chapter 5).

The business motivation also affected the regulators. The CAB has at times been concerned with low profits of the airlines (Chapters 5 and 6). It set a very generous earnings standard (Chapter 5). The congressional regulators had earlier accepted the argument for regulated competition, which—it was argued by the industry—was necessary to avoid losses in airline investments (Chapter 2).

The consequence of the business motivation on the operation of a system of regulated enterprise merits re-emphasis. Automatic limitations restrict the regulators. They must not destroy the profit motivation; they must not impair managerial initiative; they will be encircled with influences which prevent them from going "too far" in these directions. In particular, too severe regulation of prices will jeopardize further investment in new equipment necessary for technological progress.

Hence, regulatory agencies will always have one eye turned inward to the health of regulated companies. In spite of stated public objectives, there will be a certain inwardness—an attention to business facts—in regulatory perspectives. This inwardness will be increased by the dependence on private initiative through the choice of enabling powers—powers of approval or disapproval of private petitions—as the means of regulation.

2. Other centers exist or come into existence through which additional values, normally called "public" interests, are incorporated into the total system.

Certain "public" interests are reflected in our studies. The needs of commerce, postal service, and national defense were specified in the Civil Aeronautics Act (Chapter 2). Safety of passengers and flight personnel, implicit in the Act of 1938, was the specific objective of the Federal Aviation Act (Chapter 4). Fair charges to customers, also implicit in the Act of 1938, were the motivation for the passenger fare investigation (Chapter 5). Adequate service to customers is reflected in the attitudes of Congress, in the extensions of competitive service in 1955, and in CAB's concern over an oversales penalty. A sound industry through which these objectives could be achieved was an instrumental public objective (Chapter 2).

These "public" interests are represented through two kinds of structures—the first comprehensive, the second limited, in scope. The first includes the President, the party leaders, the Congress as a whole and all congressmen individually, and the forums (press, community organizations, the ballot) for influence upon these. The second includes the administrative and congressional centers that have responsibilities with respect to commercial aviation service specifically.[10]

Two consequences of the coexistence of these public representational centers and of centers with a dominant business motivation are of special significance:

a. A plurality of goals is embodied in the public-private system which emerges; this is an inherent feature of regulated private enterprise. Necessarily then, an evaluation of such a system must take note of multiple, perhaps conflicting, goals.

b. Tensions are created between established centers representing different goals, or representing these with different degrees of concentration and intensity. Private centers may share public values and, as has been stated, public centers may adjust to private objectives. Nevertheless, differences in intensity of particular motivations in private and public centers exist, and hence tension, erupting sometimes into open conflict, is inherent in the system of regulated private enterprise. Tensions were of low intensity in the studies in this book—except during the course of the General Passenger Fare Investigation and of the inquiry of the Celler Committee and the CAB into the organization and practices of ATA. Regulators for other industries, however, have learned that forceful action for public objectives conflicting with industry objectives brings to the surface the latent tensions.

3. Public power and influence are dispersed widely among many institutional centers.

This is not, of course, a feature peculiar to regulated enterprise. It is partly the result of the requirements for functional institu-

[10] For elaboration on the nature of politics at the first level, called "macropolitics," and at the second level, called "subsystem politics," see my *American Government and the Economy*, pp. 54–62.

tional specialization in a complex society. It is, additionally, the result of institutional features of American government: the sharing of powers between the executive and Congress and the fragmentation, forced in the main by the sharing, within the executive branch. It is possible, however, that any tendency toward the decrease of public influence produced by this sharing may be magnified by the public-private conflict inherent in a system of regulated enterprise.

The consequences of the dispersion of influence in the public sector must be a concern of the policy scientist. It has often been argued that dispersion within the government diminishes the vigor of regulation. The evidence in this volume is insufficient to confirm or demolish that argument. There is no hard evidence here on what the results of an alternative system of concentrated executive leadership would have been. In the system which does exist, two of our studies show that congressional units can be centers for invigoration of public action. Provision for safety was strengthened by Monroney's leadership (Chapter 4) and the push for a rate investigation came from the Celler Committee (Chapter 6). Congress may also be the scene for decision on long-standing issues, for example, on the allocation of military transport to commercial lines and on the rights of the nonskeds (Chapter 3). One study (Chapter 2) showed that a congruence of belief patterns in executive, congressional, and industry centers can produce an easy coordination among power centers. On the other hand, courses of events recorded in other studies show that conflict, confusion, and inaction were apparently produced, or were contributed to, by the sharing and deconcentration of powers.

4. Decision making is largely a search for concurrence (through accord or adjustment) among and within established centers representing different values or values held with different intensities. Institutional collaboration, within and across institutions, is the requirement.

The clearest illustration in this volume is the no-show–oversale agreement. Collaboration was achieved within the institutional structure of ATA, itself acting as a coordinator of business organizations. Collaboration was achieved also between CAB and ATA. The agreement procedure is atypical in regulatory decision making, but the processes of search for concurrence are shown in other studies. The passage of the Federal Aviation Act resulted from agreement between ATA and congressional committee leadership, between congressional committees and the Presidency, and between civilian and military leaders. Where accord could not be attained, decision was avoided, as on several issues in the passage of the Federal Aviation Act; or a compromise was effected, as in the unstable resolution of the military air transport issue; or adjustment was forced, as on oversales. It may also have been a constrained adjustment rather than a true accord which led CAB to initiate the passenger fare investigation. Where basic accord already exists, decision is simplified—as in the passage of the Civil Aeronautics Act. There is, in one way or another, much evidence in these studies of the importance of mutual adjustment in decision making.[11]

The consequence to be stated is this: decision makers are in practice limited to the area of operational concurrence, that is, of sufficient concurrence to obtain a decision that can stand. Willing concurrence by all centers of influence is not essential (constraint or coercion may effect acceptance, and some nonacceptance—noncompliance—may exist), but substantial concurrence determines the viability and durability of a decision or policy. This says again that decisions are substantially determined, and not alone by technology and resources, but by the representional strength of values.

5. Manipulative influence in decision making is exerted through a competent search for technical and policy rationality, through leadership, and through leverage exerted on the available choices.

Technical rationality—workability on the technical plane—is particularly illustrated by the no-show–oversale experience. The policy makers were dependent upon the success of an *ad hoc* committee of experts in devising a feasible operating plan. Policy rationality—the reasonableness of policy solutions—is well illustrated in the exposition of the passage of the Federal Aviation Act. Study commissions appointed by the President, and the analysis of other groups, showed the policy choices on organization and allotment of powers by which the objective of safety could be attained.

I have already noted the manipulative capacity of leadership issuing from strategic institutional positions. Leadership achieved

[11] See Charles E. Lindblom, *The Intelligence of Democracy: Decision Making through Mutual Adjustment.*

accord within and among the established representational centers. By persistent use of their positions, Slichter and Brack achieved accord in the no-show–oversale deliberations. In the passage of the Federal Aviation Act, Monroney and Tipton supplied the leadership for staffs preparing a bill, and Monroney provided the leadership necessary to reconcile differences in Congress and obtain final passage. In the enactment of the Civil Aeronautics Act, Eastman provided the leadership of ideas necessary to produce a coherent policy.

Manipulative capacity accrues, also, from the power to impose a choice among alternatives of action or inaction. The power of Congress, acting through committees and subcommittees, set—in the organic acts of 1938 and 1958—the perimeters within which future adjustments among values would be made. The power of the CAB to impose a choice determined the inclusion of oversales penalties in the no-show–oversales agreement. However, the effect of the legal power to determine the level of earnings on the actual earnings achieved is not so clear. Ability to impose choices does not arise automatically from hierarchical status or formal delegation; it is, nevertheless, the result of advantage in position, which will be affected by hierarchy or delegation.

If I have assessed correctly the manipulative factors, then the policy scientist searching for means to achieve desired ends will be interested in two things:

a. Provision for rationality, that is, for correct analysis of the consequences of courses of action—*for tracing out the possibilities of courses of action and their results so that the decision may be a reasonable one in terms of all the values to be served.* This does not imply that the decision will be correct or perfect by any ideal standard, but only that it may be assumed to be the correct decision because it is a carefully considered one. This calls for the application of creative intelligence to both the clarification and choices of objectives and the discovery of effective means for their attainment. Included will be analysis of costs, benefits, side effects, and potential future implications—as, for example, through the creation of precedents. Not all the costs and benefits will be measurable; intangibles, such as symbols, may enter the calculus of rationality.

b. Creation or strengthening of political "muscle" (comparative advantage) in those institutional centers which represent desired values. This was what Monroney and the ATA were trying to do when, to ensure greater safety, they set out to get a new agency with a strong strategic position and with powers over both civil and military flying. This is what Congress has had in mind as it sought to give adequate legal powers to regulatory commissions; but the evidence in this volume does not demonstrate any strong comparative advantage in the position of the agency (CAB) to which Congress delegated powers of economic regulation.

6. In spite of internal pluralism, order—continuity and stability—is characteristic of the system.

It was said in Chapter 1 that "pluralism is the central fact in the anatomy of regulation," and this has been confirmed in the case studies (particularly in Chapters 3, 4, and 6) and the conclusions therefrom stated above.[12] It has been noted, also, that technology, and available resources for its use, creates volatility. What then creates order, regularity, stability: What gives coherence to the system?

Order may come in part from specific decisions. Thus, it is reasonable to say that Congress substituted order for confusion in passing the Civil Aeronautics Act and that the CAB contributed to the same result through route limitations. Order may be achieved by maintenance of positions of differential advantage with respect to specific functions, for example, CAB with respect to route allocation, or FAA concerning safety. But these are incidents of a moment or are particulars within the system.

Giving coherence to the system as a whole are three general

---

[12] In a profound and insightful discussion, Theodore J. Lowi classifies government functions as distributive (individualized decisions that only by accumulation became a policy, for example, tariffs), regulatory (involving a "direct choice as to who will be indulged and who deprived," for example, licensing of television stations), and redistributive (unlike regulatory in that the "categories of impact are much broader, approaching social classes," for example, income taxes). He finds that the pluralistic explanations of political issues are substantiated only for the second of these so-called arenas of power. This is, of course, the only "arena" discussed in this volume. (Theodore J. Lowi, "American Business, Public Policy, Case-Studies, and Political Theory," *World Politics*, XVI [July, 1964] 676–715.)

factors. The first is the set of belief patterns. Thus, the belief that private responsibility should be preserved and public action restrained and limited maintains a large measure of constancy in the balances between public control and private initiative; the belief that destructive competition should be avoided bounds the exercise of power to grant certificates; and the belief that procedures should conform to judicial standards of fairness fixes certain requirements in formal process. The second is firm lines of policy. For example, there has never been a departure from the policy of limiting trunk-line business to carriers that were certificated before 1938. It is not too much to say that the main lines of policy for commercial air transportation have been stable, and have not been seriously threatened by such modifications in policy as the congressional acts giving permanent certification to local-service and irregular carriers and the decision of the CAB in 1955 to increase competition in trunkline service. The third factor is the relative firmness in the allocation of functions and the relationships among the institutional centers representing continuing values. Specifically, this includes settled understandings about who is entitled to participate, the allocation of functions and the division of labor, the procedural routes for the flows of transactions to be processed, and the degrees of deference to be accorded, at least formally, to the several participants.

The system will, of course, be only more or less stable, for it will be vulnerable to external changes in circumstances, to intensifications of tensions within, and to the rise or intrusion of new actors. One consequence of ordered relationships is that participants struggle constantly to maintain their positions vis-à-vis other participants. Companies fight to preserve their management prerogatives and ATA represents them in the fight; congressional committees repeatedly state that commissions are "arms of Congress"; and CAB asserts its jurisdiction and issues regulations to protect itself from industry influence. The maintenance of a position is often a stronger objective than immediate gain. Similarly, appeal is made by participants to belief patterns favorable to them, and the policies resulting therefrom are jealously guarded. Thus, the airlines in the GPFI emphasized rights of private judgment on depreciation, financial structure, and other matters, and in public relations campaigns the ATA has stressed the dangers of excessive competition. Thus, also, the trunklines have fought to preserve the policies which prevented or limited competition from local-service and irregular carriers.

7. In procedure, there are continuous tendencies in opposite directions—toward formality and toward informality.

An effort to formalize procedures in economic regulation has existed since the creation of the Interstate Commerce Commission. In Chapter 2 we found, as an operative part of the belief patterns behind the Civil Aeronautics Act, the idea that fairness to parties required judicialized proceedings. In Chapter 5 the requirements in law for use of the judicial model, and the practice of the CAB in conformity with the model, were shown. In Chapter 6 the formalization of relationships, though without judicialization, was illustrated in the procedure for approval of agreements. The same formalization was shown in the efforts to regularize the contacts of ATA with CAB (also in Chapter 6).

Yet tendencies toward informal action were revealed in the same examples. Temporary determinations of rates without formal procedures paralleled the formal investigation. The initiation of the no-show deliberations, the belief in the industry that the CAB desired a no-show agreement, and the understanding of the industry that the CAB would require the addition of an oversales penalty, all grew out of informal discussions between the CAB and industry leaders.

The consequence of this dualism in methods, growing out of various and sometimes conflicting needs, is to produce for the policy scientist a problem of adjustment of methods to needs in different kinds of situations. Apparently, it will be a continuous problem.

8. A system of regulated private enterprise is a political system.

In Chapter 2 the beliefs in economic motivation and in nonpolitical regulation were stated, and the first of these has been reemphasized in this listing. Nevertheless, the attributes of the social system mark its political character. Multiple values—economic and noneconomic—represented in strategic centers of power and influence, decision through accord and adjustment, leadership, order through stabilized interrelationships—these are qualities of an open and pluralistic political system. Representation, power and influence, leadership, and institutional coordination are key terms; they are also political terms. The economic game—the pursuit of private gain—is enveloped in a more comprehensive system. The consequence of this for our evaluation of *results* is important, as will appear in the next section.

The Beneficence of the System

The studies in this volume were designed to increase understanding of the qualities of a system of regulated private enterprise, and only incidentally to appraise the results of the system. More comprehensive research is needed for a satisfactory evaluation of results. Some judgments, however, are possible here, and some comments on the problems attendant on evaluation are appropriate.

What is desired is evaluation of the beneficence of the system to the people it serves, or could serve. The difficulties in such evaluation are imposing and only partially surmountable. The first is the limited isolatability of crucial phenomena. Analysis of any social subsystem must take account of external things which impinge upon it. Evaluation becomes, to some extent, either an evaluation of the social system or culture in its entirety, or of the subsystem in terms of constants within the culture which would affect equally other kinds of subsystems that could be feasibly considered as alternatives. Thus, evaluation of the beneficence of a particular method of supplying airline service for the United States and for the USSR could not be made without consideration of the different values to be served and of different resources available for allocation to airline service. Nevertheless, concentration on a subsystem—with an understanding of its boundaries, its qualities, and the ways external inputs affect it—is one method of bringing evaluation into manageable dimensions.

Second, opportunities for comparisons are limited. It is not possible to supply airline service by one method for a period of years, then try another method for a like period, and repeat this until a comparison of the results becomes meaningful. Even if courses of social events could be provided such a laboratory test, the circumstances in different periods would probably vary too much to allow comparisons to be made with confidence. Comparison with systems in other countries is possible, but subject to the limitation noted above. This could still, however, be of considerable utility, if the researcher ever had the enormous time and patience required for it.

Comparison with similar regulatory systems is also possible, for example, of the effects of limited entry into airline service and motor carrier service. But the differences between the two types of service restrict the value of the comparison. I have asked my students to make this comparison and the majority found the experience in motor carrier regulation unconvincing as a test for airline service. It is possible, also, to compare publicly regulated service with the results which might be expected from unregulated service. This has been done for airlines by Professor Richard E. Caves with considerable ingenuity, but the conclusions are made on the basis of an assumption of the priority of economic over political goals—a quite unrealistic assumption.[13]

The hazards in selecting a dominant goal, or in setting up a scale for measurement of goals, constitute the third difficulty of the researcher and analyst. It is a society that is being served and not the policy analyst. It is a political system that is being evaluated, and such a system serves multiple goals. The analyst must not inadvertently or implicitly substitute his own scaling of values, and it is doubtful at this point in time whether polling techniques can measure society's scaling: Whose goals? Each group's goals to what extent? Goals accepted without knowledge, or goals accepted by those able to estimate their utilities?

What we seek is enrichment of awareness, not definite measurement; informed judgment, not certainty. For achieving this purpose there are—in addition to some limited ability to isolate phenomena, to compare systems, and to order priorities—several standards of judgment from which evaluation may be approached. The ensuing discussion illustrates possibilities.

One standard is the purely political one of survival of the system. Avery Leiserson stated what I once called "the acceptance theory of the public interest." Leiserson wrote:

It is suggested that a satisfactory criterion of the public interest is the preponderant acceptance of administrative action by politically influential groups. Such acceptance is expressed through compliance on the part of such groups affected by administrative procedural requirements,

[13] Richard E. Caves, *Air Transport and Its Regulators: An Industry Study*, Chapters 17 and 18.

regulations, and decisions, without seeking legislative revision, amendment, or repeal.[14]

Leiserson's last words must be understood as he stated them—as a test of administration. If they were broadened to the point of becoming a test for a social system, they would mean that the system is operational in the public interest if it is accepted without serious and significant effort toward revision or abolition in the established forums for legislative, administrative, or constitutional decision, or by extraconstitutional means.

The merit of Leiserson's definition is that it measures utility by the affected society's own satisfaction with it. If we could assume an open society with no institutional overloading of interests in representational positions, this would be a democratic definition of the public interest. It is not a purely *status quo* position, for it assumes that those operating within the system will make such changes as will prevent major reformation or destruction of the system itself.[15]

Applied to the system of commercial airline service the suggested test apparently yields the answer that the system has operated in the public interest. The system itself—the system of regulated private enterprise—has not been seriously challenged. Conflicts within the system have been reconciled, problems have been solved or bypassed, and changes have been made without radical reconstruction of the system.

Yet survival alone is an inadequate criterion of beneficence. Motor carrier regulation and railroad regulation meet the same test in the same way, but the efficiency of each is widely questioned.

[14] Avery Leiserson, *Administrative Regulation: A Study in Representation of Interests*, p. 16. The merits of Leiserson's view were too lightly dismissed by me in *Administration of National Economic Control*, pp. 223ff. They have, I believe, been too heartily embraced by Glendon Schubert in *The Public Interest: A Critique of the Theory of a Political Concept*, pp. 184–185, and Frank J. Sorauf in "The Public Interest Reconsidered," *The Journal of Politics*, XIX (November, 1957), 616–639.

[15] Leiserson says, "The administrator who conceives his task solely in terms of executing a legislative mandate has but a limited view of his public and social functions. Such a view does not consider the opportunities for differential and discriminatory treatment of group interests . . ." (*Administrative Regulation*, p. 13).

There are three deficiences in the survival test. First, the initial choice in favor of a system, by creating institutions and confirming belief patterns, loads the dice in favor of its retention. It is difficult to alter a going system substantially, and more than a moderate amount of dissatisfaction is required before this can be seriously contemplated. Second, the creation or strengthening of centers of influence aggregates the representation of particular values and solidifies a balance among the contending groups, and in these ways affects decisions on the retention or modification of the system. Thus, the aggregation of influence in established positions within the existing system in airline regulation may over-represent the interests of certificated companies as against uncertificated companies or inchoate "public" interests. By drawing an illustration from outside the realm of this study, it can be said that it may have been in the public interest, and certainly in the interest of substantial portions of the public, to have moved earlier toward desegregation and the creation of more equal opportunities for Negroes, even though the established power positions for a long time had inhibited breakthroughs in this direction. By turning to an illustration from the field of economic regulation, it can be stated that it may have been in the public interest to move away from the narrow allocation of operating rights to motor carriers, as was the purpose of the Interstate Commerce Commission in Ex Parte No. MC-55 in 1959, but the motor carriers had enough strength to prevent any toying with the existing balances among themselves in operating rights.

Thus, while the survival standard provides a measure of the existence or nonexistence of strong and aggressive dissatisfactions, it must be discounted to reflect the staying power of going systems and the distortion in the representation of values by the establishment of strategic centers through which particular values can be aggregated and strengthened. This explains why the policy scientist will be interested, not only in judging systems as a whole, but also in permissable reallocations of representational strength within going systems that are judged by him, or those he assists, to reflect society's values. He may suggest to the decision maker changes in the representational system which he concludes will maximize the desired advantages in value allocation.

Another defect of the survival test is that it says nothing about the rationality of outcomes. It is a test only of the correspondence of a system with the relative political strength of contending parties, and does not measure whether the outputs of policy best satisfy their interests. It does not show whether there is a sufficient infusion of intelligence into the policy-making process to ensure that the decision makers have a clear vision of the interests of those they serve and the means available for attaining these interests. The survival test in effect measures outputs by inputs. But only on the assumption of the infusion of intelligence into policy making could one have confidence that the political inputs in the decision-making process would generate beneficent results—that is, that survival in the political process was a test of the public interest. This explains why the policy scientist will be interested, not only in the representational system through which interests are aggregated and asserted, but also in the structuring of the policy-making process in such a way as to increase the rationality of decisions— that is, the equating of outcomes with the interests (real or fancied) of persons affected.[16] It explains also why the policy scientist will search for tests of the rationality of particular kinds of systems, for he will hope that this search will produce intelligence to be infused into the decision-making process.[17]

A more familiar standard for judging a system is that of efficiency in the allocation of resources. Maximum utility is achieved in a system that allocates resources among various uses in such a way as to insure the total use of technology for human welfare. A system is efficient, and therefore beneficent, to the extent that its results approximate this ideal. The efficiency test is a rationality test, in

[16] One great difficulty will be the infusion of understanding of long-run consequences. Decisions are rarely made for this day only, for they set precedents, tend to be repeated, or are the base for incremental decision building. But it may be that we often make decisions as though they were for this day only, even though the consequences are long-range. And if we try to decide for the future ("colonial domination of the future by the present"), the difficulties of anticipating the effects, when we don't even know the technological and social context, are tremendous. See Edwin A. Bock, *The Last Colonialism: Governmental Problems Arising from the Use and Abuse of the Future.*

[17] Glendon Schubert has attacked those, including me, who are interested in "good" decisions, as being Platonists. See his *The Public Interest,* Chapter 3. This grossly misrepresents my views and I think those of others. All I have ever said is that one condition for policy in the public interest is the infusion of creative intelligence into policy making; never have I said that "philosopher kings" should be "on top."

contrast to Leiserson's political test, which emphasizes responsiveness.

This kind of evaluation entails judgments on the means of realization: whether a system with business motivation dominating, one with public motivations dominating as exclusively as can be provided by human ingenuity (public ownership and management), or some combination of the two—and if so what—will yield greater attainment of the goal. There are, of course, various kinds of combinations of public policies with private activities, such as safety measures without economic controls, general economic controls and services affecting economic enterprises generally and largely indiscriminately, and special economic controls and services of selected types for a particular industry. The system we are discussing results from a choice in favor of the last of these, specific controls being imposed on entry, expansion, service, and price, and specific services being given through operating and airport subsidies and a system of traffic control.

Judging the existing system as a whole by the efficiency standard is extremely difficult, and this study has neither sought nor produced significant data for that purpose. It is probably true, as Richard Caves concludes after careful and exhaustive study, that the system has allocated more resources to commercial aviation than would have been allocated by market controls uninfluenced by public economic regulation. Caves also shows how the system has allocated resources internally in a way different from what an unregulated market would have afforded. It has forced traffic in high-density city-pairs to carry costs of service to low-density city-pairs. This not only misallocates resources according to an economist's standards (as does also the subsidy to local-service carriers), but it prevents service expansions and diversification to meet various passenger needs in high-density, city-pairs. Caves concludes that:

[the] major standing policies [of CAB] do not coincide with the economist's usual criteria of efficiency. The Board aims at more than a normal amount of resources in the air-transport industry, service in more city-pair markets than can sustain it commercially, and probably a faster rate of development of new aircraft than unrestricted market forces would produce.[18]

18 Caves, *Air Transport*, p. 433.

Caves' analysis shows how the efficiency test is used in economic analysis. The economist's criterion of efficiency in allocation of resources is the ability of a service to survive in a free market, or the nearest feasible approximation thereof. It is the willingness and ability of the consumer of a service to pay for it through the price system. It contrasts with a political test of acceptability, as offered by Leiserson, which tests a system of consumer vote through the instruments of political influence.

Evaluation by the economist's criterion of efficiency, although highly useful as an ingredient in evaluation, will not answer fully the question of beneficence of the existing system of airline service. Rationality, of course, includes the test of means, and efficiency according to the economist's standards is a specific means test. But the problem of multiple goals, which creates political issues, remains. The goal of human welfare, taken for granted in the definition of the efficiency test, may be, as Justice Frankfurter said in talking about the "public interest," "a texture of many strands."[19] Caves notes the following objectives affecting the allocation of resources to airline use that lie outside "the usual norms of economic welfare":

1. Contribution to military potential.
2. Maintenance of a regular network of air routes uniting the nation's cities and towns.
3. Speeding the development of transport aircraft.
4. Maximizing the safety of air transport.
5. Keeping fares as stable as possible, and restricting the use of price discrimination.[20]

Caves finds that none of these "special objectives seems very compelling," but that "not all of them can be dismissed as worthless."[21] Other competent authorities may, however, rate objectives differently. Thus, the Task Force on National Aviation Goals, constituted by the FAA in response to President Kennedy's request, listed as foremost national aviation goals: "national economic growth," "national security," "national culture and a more closely knitted social fabric," and a series of objectives with respect to interna-

[19] Federal Power Commission v. Hope Natural Gas Co., 320 U.S. 591, 627 (1944).
[20] Summarized from Caves, *Air Transport*, p. 434.
[21] *Ibid.*, p. 438.

tional understanding and commerce and United States leadership in world affairs.[22] Although these goals are stated without the precise analysis of their value which characterized Caves' analysis, they do indicate the proclivity of national policy makers toward superordinate national goals. Also, individuals may not accept the supremacy of economic values in the determination of issues concerning their welfare. They may find legitimacy in claims for more service than is justified on purely economic tests. And it may be impossible for the analyst to determine whether the satisfaction of a traveler in a thin city-pair in having some service is less worthy than that of a traveler in a dense market in having more service or lower price.

In his discussion, Caves carefully avoids saying that economic standards should prevail and concludes that "the decision ultimately is a political one."[23] Political authorities in 1938 had in mind a combination of objectives, some of which were noneconomic and were specifically stated. The misallocations of resources according to a purely economic standard of welfare cannot demonstrate the failure of the system, in terms of its avowed objectives. It is likely that public regulation of an industry will ensure a greater representation of noneconomic values than unregulated private enterprise would; this may be its very purpose. Public ownership and management may do this to a still greater extent, but belief patterns inhibited consideration of this choice in 1938.

This discussion may now be refocused on the position of the policy scientist. He works within two kinds of framework. Responsiveness to human needs is the ultimate criterion and within a democratic society this must be determined within the limits of what is desired by or is acceptable to the people. This will of the people can be expressed in two kinds of balloting: in the market and in the political system, each with its imperfections. The policy scientist should be prepared to examine and compare the democracy of the market and that of the polity. My own conclusion is that the polity often provides more effective opportunity for representation

---

[22] *Report of the Task Force on National Aviation Goals,* Federal Aviation Agency (September, 1961), pp. 4–5.

[23] Caves, *Air Transport,* p. 449.

of men's interests than does the market.[24] Irrespective of the correctness of this judgment, however, mechanisms have been provided through which the preferences of society can be expressed through the political system, and hence the policy scientist will offer his wisdom to the political policy maker. He will be constrained to recognize multiple values which are expressed through that system, but without assuming that the representation of these values in existing institutions is the most acceptable one. He must also search for rationality, which includes assessment of cost and benefits. This he will do without clarity on the relative weight of goals. He is provided with a rationality test which is open-ended, because it cannot conclusively define human welfare in specific terms. The economist's standard for defining the end is so important that the policy scientist should assume that no decision ought to be made without measurement by that standard. The measurement, however, cannot be conclusive, for it is only the evidence on one kind of value to be served.

Unfortunately, not many policy scientists have, as Caves did, given hard-headed attention to system evaluation. Among the apparent reasons are the assumption that going systems will remain, the difficulties in setting priorities among goals, and the inability of the analyst—given his specialized methodological equipment and the bias of his attention toward a certain kind of analysis—to combine political and economic analyses.

Another form of evaluation needs to be considered. This is the examination of the effects of a particular aspect of a system, something most social scientists do in their studies. In the main, such evaluation has three aims. The first is to determine the effects of a decision or series of decisions. Great decisions, like great men, have an attraction for scholars. They like to study the causes and the logic of decisions, and sometimes also their effects. Most of this is history and often of little value to the policy scientist, because there are no possibilities for reversing the effects of the decisions. *Marbury v. Madison* and *McCullogh v. Maryland* are, in their larger effects, irreversable. But *Plessy v. Ferguson* and other decisions have been reversed. We are now trying to learn more—through

[24] "Business as Government" in Roscoe C. Martin (ed.), *Public Administration and Democracy*.

case studies particularly—about the process of decision making in legislatures and administrative agencies, and it might be useful to select for study the effects of some major regulatory decisions. The decision of 1941 by the CAB to admit no more airlines to trunk service may, for example, be one that should be reconsidered for the conditions of 1968 and beyond.

A second focus for study is the effects of an existing system on the achievement of single, discrete goals. Although the studies in this volume were not intended to supply a basis for evaluation of discrete goals, illustrations of the kinds of judgments that can be founded on analysis are offered. The following conclusions appear to be reasonably well substantiated from experience with commercial airline service:

1. On safety: a remarkable, indeed phenomenal, record of safety in air flight on certificated airlines has been achieved. The year 1965 was the fourteenth consecutive year in which the passenger fatality rate was less than one per 500,000,000 passenger miles flown on certificated route carriers in scheduled passenger service. It is reasonable to conclude that the maintenance of stable, solvent airline companies through economic regulation has contributed something to this result. Certainly, the safety-regulation features of public control have contributed to it.

2. On rates: rate regulation has not produced stability of earnings (a debatable goal), effective protection for the public against excessive rates, nor standards of judgment on the structure of rates. The GPFI, influenced by temporary factors, established a standard for earnings, and thus for rate levels, which is excessive in terms of what is allowed to other regulated industries or would probably be realizable if the industry were unregulated.[25] The Board thereafter set 21.35 percent as a standard for return on equity in local-service airlines. Caves remarks, "Can anyone believe that firms which actually earned this return over a period of time would find it only sufficient to attract new capital?"[26] The objectives in rate structure are too closely allied with issues of service to be easily defined, and the initiatives of the CAB on the rate structure have been quite limited.

[25] For Caves' discussion and general agreement, see his *Air Transport*, pp. 391–402.
[26] *Ibid.*, p. 402.

3. On coordination of services: assisted by the procedure of the regulated agreement, the airlines have worked out generally satisfactory arrangements for interline service, extending to ticketing, baggage handling, and passenger transfer.

4. On amount of service: analysis on this runs into the broader questions already discussed. Limited propositions or hypotheses can, however, be stated: Regulation and promotion have probably contributed materially to increasing the amount of airline service. On the other hand, it may be hypothesized that concentration on high-quality service has delayed the development of a mass air transportation system, that airline service potentialities have not been realized in dense traffic areas, and that there have been errors in timing (for example, expansions of service rights in 1955).

5. On quality of service: the quality of service—judged by such standards as safety, comfort, dependability, and speed—has been high. In spite of some inconveniences to passengers, concern over their welfare has been notable. The main issue is whether the quality of in-flight service has been emphasized too much in comparison with its quantity.

A third type of objective, and one for which this study offers quite substantial data, is to evaluate the utility of particular mechanisms and processes.

Looking first at administrative procedures, two kinds of procedure have been illustrated. The first is that for industry coordination by private action and supervision thereof by public authority, described generally in Chapter 6 and illustrated particularly by the no-show–oversale deliberations. I conclude that both public and industry utilities are served by a remarkably effective system of industry coordination and public supervision on minor policy and administrative matters related to airline service. The experience with procedures of collaboration and supervision in this industry demonstrates to the policy scientist and policy maker possibilities for fruitful private-public cooperation. It shows, however—especially in the investigation of the Celler Committee—the delicacy of the balances between private collaboration of interests and public supervision thereof. The public supervision may be too loose to protect "public" interests, in which case some congressional committee is likely to intervene; it may be too tight, in which event the antagonism of the private interests will be aroused. Our story did not examine the results of regulation of travel agents by the airline industry, and hence no conclusions are stated concerning the delegation to one set of private interests of regulatory powers over another set.

The other kind of procedure is that for rate making, portrayed in Chapter 5. I conclude that policy makers have not yet worked out procedures that permit effective use of price fixing as a major technique in economic regulation. If this conclusion is correct, then the policy scientist—particularly in the disciplines of law and political science—is under serious challenge to outline innovations for policy makers to consider. President Kennedy named three tests for procedure: "efficiency, adequacy, and fairness."[27] Simplification to speed the process is the need in price regulation. Steps in that direction have been taken—for example, the prehearing conference and the written exchange of information—but other steps are needed to achieve efficiency and adequacy without sacrifice of fairness.

Turning to processes for determining basic policy, two illustrations of the making of decisions that could be called organic are offered in this volume. Chapters 2 and 4 tell, in different ways, about the passage of the two organic acts with respect to commercial aviation—the acts of 1938 and of 1958. There is much basis for satisfaction about American legislative processes in these descriptions. The process was in both cases open, that is, all interests had opportunities for access to decision-making forums. In 1938 comparative experience in regulation of other forms of transportation was evaluated. Whether or not the decisions were correct, rationality was sought by drawing on Commissioner Eastman's expertise. The objectives were clearly understood. There may have been a need for intensive studies of the belief patterns which lay behind the legislation; but, in terms of knowledge available, the legislation of 1938 was certainly a reasonable response to felt needs. The story of the enactment of the legislation in 1958 shows that potentialities for initiative exist within the Congress, that expert analysis and expert draftsmanship can chart means for social utilization of technology, that latent interests can be represented, and that leadership can bring concurrence among power centers. Although

[27] Executive Order 10934 (April 13, 1961).

circumstances were extremely favorable and some issues were left open, the possibilities for coordination in a system of shared powers and influences were shown.

The several accounts herein do, however, leave a concern on the central issue. Do the mechanisms that exist provide sufficient assurance of re-evaluation and innovation? Passenger fares were not considered in a comprehensive investigation for approximately twenty years after CAB's creation, and the consideration that was given to them was the result of chance in the directions of inquiry by a congressional investigating committee. The subject of improvements in safety protection was tossed about in the interagency and congressional committees for years before spectacular events created the moment for action. The Celler Committee's study was adventitious, the various and repetitious concerns of Congress related frequently to relatively minor matters, and only the budget served as a means of continuous executive attention. Large issues of procedure in route and rate cases, of policy on user charges (such as airline payment for airport and safety services), of the place of airline service in a transportation system, and of the allocation of resources (such as Caves discussed) do not get concentrated attention at centers from which initiative, innovation, and leadership might be expected. In regulatory matters, at least, the normal tendency of things is to move in beaten paths; chance has a large influence in determining what gets attention; and there is a lack of executive centers for study and initiative comparable to those in many other areas of public policy.

Bibliography of Cited Materials

Almond, Gabriel A. *The American People and Foreign Policy*. New York: Praeger, 1950.

Anderson, James E. *The Emergence of the Modern Regulatory State: A Study of American Ideas on the Regulation of Economic Enterprise, 1885–1917*. Washington, D.C.: Public Affairs Press, 1962.

Bailey, Stephen K. *Congress Makes a Law: The Story behind the Employment Act of 1946*. New York: Columbia University Press, 1950.

Bernstein, Marver. *Regulating Business by Independent Commission*. Princeton: Princeton University Press, 1955.

Blachly, F. F., and Miriam E. Oatman. *Federal Regulatory Action and Control*. Washington, D.C.: Brookings, 1940.

Bock, Edwin A. *The Last Colonialism: Governmental Problems Arising from the Use and Abuse of the Future*. Bloomington: Comparative Administration Group, American Society for Public Administration, 1967.

Brandeis, Louis. *The Curse of Bigness: Miscellaneous Papers of Louis D. Brandeis*, edited by Osmond K. Frankel. New York: Viking Press, 1935.

Caves, Richard E. *Air Transport and Its Regulators: An Industry Study*. Cambridge: Harvard University Press, 1962.

Chapin, F. Stuart. *Cultural Change*. New York: The Century Co., 1928.

Civil Aeronautics Authority. *Annual Report*, 1939.

Cushman, Robert E. *The Independent Regulatory Commissions*. New York: Oxford University Press, 1941.

Dahl, Robert A., and Charles E. Lindblom. *Politics, Economics, and Welfare*. New York: Harper, 1953.

Dicey, A. V. *Lectures on the Relation between Law and Opinion in England, During the Nineteenth Century*. New York: Macmillan, 1905.

"Does Federal Aviation Act Snub Civil Aviation," *Business and Com- merical Aviation*, XII (July, 1958), 7.

Fainsod, Merle. "Some Reflections on the Nature of the Regulatory Process" in Carl Joachim Friedrich and Edward S. Mason (eds.), *Public Policy, 1940*. Cambridge: Harvard University Press, 1940.

Fenno, Richard F., Jr. "The House Appropriations Committee as a Political System: The Problem of Integration," *American Political Science Association*, LVI (June, 1962), 310–324.

Fisk, Winston M. *Administrative Procedure in a Regulatory Agency: The CAB and the New York-Chicago Route Case*, Inter-University Case Program Study No. 85. Indianapolis: The Bobbs-Merrill Co., 1965.

Freeman, J. Leiper. *The Political Process: Executive Bureau-Legisla- tive Committee Relations*. Garden City: Doubleday and Company, Inc., 1955.

Freund, Ernst. *Administrative Powers over Persons and Property*. Chicago: University of Chicago Press, 1928.

Gaus, John. *Reflections on Public Administration*. University, Ala- bama: University of Alabama Press, 1947.

Griffith, Ernest S. *The American System of Government*. London: Methuen, 1954.

———. *The Impasse of Democracy*. New York: Harrison-Hilton, 1939.

Herring, E. Pendleton. *Public Administration and the Public Interest*. New York: McGraw-Hill Book Co., Inc., 1936.

"The Inside Story of the Aviation Act," *American Aviation*, XXII, No. 2 (June 16, 1958), 41–43.

Kluckhohn, Clyde: *Mirror for Man*. New York: Whittlesey House, 1949.

Leiserson, Avery. *Administrative Regulation: A Study in Representa- tion of Interests*. Chicago: University of Chicago Press, 1942.

Lerner, Daniel, and Harold D. Lasswell. *The Policy Sciences: Recent Developments in Scope and Method*. Stanford: Stanford University Press, 1951.

Lindblom, Charles E. *The Intelligence of Democracy: Decision Mak- ing through Mutual Adjustment*. New York: The Free Press, 1965.

———. "Policy Analysis," *American Economic Review*, XLVIII (June, 1958), 298–312.

Lowi, Theodore J. "American Business, Public Policy, Case-Studies, and Political Theory," *World Politics*, XVI (July, 1964), 676–715.

Maass, Arthur. *Muddy Waters*. Cambridge: Harvard University Press, 1951.

Maclay, Hardy K., and William C. Burt. "Entry of New Carriers into Domestic Trunkline Air Transportation," *Journal of Air Law and Commerce*, XXII (Spring, 1955), 131–156.

Mill, John Stuart. *Principles of Political Economy*, edited by W. J. Ashley. New York: Longmans, Green, 1909.

Mills, Warner E., Jr. *Martial Law in East Texas*. University, Alabama: University of Alabama Press, 1960.

Redford, Emmette. *Administration of National Economic Control*. New York: Macmillan Co., 1952.

———. *American Government and the Economy*. New York: Macmillan Co., 1965.

———. "Business as Government" in Roscoe C. Martin (ed.), *Public Administration and Democracy*. Syracuse: Syracuse University Press, 1965.

Report of the Task Force on National Aviation Goals. Washington, D.C.: Federal Aviation Agency, 1961.

Riggs, F. W. *The Ecology of Public Administration*. New York: Asia Publishing House, 1961.

Schubert, Glendon. *The Public Interest: A Critique of a Political Concept*. Glencoe: Free Press, 1960.

Sharfman, Isaiah. *The Interstate Commerce Commission*. New York: The Commonwealth Fund, 4 vols in 5, 1931–1937.

Simon, Herbert A. *Administrative Behavior*. 2nd ed. New York: Macmillan, 1957.

Snyder, Richard C., and Glenn D. Paige. "The United States Decision to Resist Aggression in Korea: The Application of an Analytical Scheme," *Administrative Science Quarterly*, III (December, 1958), 341–378.

Sorauf, Frank J. "The Public Interest Reconsidered," *The Journal of Politics*, XIX (November, 1957), 616–639.

Tillett, Paul D. *The Army Flies the Mails*. University, Alabama: University of Alabama Press, 1954.

Truman, David B. *The Governmental Process: Political Interests and Public Opinion*. New York: Knopf, 1951.

Wilson, Woodrow. *The Crossroads of Freedom: The 1912 Campaign Speeches of Woodrow Wilson*, edited by John Wells Davidson. New Haven: Yale University Press, 1956.

INDEX

accidents: investigation of, 85, 106, 117–118, 127. SEE ALSO collisions

Adams, Joseph P.: and GFPI, 153 and n., 156, 158–159, 164, 165

Adams, Sherman: 79

administrative agencies: 3, 318

administrative centers: staffing of, 65

Administrative Procedure Act (APA): 33, 88; safeguards in, 116; rule making in, 138–139, 171 n., 284; Bureau of Hearing Examiners and, 168–169, 184, 236

Advisory Committee on Government Organization: 78, 96

Advisory Committee on Transport Policy and Organization: 78–79

AFL-CIO: airline industry groups and, 59–60

air-cargo transportation: 46, 58

air carriers: economic regulation of, 142–153

Air Commerce Act: 74

Air Coordinating Committee: 48, 53, 76, 88

Aircraft Owners and Pilots Association: 59, 110

air defense systems: 104

Air Force, Department of: 40, 97, 173. SEE ALSO MATS

air freight: rates, 150, 158; shipment, 267

Air Line Pilots Association (ALPA): functions of 11; at hearings, 55, 58, 59; on air space, 78; and CAA, 82, 87, 110, 128, 134

airlines: as centers of influence, 11–12; private v. public management of, 22–38; comparison of, with other industries, 193–196. SEE ALSO Con-

gress; rates; specific act, agency, airline, association

Airlines Clearing House: 253

Airlines Operations Conference (of ATA): 264–265, 268

Airline Stewards and Stewardesses Association: 110

air mail: 23, 25, 28, 143–144, 147–148, 158, 206–207, 222

Air Navigation Development Board (ANDB): 77

air navigation facilities: establishment of, 53, 54, 76

Airport Act. SEE Federal Airport Act

airport construction: 47–48, 59–60, 109, 122–125, 128, 130

Airport Operations Council: 110, 121

Air Safety Board: 74, 75. SEE ALSO safety

airspace, use of: 74, 82, 83, 85, 86, 98, 107–108, 124, 130, 232

Air Traffic Conference (of ATA): 257, 264–265, 266–267, 271, 273, 275, 285–286, 287 and n., 288

Air Traffic Control Association: 110

air transport: as consumer-service organization, 4, 247–251; and public v. private enterprise, 25–32; pluralism of interests of, 58–59, 298

Air Transport Association (ATA): functions of, 11, 55, 247, 250–251; as interest center, 59–60, 78, 100, 248, 297; Board of Directors of, 60, 89, 252, 254, 256, 261; and CAA, 82–83, 89, 90–91, 93, 101, 102–104, 110, 250; and CAB, 118, 252, 255, 256, 258, 269–289 passim, 303–304, 308; and GPFI, 150, 151, 166, 173, 192–193, 210, 217, 219, 237, 261–262; Articles

117–118, 127; public interest under, 109–110, 113–114, 299; on personnel, 108, 119–120, 125–126, 133, 134, 226 n.; Senate debate on, 127–131; in the House of Representatives, 131–135; on rates, 148, 149

Federal Aviation Agency (FAA): functions of, 12, 73–74, 103, 106–107, 108–109, 112–115, 118, 119, 127, 136–137, 297; establishment of, 53, 111, 112, 127; personnel for, 121–122, 125–126

—Administrator: responsibilities of, 103–108 *passim*, 111, 113, 116, 120–136 *passim*; tenure of, 111–112

Federal Communications Commission: 140

Finance and Accounting Conference (of ATA): 264–266

Finney, Thomas: 90, 93, 100, 101, 102, 111, 112

Fitch Publishing Co.: 204

Flemming, Arthur: 78

Flood, Daniel J.: 42, 49, 50

Flynt, John J., Jr.: 131–132, 133

foreign transport: facilitation of, 262–263

Foster, J. Rhoads: 195

FPC v. Natural Gas Pipeline Co.: 229

Frankfurter, Justice Felix: 296, 315

Freeman, J. Lieper: 298

Gaus, John: 6 n., 299

General Passenger Fare Investigation: substantive issues in, 34, 139–142, 154–155, 156–157, 158–159, 172–173, 175–176, 186–220; Celler and, 45, 52, 159; CAB and, 139, 151, 153–155, 160–164, 167, 168–219 *passim*, 220–228, 235–243, 304; Congress and, 140, 159–160, 163–164, 187; public interest and, 141–142, 298, 302; procedures in, 168–220; examiner for, 174, 175–186 *passim*, 228–235; ATA and, 173, 261; airlines and, 173, 177–178, 180, 181–182, 182–186; ground

rules for, 178–180, 182; Six Percent case and, 180–181, 182, 183, 221–222; influence of technology on, 299

General Services Administration (GSA): 187, 237, 279

Gewirtz, Stanley: 150

Gilliland, Whitney: 237–238

Gilman, W. C.: 197, 200, 202, 203, 206

goals: tensions as a result of, 302; for aviation, 315–316

Gorrell, Edgar S.: 28, 32

Government Operations, committees on: 40, 44, 49, 50–51, 65

government regulation: perspectives for study of, 3–21

GPFI. See General Passenger Fare Investigation

Griffith, Ernest S.: 10 n.

Gross, H. R.: 133

GSA. See General Services Administration

Gurney, Chan: 153, 156, 165, 224, 237, 238

Harding report: 83

Harris, Oren: 41, 62, 63, 95, 131

Hayden, Carl: 49–50

Hayward, Carlton: 82

Hector, Louis J.: 34, 185 n., 188, 226–227, 237

helicopter carriers: represented in ATA, 256

Herring, Pendleton: 268

Heselton, John: 56

Hester, Clinton M.: 36

Highway Contractors Division of the Associated General Contractors of America: 60

history consciousness: and regulatory policy, 18

Holifield, Chet: 49

Holland, Spessard: 42, 53

Holmes, Justice Oliver Wendell: 22

Hoover Commission: 48, 50–51

Hope case: 190, 191, 229

Opinion Writing Division. SEE Office of General Counsel

Parker, Charles A.: 82

passengers. SEE General Passenger Fare Investigation; in-flight services; rates; safety

Pastore, John: 166

Patterson, W. A. (Pat): 61, 92, 115, 119

Payne, Frederick: 42, 128

Pearson, Drew: 161

Perley, Allen H.: 131

Personnel Relations Conference (of ATA): 263–264

Piedmont Airlines: 271, 274, 276

pilots. SEE Air Line Pilots Association

Player, Willis: 261

Plessy v. Ferguson: 317

policy: processes of, 15–16, 313, 320; study of, and regulation, 16–19; scientist, 293–294, 313, 316–317, 319

postal service: 24, 143, 147. SEE ALSO air mail

Preston, Prince H.: 42, 53, 54, 56, 118, 165

private agents. SEE public-private collaboration

private enterprise: regulation of, 25–26, 246–247, 308–309

private *v.* public enterprise: 24–38

profit (margin-of-return) method: 188, 193–196

public, interests of: 24, 26–29, 32–33, 143, 301–303

Public Affairs Department (of ATA): 259, 262

public-private collaboration: 246–247, 289, 302

public regulation: 25–26, 138–139

Public Relations Service (of ATA): 260–261

public responsibility: extent of, 189, 218–219

Pyle, James T.: 98, 116, 118

Quesada, General E. R.: as assistant to the President, 93, 95; and Depart-

ment of Defense, 96–97; and Monroney, 97–100, 111, 117, 119, 131; and position of CAB Administrator, 133

Quigley, James M.: 159, 163, 167

radar approach facilities: 119

Radio Technical Committee for Aeronautics (RTCA): 77

railroad regulations: 32

Rates Division (of BAO): 164, 169–171

rate making: governmental, 141–142, 245; elements of, 188, 320; standards for, 189, 219–220; cyclical theory of, 224; bulkline theory of, 241

rate of return: 188, 196–208, 222, 229, 234, 239, 240, 242

rates: regulation of, 138–142, 232, 243–245, 308; level of, 138, 149–150, 154–157, 228, 241; change of, 141, 147–150, 216–218; structure of, 154, 188, 228; base of, 205–207, 231, 239–240. SEE ALSO General Passenger Fare Investigation

rationality, provision for: 305

Reconstruction Finance Corp.: 169

regulation: study of, 3–21, 318

regulatory agencies: 301

regulatory system: institutional attributes of, 300–309; beneficence of, 308–321; survival test of, 310–313

Rentzel, Delos (Del): 81, 92, 93, 94, 99, 115

reorganization plans: 75

research: purposes of, 5–6

Rhatigan, E. K.: 271, 274

Riggs, Fred: 299

Rivers, Mendel: 51, 63

Rizley, Ross: 163, 164, 165

Roberts, Kenneth A.: 131

Rockefeller, Nelson: 78, 79

Rogers, Ed: 89

Roosevelt, President Franklin D.: 75

Roth, Irving: 163, 270, 276, 277, 286

Rothschild, Louis S.: 82

routes: control of, 168, 243
rule making: 118
runway layout: allocation of, 130
Ryan, Oswald: 153, 156
Ryan, William F.: 279

Sadowski, George: 27
safety: legislation for, 52–53, 73, 74,
    321; under the FAA, 74, 100–101,
    114–117, 136–137, 297; regulation of,
    75–78, 107, 136, 318; Curtis report
    on, 85–86, 89; ATA on, 102, 104
*Sangaman Valley Television Corp v.
    U. S.*: 140 n.
Sayen, Clarence: 82, 87, 99, 115–116
Schoeppel, Andrew: 42, 100, 119, 123–
    124, 128–130
scheduled service: 30–31, 146
Schubert, Glendon: 20 n., 313 n.
Scott, Hugh: 159
Scrivner, Errett: 56
Securities and Exchange Commission:
    31, 140
Senate: and FAA, 127–130, 110–127
—Committee on Appropriations: 51,
    60
—Committee on Government Opera-
    tions: 40, 46
—Committee on Interstate and For-
    eign Commerce: 40, 44
—Judiciary Committee: 40
—Small Business Committee: 51
—Subcommittee on Aviation: 40, 41,
    44, 64
Seybold, Leo: 89, 91, 93, 260
Simon, Herbert A.: 17, 18
Six Percent case: 180–182, 221–222,
    224–227
Slichter, Jack M.: 270, 271, 274
Slick Airlines: 92
Smathers, George: 41–42, 115
Smith, C. R.: 208
Smyth v. Ames: 191
Snyder, Richard C.: 6 n.
social action: universe of, 4–5, 9–10,
    19–21, 294

social policy: 294–299
social scientist: 317
Sparkman, John: 50
Supreme Court: on rate making, 138–
    139
survival test: of systems, 310–313
Suspended Passenger Fare Increase
    case. SEE Six Percent case
Symington, W. Stuart: 129

TACAN: 53, 77–78, 83
Tariff Corporation: 257
Task Force on National Aviation
    Goals: 315–316
taxes: CAB on, 241
technical rationality: 304
technology: influence of, 13, 298–299,
    306
Thomas, Albert: 42, 165, 167
Thye, Edward J.: 127–129
Tipton, Stuart G.: and 40–20 formula,
    60; on revision of CAA, 82, 89, 91;
    on rule making, 115; on the mili-
    tary, 119; on CAB, 150, 151–152;
    and Denny, 159, 160, 161–163; and
    GPFI, 166, 183, 262, 271; influence
    of, 260, 297, 305
tower operators: 57–58, 75, 106
traffic. SEE airspace, use of
Traffic Department (of ATA): 251–
    252
Transport Workers Union of America:
    60
transportation: study of, 78–80; Under
    Secretary for, 86; regulation of rates
    for, 138–142
Trans World Airlines (TWA): 183,
    187, 199, 200, 201, 203, 217
travel agents: and CAB, 266
Treasury Department: 60
Truman, David B.: 7, 295
Truman, President Harry: 37, 75, 81
trunklines: number of, 18, 145–146,
    173; subsidy for, 56, 147, 151; rates
    of, 139, 152, 153–155, 183–184, 238,
    241; certification of, 144–147, 151;